Mentors in the Garden of Life

Colleen Plimpton

Park East Press, Inc.

Printed in the United States of America.

For information address:

Park East Press, Inc.
The Graybar Building
420 Lexington Avenue, Suite 300
New York, NY 10170

Library of Congress Cataloging-in-Publication Data

Plimpton, Colleen

Mentors in the Garden of Life/ Colleen Plimpton

Library of Congress Control Number: 2010927706

p. cm.

ISBN: 978-0-9825292-0-1

First Edition

10 9 8 7 6 5 4 3 2 1

To Jerry Shike, my partner in gardening and in life.

Acknowledgments

This book would not have been possible without the clarity, kindness and ongoing vision of my writing teacher, Linda Chiara.

Editor extraordinaire Bob Middlemiss, with his thoughtful suggestions and vast experience, helped to gently shape this book into a coherent whole.

My gratitude to Sue West, whose professional photography shows my garden in its best bib and tucker, no matter what it really looks like.

And thanks to my many gardening friends, and to readers of my column, all of whom inspire me again and again with their comments, insight and wisdom.

A briefer version of Chapter 2, "Uncle Arthur," appeared in the Summer 2006 issue of *The Litchfield Review.*
A slightly different form of Chapter 22, "Ann Tibbatts," appeared in the May/June 2009 issue of *Connecticut Gardener.*
A version of Chapter 26, "Bernice Shike," appeared in the Autumn 2006 issue of *GreenPrints.*
A similar, but not identical rendering of Chapter 28, "Paul Young," appeared in the Early Summer 2007 issue of *People, Places & Plants.*

Photography by Sue West and Jerry Shike.

Contents

The Farm

Louise Schoonover

The smooth granite of the tombstone lay cold under my hand that chilly afternoon in 1990. Faded November crabapples hung desiccated from the tree next to the grave, and a determined breeze lifted the collar of my pea coat. A jay scolded from lank rhododendron. The air smelled wintry. I stomped my feet, damp from traversing the confusing, rutted lanes of the hilly country cemetery. The paths circled back around themselves, encompassing the modest markers of the generations of sturdy upstate New York yeomen and women who lay among the bigleaf hydrangea and the liveforever.

My fingers lingered in the grooves of her name.

Louise Plimpton Schoonover, 1894 - 1982

Rest in peace, gentle soul.

Aunt Louise, short and round, her pink face always wreathed in a smile, sparse white hair gathered in a net, was a remarkable part of my youth. A farmer's daughter who'd moved to town when her dad retired in 1913, she'd been my father's primary childhood caretaker. She'd shepherded him through abusive, neglectful parents, comforted him when local bullies tormented, and monitored his ups and downs with schooling. Her duty complete when he volunteered for service in World War II, she married a man she knew from church. Uncle Willard owned a dairy farm one town south.

No children were granted to their late-in-life union, and so my siblings and I, when we came along in the 1940s and '50s, became her de facto grandkids.

She'd died almost a decade prior to the brisk autumn day when I located her marker. At the time of her passing I'd been in the midst of second year graduate school examinations in far-off New York City and couldn't be at her deathbed, nor attend her funeral. In the intervening years, with the callowness of youth, I'd never visited her grave. Time passed, life grew busier yet. Now, with middle age rapidly looming, and my children growing more independent, I found I increasingly missed my Aunt Louise. I recalled her unmitigated joy at our mere presence; I longed for the sweet taste of her Sunday dinner sticky buns. Most of all, I missed her wise counsel concerning matters of the land.

I needed to see where she lay under that thin, stony upstate New York soil.

Sometime during that hour spent by her grave, deep in conversation with my memory of the kind woman who'd been mentor as well as great-aunt, I understood why gardening, that sweet skill of producing beauty and plenty from the earth, had become more and more primal to me. Neither of my parents was wedded to the soil, and I'd wondered at the increased importance I attached to making things grow. Over Aunt Louise's grave that afternoon I finally made the connection between the upstate New York farm woman who'd loved me, and my love of the land.

I perceived that I am a heritage gardener. My knowledge comes to me not solely through hard-won knowledge from countless classes and hours spent poring through garden books and magazines. Nor just from dirt-encrusted hands and the daily gleaning of the weather report. Nor simply from due diligence on the Internet and chatting up those stewards of the earth more experienced than I. No, a great deal of what I know comes to me via those I've loved who have gone before.

Individuals such as my grandmother Elva, whose clambering roses draped over her white picket fence, and whose cabbages thrived in neat tracks in her vegetable patch by the tilted garage. And my uncle Frank, whose backyard held not a blade of grass, but row upon row of prize-winning vegetables. Or the distant stories of my great-grandfather's farm in Spencer, New York, in the 1800s and the legendary gladiolus he later grew and sold from his front porch during the Great Depression. Or Grandpa Kennett's potato patch out by the cow pasture in the gone-to-seed farm on which I grew to adulthood. Even my dad, for that matter, who, though he had no truck for fancy garden beds (and would, in fact, mow over them if they were not well-maintained), nonetheless rescued and transplanted a magnificent row of bridal wreath spirea into our backyard, and tried his hand at being a vegetable farmer in the postwar era.

And there are others from whom I've learned lessons, such as my great friend Paul Young, who retired from the nurseryman trade to grow a thousand different hosta cultivars on a precious ten acres in suburban Fairfield County, Connecticut. He looked beyond his threescore and ten when he donated an additional fifteen acres to the local land trust.

And my best friend Muriel, whose unique gardening skill lies in her joy at the exuberance of nature. Her abandonment of hard-and-fast rules of what should grow where has taught me invaluable lessons about relaxation and enjoyment.

There are others who have touched my gardening life, and whose lives I, in turn, believe I have touched. But it was my recollections of great-aunt Louise which prompted these musings. Aunt Louise, whose cluttered dairy farm was ever a host to a curious child of the 1950s, the studious little person who was me. The child who became fascinated, and never forgot, that hickory nuts were to be had for the taking on bright autumn days in the lane leading to her farm. Or that chickens produce manure which stinks when gathered, but helps the soil grow the most splendid flowers. Or that stupendous view from the garden down to the pond, and across to the

Bristol Hills, which was balm to the soul of a confused college student in the 1960s.

Aunt Louise, whose name I gave to my only daughter.

It's important to remember.

I have come, therefore, to understand that some gardening knowledge is in the genes, distilled through age. I find I don't really know how much I know. Facts, anecdotes, and knowledge at times spring unbidden to my brain. How do I understand what shade of green newly-unfurling spring leaves should tint? What connects me so firmly to the soil? Whence comes the peace of autumn, of labors well-performed? Why does my heart leap at a sunny day in January and my thoughts turn to seed catalogues?

Because it's in my blood.

In the gathering dusk on that long-ago November day, sleet began to pelt against my pea coat collar. I turned to retrace my steps, find my car, exit the black wrought-iron gates of Union Free Cemetery in Livonia, New York, and return to my middle-class suburban life. But I was changed. I knew I would someday, somehow, find a way to memorialize Aunt Louise, and all the garden mentors, past and present, who, by example and experience, have beckoned to me.

This book is for them.

Photo by Sue West

Hickory (Carya ovata)

Description: Common deciduous, nut-bearing tree native to Eastern United States and southeast Canada; member of the walnut family. Can grow to 100 feet and live up to 200 years. Many types have interesting exfoliating bark.

Favorites: Shagbark, pignut. Shagbark cultivars include 'Yoder', 'Grainger' and 'Abundance'.

Zones: 5 to 10

Exposure: Full to partial sun.

Soil: Humus-rich, fertile, well-drained. Do not plant too deeply.

Water: Water well after planting and the first year.

Fertilizer: Use a slow-release granular formulation specifically for trees.

Pruning: Prune top fifth after transplanting. Prune branches that develop at a sharp angle to the trunk.

Potential Problems: Difficult to transplant from the wild due to long taproot. Grafted specimens are available from specialty nurseries. Pests include aphids, stem galls and bark beetles. Diseases include anthracnose and verticillium wilt.

Interesting Asides: Beautiful autumn coloring of red, yellow and orange and attractive canopy makes hickory a favorable yard tree choice. These trees are pollinated by wind and require cross pollination to bear fruit. Nuts are important food for wildlife and were a vital source of nutrients for Native Americans. Hickory wood is very strong and valued for furniture, baseball bats as well as firewood and use in smoking meats.

2

Lilac

Arthur Kennett

"Colleen, will you take this iced tea in to your Uncle Arthur, please?"

I hesitated, glancing at the metal tray sitting on our enameled kitchen table. That's where we generally placed items to go into the sickroom.

"Now that you're five, you can handle the glass." Mother positioned a red aluminum tumbler in my cupped hands. It was chilly and smooth and I held it out from my body, waiting. "I'll take the tray. Go on, you know how he loves to see you. I'll be right behind."

I did as my mother directed, gingerly balancing through the back kitchen and over the ragged sill onto the sun porch. I placed the container on the TV table next to the cot occupied by my mother's brother, adjacent to the egg cup stained with the remnants of soft-boiled egg and just touching the pristine box of Fannie Farmer candy. I tried to ignore the sight of Uncle Arthur's skeletal limbs and the burnt odor of rubber sheets. He smiled weakly and held out his hands for the tumbler. "Thanks, Squirt."

It was May of 1953. That summer it would take my Uncle Arthur three months to die in his sickbed on our sun porch. From Memorial Day, when the summer smell of purple lilacs filled the air, to August, when hydrangea bloomed out by the potato patch. He had cancer and had come home to die. He'd come to our dilapidated farmhouse on the edge of town, with its faded elegance and rippled window glass. With its wide, hosta-encircled front porch, and its rickety stairs leading down to the backyard my dad had carved out of cornfield. With its currant bushes and snowball shrubs and gnarled apple trees. And with its sun porch off the kitchen.

The porch, it turned out, was a good place to be. It faced southwest and caught the afternoon sun. The backyard maples were full of songbirds, and Spring Creek murmured nearby.

Uncle Art was a young man, a veteran of World War II, but he was dying nonetheless. He knew it, my mother knew it, and his parents, raging at the injustice of it all, knew it too.

His bed was arranged by an outside wall... so that through the screen, on "strong-enough" days, he'd be able to see the willow swaying in the summer breeze, and hear sparrows twittering in the English walnut. He could catch the fluttering of butterflies as they wafted from the old yellow daylilies to the tall garden phlox.

Uncle Arthur and I had been buddies even before his illness. He had a daughter, Linda, who was just my age, but who lived far away in Rochester with her mother, Arthur's estranged wife. Relatives said we looked alike. He didn't see Linda much. Perhaps I reminded him of happier times.

As the weeks wore on, his strength waned. And yet, there were days when he raised himself on his elbow, stared out the screened window, and with a bony index finger, pointed the out the sights to me.

"Look, Squirt, see the elm tree?" I hung back, unsmiling, my left foot scratching my right leg under the brown checked cotton dress. "It's OK," he said. "C'mon and look. I'm still Uncle Art, and I don't bite, you know. Never did."

I leaned over and looked out the window. He meant the tree with the swing.

"That's the swing my dad, your grandpa, hung when I was a pup. He made it out of a slab of wood and a couple of chains. You still use it?"

I nodded. "But not a lot, 'cause there's bugs on the tree. Yellow wormy things."

"Dutch Elm disease. I heard it's gotten this far north. Too bad, too bad. The trees don't last long with that."

On this and subsequent days, as he lost his ability to climb stairs, he increasingly toured a familiar yard from his bed. "There's my mother's rose, over where the barn used to be," he announced one day. "It's getting big, just like you girls. Are you helping her take care of it?"

I'd never really noticed the brambly bush, except to the extent it got in the way of hide-and-go-seek games. It bloomed a few days later, a wide-flung spectacle of yellow. That morning, after running around the yard in my swimsuit, reveling in the warmth of a summer rain, I buried my nose in the flower's bouquet and glanced up at the sun porch window.

Uncle Art waved.

Another good day came the following week, sandwiched between ambulance visits to the hospital. Uncle Art had been eating less and less from the plates on the gunmetal-gray tray. He was past rejoicing at the end of the Korean War, or the fact that Ted Williams would now be returning to Major League baseball. He was always cold, despite the heat of summer.

One day he grasped my wrist as I brought him his tea. "Don't take all this for granted, Colleen." He waved weakly at the pastoral scene spread before him, unavailable now, beyond the screen. "You're lucky to have it. I was a city kid myself, like your mom. But I've had some good times here, after the war, with your mother and dad. Some good parties in that backyard."

He seemed very far away.

His death in that place is my earliest memory of a sun porch, and my earliest memory of a much-loved backyard. A backyard, long gone now, but which nonetheless lives on in my memory.

It's a gentler time now for me. I am decades older than my Uncle Art when he died. From my own sun porch, hundreds of miles and a generation removed from that sad summer, I watch the seasons reel and pass. My particular piece of architectural after-thought is also situated off the kitchen, high above my sloping back-yard domain.

It is my sanctuary, just as the last months of Arthur's life were spent in his sanctuary, in a beautiful place, among people who loved him.

From my Connecticut sun porch I can reflect on a life joyfully lived in and among the northeastern forest and glacial drumlins. I can see the fruit of my labors evident in much-loved garden beds now surrounding the house. Among many other plants, a yellow rose dwells there, descended from my grandmother's.

From there I can catch a glimpse of the compost, in which the annual cycle of death and renewal is so obvious. The farm pond, far below, glistens celestial blue in spring and pearl white in winter. From the porch, years ago, I laid out in my mind's eye the swirling paths of the backyard garden, and the placement of the berms. I planned the perfect selection of woodland-edge plantings—the cornus mas, amelanchier and viburnum. Just as my childhood back-yard was ringed by pasture gone to meadow and planted by nature, I orchestrated the colors of the perennials, the height of the shrubs.

And it all came to be.

Now the porch is the first place I go in the morning, coffee cup in hand, to watch daylight climb over the ridge. It's often the last place I sit in the evening, listening in spring to the peepers and in summer to the goodnight calls of neighborhood birds. It's where I have my lunch, temperature permitting, overlooking the gardens, watching soaring hawks, scolding jays and scurrying chipmunks. It's where guests sink into the forest-green wicker furniture with a sigh, their eyes drawn to the boughs of the beech in which the porch seems to rest. It's where Book Club congregates for our July meeting, candles lit against the dusk, ears attuned to the *whoo whoo whoo* of owls and the faraway yips of coyotes. In the autumn, bundled up on the porch against the New England chill, the rustle of maple and oak leaves is my dawn song and my lullaby. Deep in the throes of a northern winter the porch serves as both a repository for recycling and a winter feeding room for my cats, restive at the length of their confinement. During that frosty season, possums and raccoons will often visit just as day turns to night, to sample what leftovers the cats might have abandoned in their dishes.

My porch is my respite, much the same as the one that served as a respite in the summer of 1953, a respite from the hard work of dying.

What did I learn from that long-ago summer? I learned, and have never forgotten, to look, really look at one's surroundings. I learned that there is loveliness even in a weedy, overgrown back-yard full of hand-me-down plants from other lives. I learned to look through another's eyes.

Uncle Arthur lives on for me in the memory of that wild back-yard. Long since gone, the yard, and Uncle Art, are as real to me as they were in a lingering sorrowful summer in 1953.

One never knows how long one will be on this earth. One never really knows what opulence and bounty surround us.

It's time to look.

Lilac (Syringa vulgaris) Photo by Jerry Shike

Description: Deciduous flowering shrub or multi-stemmed small tree; member of the olive family.

Favorites: 'Alba', 'Charles Joly'.

Zone: 3 to 7.

Exposure: Full sun. These woody shrubs can grow to 20 feet and will bloom in less than full sun, although more sparsely.

Soil: Neutral to alkaline; amend with compost at planting.

Water: Drought tolerant, but water regularly the first year.

Fertilizer: None needed if grown in good soil; add supplemental lime if soil is acid.

Pruning: Immediately after bloom, so as to not sacrifice next year's blooms. If overgrown, shrub can be pruned for structure and height by taking out 1/3 of branches each year for three years.

In the vase: For longest life, pick in evening, not during heat of day. Strip leaves, split stems. Plunge into deep vase of lukewarm water. Keep in dark place overnight, then display.

Potential Problems: Powdery mildew can appear on leaves in midsummer in crowded or shady conditions. Though unsightly, it does not generally affect health of plant. Use a baking soda mixture for control.

Interesting Asides: Lilacs are prized for their spring fragrance. They make a nice addition to the shrub border, as an allee or a specimen plant. With careful planning, it's possible to have lilacs in bloom for two months. The wood of the common lilac is quite dense, and has been traditionally used for engraving, for musical instruments, and for knife handles.

3

Apple Tree

William Kennett

A forgotten former farm at the edge of a small town in western New York State was my childhood home. Though Lima was also my dad's hometown, my mother was a transplant. A city girl, she'd come to town as a teenager when her parents bought a decrepit farmhouse for their summer use. When my parents married, the house was rented to them for the ridiculously low price of $25 per month. To their sorrow, Grandpa Kennett stubbornly refused to sell it to them.

"No, Dolly," he'd say. "You'll get it when I die. There'll be a house for each of you kids then, you know that. Why do you want it now?"

Mother never could explain to him that our family wanted our own home. Right then, not at some future point.

We four kids—Debbie, Jennie, Ricky and me—all loved the old place. It'd ceased to be a working farm some decades before, and the barn had fallen in, but the acreage was still there, with the creek, the overgrown fields, and the Big Hill out back. My siblings and I rambled around the rough land. We swung on the elm trees, waded and skinny-dipped in the creek (risking the glossy black smoothness of bloodsuckers), picked sweet wild roses in the back lot, and tromped through the neighboring horse pasture.

Grandpa had told us to stay out of the pasture, that it belonged to the Fays, our neighbors up the hill. That we shouldn't disturb the horses. But we didn't always listen to him. Not about that, and not about other things.

A tall, stooped fellow, Grandpa had a narrow, handsome face framed by an undomesticated mane of wavy white hair. A veteran of WWI and retired from the Railroad Postal Service, he lived to putter in and around his various houses. Of a summer evening he enjoyed smoking a pipe in his slide rocker on the porch, attended by an audience listening to his stories of long ago. During the day he'd sometimes allow us to help him in his potato patch, or take us for rides in the bed of his makeshift truck. He'd jerry-rigged it out of a 1940 Plymouth, a two-wheeled trailer constructed from discarded wood, and the base of a model T pickup truck. We'd swing ourselves over the wheel well and onto rough planks, arguing who got the backrest against the cab. Up East Main Street we'd go, usually just half a mile to the insulator factory for a load of ashes for the ongoing driveway-paving project.

The wild property made for an idyllic childhood. In the mid '50s polio was still a threat, so we didn't attend many community get-togethers, but with splintery bamboo poles and rusty hooks, we kids fished the creek, waded up it as far as we dared, stood under the highway bridge and listened to the echoes of the traffic overhead on Route 5 and 20. Once a summer we'd venture as far as the railroad trestle, high above Spring Creek and a mile or so south into the woods. We'd stride halfway across, then decide we'd better place an ear to the ground and listen for the *chunk-a-chunk-a-chunk-a* rumble of the daily Lehigh Valley freight train. We were poised to race to the other side of the trestle and hit the dirt if the sound was too close.

We climbed trees, picked wildflowers, slid down the Big Hill. We flew kites on the ridge high above the creek. We scooped up minnows and frogs in our cupped hands, letting them go after hauling our trophies home in tin cans to show Mother. We romped through the meadow and slogged up the muddy banks of the creek.

When we felt particularly restless or adventuresome, we'd hike southwest and end up at St. Rose School.

Tossed out of the house each summer day, we'd be told to "go outside and play" by both my mother and my grandmother, Nana. A favorite place after lunch was the wobbly swing set in the far back, by the burn barrel. We older ones had to be careful; the anchoring poles, not well secured, leapt out of the ground with a vigorous swing.

We discovered cow bones in the cow pasture and displayed our archeological findings on the front porch. We went barefoot all summer and had an ongoing contest to see whose feet were most calloused. By the end of summer, even the driveway's coal cinders didn't hurt.

We all had various hideaways in our backyard wilderness. Nests in the grove of white pines, lined with the surprisingly soft down of pine needles. A nook under the row of bridal wreath spirea, their branches pure white in spring. A patch of sunny, dimpled ground at the edge of the meadow, out by the sumac.

In what became our lawn, six or seven peach, pear and apple trees in various stages of antiquity and disease adorned the slope, a residual orchard from farming days. The biggest of them, a huge apple tree at the top of the yard, was crooked with age, bore a yearly abundance of spotted apples, and was great for climbing. I received my first kiss under that apple tree one May when it was in full bloom, but that's a story for a different time. Of unknown provenance, the tree's spreading branches gave the climber a vantage point to survey the entire domain of the backyard.

The apples that dropped early were small and green and hard, but we ate them anyway. By midsummer they were larger, with scabby patches, and we learned to gnaw around the worms. When the apples fell to the ground below they became soggy mush, splitting open to emit a rich vinegary smell, a smell which is reminiscent of my childhood to this day.

Deep into one July afternoon, prickled, stained and mosquito-bitten after a stint of plucking blackberries in an unsuspecting neighbor's patch, four or five of us decided to make "homes" in the scaffolding of the old apple tree. Those who dared climb high, myself included, got the forks, with their resting places and wide vistas. The littler kids got the lower branches, easier to grasp and descend from.

Once claimed, our individual territories needed to be marked. But how? We decided to strip a ring of bark off the first branch of each kingdom. That would be the door, over which no fellow tree-dweller might pass without permission. We started on the lowest limb, which was Ricky's, gouging off a slick peel of bark, exposing the smooth, wet underbelly of the tree branch. We worked assiduously, oblivious to an approaching elder.

"What in the Sam Hill are you youngsters doing?"

Obscured in the apple foliage, I'd heard Grandpa Kennett before I saw him, his boots swishing in the overgrown grass below the tree. I froze. He was clearly upset by something.

Debbie's eyes found mine, darting anxiously from Grandpa to the other kids. We were in trouble, but we didn't know why.

Grandpa looked up at us, then pointed at the ground, littered with fallen apples. "Get down here where I can see you. All of you."

I detached myself from my secure perch high in the boughs, toed the crotch of the tree, and jumped down to where Grandpa, old soldier that he was, waited. He was dead silent for about 30 seconds... a long time for a gaggle of kids.

He patted the lowest branch of the tree where it met the stout trunk. "What's the meaning of this?" His hand, as knobby as the old tree, indicated the shiny white strip where we'd peeled back the bark to mark our turf.

Jennie silently glanced at me, then back to Grandpa.

I stuttered. "We just... we thought... we need to mark our houses..." Debbie tugged on her left pigtail, her wide blue eyes fearful.

Grandpa spoke slowly. "You'll kill this tree with your shenanigans." He pulled his bandana handkerchief out of his back overalls pocket and wiped his brow. "I don't think you want to do that. Each branch needs to be connected to the trunk; it breathes through the bark. What you've done here, you've stopped this branch from breathing."

We kids looked at each other, hot with humiliation. I scrubbed my bare feet in the grass. We sure didn't want to kill our tree. And we certainly didn't want to get on the wrong side of Grandpa.

His bushy white eyebrows beetled over blue eyes. "I know you kids can figure out a way to play without hurting a tree that's older than the lot of you together. Now do it. Make me proud."

As he strode down the hill towards the garage, we looked at each other and scattered, the lure of the apple tree somehow gone for that day. But days later, when we climbed the tree and sought our homes, we respected each and every branch. We never harmed another living limb.

I didn't forget. Though I don't grow apples or other fruit trees, I do grow crabapples and hemlocks, sassafras and dogwoods. I grow tulip trees and junipers, river birch and beech trees. I transplant maples from the woods. I seek out and relocate white oak seedlings threatened by hungry deer.

I care for and about the trees in my garden. I plant them with the correct exposure and in good soil. I provide ample water and a judicious amount of fertilizer. I stake them when necessary, but not for too long. I bind their wounds when the woodpeckers get overly enthusiastic, and I apply deer repellent regularly. I consult the professionals on issues of insects and pruning. I recognize that trees are essential to the well-being of each and every citizen of the world.

Does all of this stem from a time long ago when Grandpa Kennett assembled a bunch of kids under the boughs of an old apple tree? Does the lesson he taught us—how to get along not only with each other, but with Mother Nature—linger to this day?

Of course it does.

Crabapple (Malus)

Photo by Sue West

Description: Deciduous spring-flowering tree of varying habits; pendulous, spreading, upright, vase-shaped or pyramidal. Flowers may be white, pink or red. Most cultivars grow from 8 feet to 20 feet but may be larger.

Favorites: 'Scarlet Brandywine', 'Prairie Fire'.

Zones: 4 to 8.

Exposure: Best in full sun. Will grow in less light, but sparsely, or may lean.

Soil: Slightly acidic. Incorporate compost at planting.

Water: Regular deep watering for first year and in times of drought otherwise.

Fertilizer: None needed in good soil. Mulch to conserve water and suppress weeds, but do not pull mulch to the base of the trunk.

Pruning: Regular removal of suckers, water sprouts and crossed branches.

Potential Problems: Apple scab & fire blight will defoliate trees. Purchase resistant varieties. If deer are an issue, spray branches with repellent.

Interesting Asides: If the homeowner doesn't use the fruit, it provides food for wildlife such as birds, squirrels, fox, and raccoons. The fruit also provides winter interest, as long as it lasts. Fruit persists on some trees until March. Fruited branches can be used for the vase or outdoor ornament. Use small crabapples as an allee, to grace the front entrance or to focus on an important point in the garden.

4

Potatoes

Dorothy and Sylvalan (Fred) Plimpton

During the Great Depression of the 1930s, families did what they could to keep body and soul together. They recycled before that word entered the vernacular. They took in boarders. They put the car up on blocks and traveled by shank's mare. They darned socks, donned hand-me-downs and saved pennies in glass pickle jars. They wore holes in their shoes and turned dog-eared towels into supports for next summer's squash.

My grandparents in western New York State were among the multitude. Ralph and Elva Plimpton, Dad's parents, lived in the small town of Lima and cultivated a large vegetable garden. Apple and walnut trees dotted side and front lawns of their old brick house. Chickens clucked in the converted garage, earning their keep by pecking the hornworms out of the tomatoes and providing the family a nutritious dinner each Sunday. Ralph, in addition to his full-time factory employment at the Porcelain Insulator Company, took odd jobs. And he subcontracted his two sons out before and after their schooldays to shovel snow and coal, mow lawns and clean out cisterns. Both boys were also expected to work in the garden and to care for the hens. Backyard farming was not my dad's favorite work, but despite himself he learned a thing or two about agriculture.

My mother's folks, Nana and Grandpa Kennett, on the other hand, lived 20 miles north of Lima in Rochester's 19th ward, where they grew fruits and vegetables on their large city lot. Nana took in foster children from Catholic Charities and occasionally worked at F.W. Woolworth in the nearby Bull's Head neighborhood. Grandpa was a railroad man; his job took him away from home three weeks out of four, but he prided himself on doing most of the family's handyman chores when he was back at Hawley Street. My mother, unlike my dad, acquired not a whit of expertise in gardening.

Fast forward to the middle 1950s. My parents, who'd met in Lima as berry-picking teens, married in 1947, produced four children in seven years, and struggled financially. Mother had left her teaching career to raise the family. Dad didn't earn much as an office machine repairman for A.B. Dick Company. In spite of a low rent on the big old farmhouse leased from my maternal grandparents, and lessons learned from the Depression, their money didn't stretch far enough.

In the early winter of '56, Mother hatched a plan to assist with our ever-expanding grocery bill. The family would grow vegetables on a patch of weed-infested ground beyond our lawn. Though long fallow, the chosen field looked suitable. It faced east and sloped down to Spring Creek, a small tributary out of Honeoye Lake. Dad surmised that the chocolaty clay earth had soaked up overspill from a millennium of creek flooding and was organic enough to produce for us.

Upon closer examination the soil turned out to be sour, and thus good for growing potatoes, but unfortunately also good for growing comfrey. Our property was chock full of that perennial herb. Comfrey had been a valuable incidental crop in colonial America, considered valuable forage for livestock; its large leaves added fertility to the soil, and its tuberous, turnip-like roots had medicinal value. It thrived along the banks of Spring Creek.

At three feet or more in height, comfrey is a large plant, and thick greasy leaves prickle the fingers of whoever touches it. Its deep and expansive root system resists removal, though, and new plants can spring from snippets. All in all, it's difficult to eradicate.

My dad tried. In preparation for the vegetable endeavor, Grandpa Kennett, who spent summers at our house, loaned him an obsolete, two-wheeled, walk-behind garden tiller, powered by a Briggs & Stratton engine. Dad labored mightily to break up soil that hadn't been plowed in 50 years.

"Gol-durned thumping thing!" My dad stumbled through the coarse field behind his mechanical nemesis. Baptist-raised and Catholic-converted, he didn't actually swear much, at least around us. I suspect that when we weren't in earshot, though, he could sling curses with the best of them.

He fought that field evening after evening during the early spring of 1957. The methane-like odor of rotting comfrey wafted up to the screen porch where Mother, ensconced with the two younger kids and her after-dinner cup of coffee, watched and supervised.

"Don't make the row so long, Fred!" she'd call. Or, "I'm sending the girls out to help you, Fred, so watch out for them."

Dorothy Kennett Plimpton might have known nothing of farming, but she was The Director, and Sylvalan, as always, did as he was bid. That was the most prudent tack to take when Mother made up her Yankee mind about something. Her job was to offer encouragement, mercurochrome our field-hand cuts, and gift us with the occasional orange Popsicle as reward for our efforts. She didn't do field work.

Debbie and I, the two oldest kids, also bent to Mother's will, but unlike Dad, we thought growing potatoes a grand adventure. I was eight that summer, Debbie almost seven, and we fancied ourselves miniature farmers. We were the only kids at St. Rose Parochial School who had their own personal potato field in their backyard, but it didn't matter.

Dad obtained his seed potatoes courtesy of his friend and former neighbor, Ernie Ziegler. Some years older than Dad, Ernie belonged to the farm across the street from Dad's childhood home on Elm Street. A lifelong bachelor, he owned some 40 acres of in-town land that had been the Dalton farm. As a brakeman for the

New York Central, Ernie didn't have time to actually grow alfalfa or keep dairy cows, as had the Daltons, but he loved his "ranch."

And he was a good friend as Sylvalan Plimpton transitioned from the blood and chaos of World War II on the South Pacific island of Saipan back to normal life in Lima. There were several months after homecoming when Dad spent much of his free time with Ernie, drinking, carousing, and raising Cain, and during which he enjoyed an innocent, brief interlude before the responsibilities of marriage, family and career closed in. After a childhood and adolescence in which he had been browbeaten, belittled, and expected to be a wage earner, this turned out to be the only time in his life Dad was to be carefree.

Ernie certainly tippled too much, but he grew fine vegetables. He and Dad remained buddies (though without so much sauce) after my parents' marriage, and in the spring of '57 Ernie took Dad along to Canandaigua when he purchased his seed potatoes.

Several days later, those seed potatoes lay in an irregular jumble under the elm as the family congregated to prepare them for planting. The lawn, whittled from brush over a series of years, had been mowed several times by potato planting time, so the grass was green and only semi-weedy. Mother in her housecoat and apron, Dad in his black Sears wash pants, Debbie with her plaited blonde hair, ever-bubbly baby sister Jennie, and Ricky still in diapers, safely stowed behind the snow fencing that served as a makeshift playpen; all but Ricky had a job.

Surrounded by Ernie Ziegler's seed potatoes, wearing my Davy Crockett coonskin cap, I was entrusted for the first time with a sharp knife. The task was to cut the spuds into pieces, each part bearing at least one arching eyebrow with an eye-hollow. Coming up out of the arch I was to look for an "eye," or dark diminutive bud. This piece would be planted in the plowed trenches. My work progressed haltingly as I stopped frequently to examine the odd contours and lumpy textures of the root vegetable; to savor their wet starchy smell, feel the moist texture of the cut edges, lick the coarse surface. I was captivated to think that each eye-bearing chunk of potato would produce a plant, and eventually, hidden in the ground, more potatoes.

The mound grew as we all chopped, sawed and plunked the chunks into a wheelbarrow. Dad muscled the load to the furrowed field, where we formed a conga line of sorts. Dad first, tossing in a potato piece; me next, covering the seed with dirt; Debbie lagging behind, scuffing dirt over any hunks I'd missed.

"Be careful, Colleen! Don't step on the potatoes; you'll bruise them." My father backtracked to show us again how the pieces should be handled. "And mind that they're only as deep as my hand. Make sure Debbie does it right, too."

Proud of my responsibility, I did as instructed, though I was distracted by the secrets of the soil revealed in the furrow. The mice running ahead of the plow, the earthworms, bugs, small clusters of soil in mesmerizing shapes. I was smitten by the sun on my back, the rush of May water in Spring Creek and the primal satisfaction of growing food.

The lure of working the land seized me that spring day and has never let go.

Weeding was a constant chore after the plants sprouted, and every few weeks we hilled. The dirt gushed up between our toes as, barefoot, dressed in hand-me-down blouses and tattered skirts, we made teepees of soil over each small potato plant. Dad taught us that any part of potato showing would be damaged, so we were careful as we walked the rows and added an additional inch or so of soil to the base of each plant.

We loved it. The getting dirty part, the in the sun part, the working with Dad part.

But a threat to our potato crop, as to all potato crops then and now, lurked: the Colorado potato beetle, known to us as the potato bug, or erroneously, "ladybug." The insect was capable of rapidly defoliating a field of potato plant leaves, and it had to be controlled.

The 1950s were not known for their organic practices, so when it came to the Plimpton family versus the potato bug, big guns were called forth. My job was to carry a rusty Maxwell House coffee can filled partway with arsenic mixture, to dip an old ruler in and flick the thin white fluid onto the plants, hopefully striking enough bugs to make a dent in the population. The insects, yellow with black stripes, were easy to aim for, and the faintly garlicky smell of the poison followed me down the rows.

Rains came steadily that summer, and only once do I remember having to carry buckets of water to the garden from the rain barrel under the downspout at the southeast corner of our house. Watering stopped a week or so before full maturation of the plants, to give the potatoes a "rest." Then it was time to harvest our hidden hoard. That was best part, finding the tubers concealed in the soil. Dad used a pitchfork, not a shovel, so as not to slice into our findings. Debbie and I bunched up the bounty in an old sheet and dragged it to the lawn, where we rinsed the tubers before lugging the load up the back stairs to the kitchen.

We used our gatherings right away, mostly because my granddad had experienced previous ill fortune in storing the potatoes he grew in his field further back on the property. Though he'd been raised on a farm near Scottsville, Grandpa Kennett had lived in Rochester for decades and apparently had forgotten the science of storing potatoes. A stubborn old coot, he wasn't going to ask for advice, either. The previous winter he'd left his crop in the stone basement of our old farmhouse, and they'd frozen. The entire crop, lost.

So Dad and Mother weren't about to attempt putting their harvest by. We ate all those potatoes as they came up out of the ground. Mother fried, scalloped and mashed our potatoes. We ate them baked, boiled, riced and fricasseed. We had new potatoes, main course potatoes, and leftover potatoes. We had Potatoes Anna, Potatoes Dauphin and Potatoes Lorette, all of which were experiments Mother tried from her wedding-gift copy of the Fannie

Farmer cookbook, stored high on a shelf in her cluttered kitchen. Mother wasn't much of a cook, and as it turned out, Dad wasn't much of a farmer, but for one brief interlude in the 1950s, our Plimpton family enjoyed all the fresh potatoes we could eat.

But in the end, growing potatoes was simply too much work for Dad. Battling the comfrey and the weather, the bugs and the weeds each day after the 20-mile drive home from the city was exhausting.

The following spring he didn't plant the field. The garden had lasted only one season, but for me the seminar on productivity and plenty has lasted a lifetime.

The only place I now raise potatoes is inadvertently in the compost, when they volunteer. But I'm still a backyard farmer. Instead of reveling in a table of harvested vegetables, I nurture a thousand different kinds of annuals, perennials, biennials, vines, shrubs, and trees in my Connecticut backyard. I grow ornamentals. My reward for a season of tilling the earth, bargaining with critters, and applying astute amounts of water, fertilizer and mulch is not Potatoes Lyonnais or deep-dish scalloped potatoes. My harvest is vases crammed with lilac panicles, rhododendron trusses, and peony blooms. It's armloads of Rembrandt tulips and English roses. It's dried sedum and nodding grasses on the bathroom counter during the bleak midwinter.

From the yellow corydalis and Johnny jump-ups of March to the Montauk daisies and oakleaf hydrangeas of November, my garden yields for me. The vases in my house and the homes of my friends are full. I furnish armloads of flowers each week in season for the altar at church. I give away flowers to friends, acquaintances and deliverymen. Anyone who admires a particular flower gets a gift.

Each spring some part of me remembers my dad and the potato field, and I reach into my soul to again find the wonder and the enthusiasm for growing things on this green earth. I'm hundreds of miles away from Spring Creek and a comfrey-filled field. But, fed by memories, my garden grows.

Comfrey (Symphytum officinale)   Photo from Wikipedia.com

Description: Perennial herb in the borage family, long recognized by organic farmers and herbalists for its versatility.

Favorites: Russian comfrey.

Zones: 3-10.

Exposure: Full sun.

Soil: Acid.

Water: Needs abundant moisture in its first year. Somewhat drought-tolerant in subsequent seasons.

Fertilizer: Nitrogen hungry; benefits from the application of mulched manure.

Pruning/Harvesting: Do not harvest first year. In late summer of second and successive seasons, cut plant to about two inches.

Wear gloves as protection against the rough leaves. Use as fertilizer in the organic garden, a compost activator, and a soil additive.

Potential Problems: Very deep rooted and difficult to remove. Be sure to plant it where it's wanted.

Interesting Asides: One of the country names for comfrey was "knitbone," a reminder of its traditional use in healing. It contains allantoin, a cell proliferant that speeds up the natural replacement of body cells. However, contemporary herbalists view comfrey as a controversial herb that may offer therapeutic benefits, but at the potential risk of liver toxicity.

Potato (Solanum tuberosum)   Photo by Sue West

Description: Starchy, tuberous crop from the nightshade family. The word "potato" may refer to the plant or the product.

Favorites: 'Kennebec', 'Red Pontiac', 'All Blue'.

Zones: Multiple. Potatoes are cropped annually.

Exposure: Plants need full sun, but never allow the tubers to be exposed.

Soil: Slightly acid soil desired (pH of 5.8-6.5). As they root aggressively, potatoes grow best in light, loose, well-drained conditions.

Water: Water well, especially when in flower, as the tubers are being set. When foliage turns yellow and dies back, discontinue watering to allow tubers to mature for a week or so prior to harvest.

Fertilizer: None necessary in good soil. Too much organic material can cause scab.

Pruning/Care: Plant seed potatoes in trenches spaced 15 inches apart. Hill every two weeks or so, as plants grow. Do not plant potatoes in the same soil more than once in three years.

Potential Problems: Grow on a three-year rotation plan to combat red wireworms. Hand pick Colorado potato beetle; practice Integrated Pest Management. Watch for potato blight.

Interesting Asides: Potatoes were first cultivated by the Incas in Peru around 200 B.C. They were "discovered" by conquistadores and brought to Europe in the 1500s. Arrived in North America in 1621. In the USA 35 billion pounds of potatoes are grown per year!

5

Currants

Bessye Kennett

"Eee-yew, Colleen, how can you eat those? They're sour!" My little sister Debbie stared at me, her skinny arms akimbo, blue eyes flashing, bare feet planted firmly in the tall grass adjacent to the hedgerow of currants.

Undaunted, I popped the cluster of translucent red berries into my mouth, tonguing out the prickly stems. "I don't care, I like 'em. Nana does too. She'll put some of that yummy Reddi-wip stuff on and we'll have a feast."

It was July 1957, and the currants were ripe. Debbie was correct—they *were* sour. But there was something about eating those tiny bright berries directly off the bush that appealed to me. And my maternal grandmother, whom we called Nana, loved them.

Tart, squishy on the inside and firm-skinned on the outside, somehow those berries were a tad similar to Nana herself. I knew that because my Kennett grandparents owned the rambling elderly farmhouse in which our family of six lived. I came to know my Nana well. Although she and Grandpa spent most of the year at their gracious Queen Anne on Warwick Avenue in Rochester, they descended upon us each summer. At the close of the school year, the rumbling old Plymouth would arrive on East Main Street in Lima, freighted with their various foster children, clothing, pots and pans, her sewing and Grandpa's tools. They'd move into the part of the house set aside for them. Considered to be theirs were three rooms; the back kitchen; Nana's bedroom, a spacious rectangular room on the second floor with windows facing the road; and Grandpa's bedroom, a small, dark room to the left of the stairs. The kids would bunk in with the four of us.

My Nana, Bessye Sheridan Kennett, was a feisty one. Born Elizabeth and called Bessie, my grandmother arrived during the summer of 1888, four months after the Great Blizzard, the daughter of an English immigrant mother who'd disembarked at Castle Garden with a son and a shady past, and a father whose family were potato famine émigrés. Nana's mother died at an early age, and Bessye shepherded the family, caring for her father and siblings. She finished school at 8th grade, and it was about that time she decided that an alternate spelling of her nickname better suited her personality.

But by the time I met her she was already an ancient 60, with hair dyed dark and fluttery hands. Old black-and-white pictures of her, however, reveal a slender young woman of the early 20th century, Gibson-girl hairdo fastidiously arranged, seated primly upon a Pope Columbia bicycle. She regaled us with tales of her girlhood, when the new fad of bicycling crowded the paths along the Genesee River in Rochester, where she was courted by tall, taciturn Will Kennett, lately come to the city from the family farm in Scottsville to make his fortune. They married behind schedule; she was 30 and he 31. And then they had to wait for normalcy, as WWI erupted and Grandpa went off to fight the Germans in France. When he came home they were ready to start a life and a family. My mother, Dorothy Eleanor, forever called Dolly, was born in 1922, the first of their three children.

By that time women had had the vote for two years, but my Nana seems in retrospect agelessly liberated. Even to 1950s kids it was obvious to us that Bessye was different. Not content to sedately sit tatting in the parlor with other grandmas, not content to let the men have their say without voicing hers, she hiked the back lot with us, expressed her concerns about social injustice and questioned us with interest regarding hobbies and friends.

Every decade or so she sailed to Britain to visit relatives, and came back with small gifts and gossip. She liked to know what was going on in the world, and fancied herself forever young.

Though a city girl, Nana loved the countryside and what it could produce. I doubt she knew the names, cultivation practices or habits of the apples, pears, berries, hostas, roses and wildflowers that grew at our place, but she was enthused and curious about them.

The currants, for instance. She'd pointed out the shrubs for us, showing where they flourished between the pear and the apple trees on the west side, the uphill side of the yard, near the fence that separated our property from the Fays' horse pasture. She admired how the berries hung in knots on the shrub with rough leaves that tickled your face. And she loved to treat herself with the sour fruit.

"You better stop eating so many and save some to put in the cup, Colleen."

Debbie brought me up short with her comment; she didn't usually give unsolicited advice.

That summer morning, Nana had promised to pay Debbie and me for picking currants. We didn't know how much we'd make, but earning anything was enticing to two small country girls who didn't receive an allowance and had no other way to make money. Of course, we had no place to *spend* it either, but that didn't matter. We worked diligently, Debbie at filling her bucket, me at alternately picking berries and eating my harvest. As lunchtime drew near and my container wasn't as full as Deb's, I grabbed a handful of tall grass from under the barbed wire fence, jammed it in the bottom of the container and replaced the currants on top.

Debbie stared at me, shocked. "That's cheating, Colleen!"

"I bet Nana won't even notice; she'll be so glad to get the currants," I retorted.

We slung our buckets over our arms and headed for the house.

"Well, look at you two!" Nana smiled down from the sway-backed porch, her flowered housecoat loose about her round little figure. She clapped her hands. "You brought me my red currants, and a whole lot of them. We can make jam!"

Debbie and I grinned at each other. We knew she was funning us; there wouldn't be any jam-making in Nana's kitchen. She and Aunt Louise were as different as daisies and daffodils.

We were familiar with homemade jam because Great-Aunt Louise was famous for her jars of the jewel-bright jellies, prepared in the shimmering summer heat of her kitchen in Livonia. She harvested the fruit, washed it, added sugar and pectin, cooked the scalding mixture, cooled it, ladled the whole concoction into clear Ball canning jars and sealed them with a dollop of white paraffin, that mysterious substance. Was paraffin animal, vegetable or mineral? we wondered as we surreptitiously scraped it with grubby fingernails and tentatively tasted. It didn't make a hill of beans' difference; what was underneath the thick, waxy layer was delicious on toast all winter long.

But unlike Aunt Louise, Nana wasn't what anyone would call "domestic." She'd rather stand on her head than fix an elaborate meal. And she wasn't much of a housekeeper. Her kitchen smelled of the bread fried in bacon grease she fixed for Grandpa and the stale Borden's sweetened condensed milk he poured in his coffee. The rooms were redolent of the floor sweepings she didn't discard in a dustpan, but dropped down the floor registers, and of garbage that stayed too long in the pail. Even as children we held our noses in her kitchen.

But even as children we also admired the room. Situated on the opposite side of the house from our kitchen, it was large and well-proportioned, with a round oak table near the cellar door, a wood-burning range in one corner, and the added intrigue of a spacious butler's pantry, complete with shelves and cupboards. The pantry opened onto the dining room, and to us it was a miniature home, little-girl-sized; perfect for playing house or spying on the rest of the family from our hidden alcove.

A woman of simple pleasures, with a deep Roman Catholic faith, Nana also had a tart Irish tongue, and could be as cranky as a bear with a toothache. She didn't always think before she spoke, even to us kids. I'm reminded of the time she nonchalantly informed me the crunchy, velvety berries I'd found on a creekside shrub and consumed were, in her opinion, poison sumac. I spent the next several hours silently reciting the Catechism, expecting to die.

We children learned to be wary of Nana's sarcasm and to double check what she told us. Where I got the moxie to try to fool her about the currants, I'll never know.

Debbie and I mounted the steep stairs to the back porch, where Nana awaited with the new can of Reddi-wip. As loyal as a puppy, my sister didn't tattle on me as we passed over our containers. But I saw the smile fade from Nana's face as she hefted the pans, one on each side.

"Whose is this?" she asked sharply, raising aloft the one on the left. Trained by the nuns, I raised my hand as my mind leapt into the immediate, uncertain future with a churning dread.

Nana cocked her head as her small hands sifted the berries onto the wide wooden ledge of the porch. "Colleen Elizabeth Plimpton. What's the meaning of this?" She poked at the dry grass spearing up from the bottom of the bucket.

I had the grace to look sheepish. I bit my lower lip and hung my head. "I was in a hurry, Nana."

"So much of a hurry that you'd want to cheat your old Nana?" There was astonishment in her voice.

She beckoned me with a pudgy hand and waved Debbie towards the backyard. "Debbie, go play. You can come back in a few minutes. Colleen, go into the kitchen."

Thankful for privacy during the verbal punishment that was sure to come, I perched on the edge of a pressed-back chair and waited.

Nana sat down and patted the oilcloth-covered table for emphasis. Her voice was steely-soft. "The Good Lord gave us each new day, child, and we should be grateful for that. But He didn't mean us to fib, or take things that aren't ours." She lifted an expository finger. "You didn't fill the pail with currants, now did you? So you haven't earned what I was going to pay you, now have you?"

I couldn't argue with her logic, but I didn't want to yield the point too soon, either. "Noooo. But…"

"But nothing." She took a folded dollar bill out of her apron pocket and set it aside. "This is for your sister. And this…" She extracted a tarnished half-dollar and pushed it towards me. "This is what you've earned. A good day's pay is worth a good day's work. It's time you learned that."

I did learn that. I learned it well.

Sorrow is part and parcel of everyone's life, and Nana was no exception. It took all her Catholic faith to forgive God for taking her son, Arthur. It grieved her grandmotherly heart to lose contact for a time with Arthur's children, grandchildren numbers three and five. But Nana lived to be 96, and even in her declining years she summoned zest for visits, food and great-grandchildren. The spunky ability to glaze a conversation with an audacious comment also remained until the end, though Alzheimer's clouded her mind.

I miss my Nana. I miss her rosary beads and her concern for the babies of the world. I miss her high spirits and love of family. And sometimes when I think of her, I even miss the sour currants. I miss the rough good looks of the shrubs, the crushed leaves that smelled of cloves, roses and rue. How the clustered berries with their tart aftertaste popped in my mouth when I bit down on them.

No one I know grows currants anymore. And since I live in a region replete with white pines, I cannot in good conscience grow them myself. Currants are now known to be an alternate host to a dreaded fungal disease, white pine blister rust, and can only be safely raised a mile or more from those trees.

Fifty years have come and gone since the summers I spent with my Nana, who taught me so many things. To be honest, and daring; to be different, and confident. Not to kow-tow to the men. To speak up, and to give a fair day's work for a fair day's wage. And especially, to try anything, even if the first taste is sour.

Every now and again what's on my daily plate *is* sour. But usually, if I look hard enough, there's something to savor.

Red currant (Ribes rubrum)   Photo by Sue West

Description: Deciduous, upright, fruiting shrub native to northern Europe. Grows 3 feet to 5 feet tall and wide.

Favorites: 'Cherry Red', 'Red Lake'.

Zones: 3 to 8

Exposure: Full sun to part shade. Space 5 feet apart.

Soil: Best grown in organically rich, medium moisture, well-drained soil. Appreciates mulch; protect from drying winter winds.

Water: Regular watering to keep soil uniformly moist, but no overhead watering.

Fertilizer: None additional if planted in good soil.

Pruning: As needed, in dormancy. Recommended that all stems older than three years be removed.

Potential Problems: May take 3-5 years to produce. No serious insect issues, but is an alternate host to white pine blister rust. Fourteen states maintain bans on various types of Ribes species. It is best to avoid planting currants in locations where white pines grow unless rust-immune cultivars are used.

Interesting Asides: Can make an attractive ornamental hedge. Focal food for birds. Spicy leaves.

6

Dandelions

Dorothy Kennett Plimpton

"Fred, I can't stand these dandelions one more day! I just want to read in peace, and all I see are those blasted weeds staring me in the face!"

"Aw, honey, you know I'm busy," my long-suffering father replied. "What do you expect me to do about the dandelions?"

"Well, *something*, anything."

Over the nine years our family had lived at 71 East Main Street in Lima, New York, Dad had successfully wrested a lawn out of the wilderness of a forsaken farm by dint of sheer willpower and a whirring push mower. Each spring he reclaimed more of the gone-to-weed fields. The resulting green sward was increasingly used by sunbathing foster teens slippery with the coconut smell of suntan oil, by my clothes-hanging mom and grandma, and by hula-hooping children. The lawn was Dad's pride and joy, but by May the turf was generously speckled with bright yellow. The other weeds, the blue chicory, ground ivy and plantains, didn't bother Mother. It was the dandelions that got to her. My pretty, petite mother was emphatically NOT a horticulturalist. But she was frustrated.

When she failed to light a fire under my father, she turned to *her* father, Bill Kennett. No luck. Next she thoroughly discussed the issue with Nana. The one thing Mother would not do was tend to the problem herself. The entire household knew that for Mother, after slap-dash caring for four kids, and dinners of Chef Boyardee, but before housework, came reading. There was no time whatsoever for the yard.

Fickle upstate New York weather permitting, she best liked to read in the backyard, on the east side of the lawn, near murmuring Spring Creek. I remember her seated primly in a squeaky, springy, metal lawn chair (no sprawling allowed for virtuous Catholic women!), dressed in demure shorts and casual cotton blouse, cup of black coffee at the ready, book in hand. We kids were allowed to play as we might—our yard and land offered endless possibilities, and as long as we responded to the ricocheting clang of the dinner bell, we were presumed to be fine. Our freedom gave Mother the liberty to read her beloved books.

But the dandelions interfered. Red Nichols' hardware store didn't yet offer weed killer in a can, and anyway, there wasn't money for frivolities like combating weeds. Most families just lived with them. Mother, perhaps because she was raised in the city and was appreciative of an expanse of cool green grass, wanted a weed-free breadth over which to gaze as she rested her eyes from her latest book. But she considered everything about the lawn except enjoying it to be Dad's bailiwick. She believed *it should be perfect.* She didn't care all that much about a clean house, but a spotless lawn; that was another matter entirely.

At ten, I, her eldest child, was next in the persuading lineup.

On a bright May morning, I clattered down the back steps, clad in shorts and shirt, with my purple poppit beads around my neck, intent on initiating the daily search for another elusive four-leaf clover. I zoomed past Mother, who was hanging clothes on the line. She waved a sheet-draped arm at the side yard, stopping me in my tracks, and said, "Colleen, those dandelions are spoiling our grass."

Preoccupied by my determination to investigate a swatch of turf by the spirea, I barely heard her. I certainly didn't know what was coming.

"What's wrong with dandelions?" I said distractedly. "They look OK to me."

"They're weeds, and they don't belong in your father's lawn. I want you to get rid of them."

"How? There's about a million."

"I don't care, pick them, I guess."

"Aww, Mo-ther!"

A heartbeat of uncomfortable silence followed, and then she added, "I'll pay you."

That grabbed my attention. "You'll PAY me? How much?"

Four-leaf clovers forgotten, we decided on a nickel for each hundred blossoms... a small fortune. Something within the burgeoning gardener that was me niggled, silently advising that simply picking those dandelions wouldn't make a heck of a lot of difference; that they'd be back. I'd already learned from *Nature and Children*, the book my foster Aunt Joyce had given me the previous Christmas, that weeds like dandelions must be pulled out by the roots.

I didn't mention that fact to Mother.

The lure of those buffalo nickels was powerful. By the next morning I'd lopped the heads off two hundred dandelions, and already the lawn looked better, though my hands were stained by sticky, bitter white sap. I mounded the dandelions at various points in the backyard. Each morning I whooshed out of the kitchen after downing my cereal and dashed through the sun porch and down the rickety steps to the backyard to see how many more dandelions were in bloom. Quickly I beheaded them and added to my stash. I counted carefully, and though the piles soon wilted, I could account for each and every weed. At the end of the week I gathered them all in one strategic spot.

All two thousand of them.

"Colleen! Are you sure I owe you an entire DOLLAR? That's a lot of dandelions!"

The prospect of financial success was now scented with dread, and I hurried to answer, my words stumbling over themselves. "Yeah, Mother, two thousand. But you said a nickel a hundred, right? So that's a dollar. I counted them every day. There they are." I pointed to the slimy black mess under the elm tree, slowly suffocating Dad's green lawn.

She paid up, and for a short time (a very short time) Mother had a clean lawn to enjoy. And enjoy it she did. Those fine summer days her eclectic stash of reading material pyramided by her outdoor chair: the *Reader's Digest* Condensed Books, the history books and biographies, the memoirs and the stories of the saints.

We children soon learned to emulate our reading mother, and it became no easy feat to keep us supplied with reading material. Debbie had her *Cherry Ames, Student Nurse.* Jennie loved *Mike Mulligan and His Steam Shovel,* along with other Virginia Lee Burton stories. Ricky, baby that he was, favored *The Poky Little Puppy,* read to him by his big sisters.

Acquired from here and there, I had my *Wild Flowers of America,* my *New England Year,* and my Gene Stratton-Porter books, *Freckles* and *A Girl of the Limberlost.* I also owned bedraggled copies of Zane Grey, the Bobbsey Twins and of course, Nancy Drew.

But there were no bookstores in Lima in the 1950s, and we seldom traveled to Rochester, where there were. If we wanted access to more books, it was a lead-pipe cinch that we would become devotees of the Lima Public Library.

It was the era of one-car families, and Dad drove the English Ford to work each day. Our modest family walked uptown to the library, on the sidewalk along wide East Main Street, with the sheltering branches of mature horse chestnut trees above us.

Lima's streets were lined with gracious old homes, many of them Victorians built by well-to-do farmers who moved to town upon retiring from farming the fertile surrounding farmland. We passed many of these houses on our way to the library. Several sported cottage gardens out front, replete with four-o'clocks, geraniums and sweet peas. The walks to the library were my introduction to America's favorite flowers of the '50s.

Mr. Tousey's home, with the fishpond in the back, was the first interesting locale. Sometimes he'd entertain us by demonstrating how his goldfish would froth to the surface, mouths gaping, as he advanced with fish food.

Then up the hill, past Mr. Hennessey's grand yellow brick home, which had been a stagecoach stop back in the 1700s and still boasted grandeur foreign to our farm town. His landscape was more formal, with clipped boxwood and twinned planters on the veranda. Mr. Hennessey was rich, everybody knew that, but we children thought it odd that he wasn't married, and that only he and his old mother lived there.

We would then pass the Murphys' turreted home. Their son, in my class at St. Rose, had been born late in life to Lima's postmaster and his wife, and was that enviable anomaly in our Irish Catholic town, an only child.

Mrs. Murphy, a gracious, literate woman of generous proportions, was given to pretty flower beds of gillyflower and pinks in front of the latticework of her Queen Anne residence. I longed to linger and inhale their delicate scent, but Mother was generally in a hurry.

"Don't dilly-dally, Colleen!" Mother at times had an undersized appreciation of my curiosity, which had me edging up their sidewalk. "And don't trespass, either. Respect other people's property, for heaven's sake!"

So on we trooped, past the homes of Mr. Malloy, the high school principal, whose pretty wife had died so young, and Dr. Kober, who'd been doctoring my father's family since the First World War. Up past the Town Hall, built in 1880 and where the annual Memorial Day parade ended, when Taps were sounded, blank gunshots fired, names of the honored war dead read, and a wreath laid at the town monument. Past the firehouse with its too-small doors constructed for horses, not trucks. Around the corner of the commercial block, with its leaded glass windows and wooden steps. We would cross Rochester Street there, at Lima's single traffic light, and round the corner in front of the elegant Presbyterian Church, set regally back on its wide lawn under the steeple clock my dad, Baptist-turned-Catholic but employed by the Presbyterians, was charged with keeping in good repair.

Beecher Brothers Dry Goods, with its maple floors and shallow shelves of goods, stood catawampus to the church, and was owned by two elderly bachelor brothers. The smell of dry old wood and dry old men lingers to this day in my mind.

And finally, to the library. A walk of nearly a mile, just to get a week's worth of new books. Our town's collection was housed in the Beale building, erected in 1875 by Robert Beale. It had done duty as the Town Hall, a two-cell jail and a community voting place before becoming the Lima Public Library in 1923. Too small by the 1950s, still, it was where the books lived, and we loved it.

Once inside the vestibule, narrow stairs led up to the main reading room, which was manned by needle-faced Mrs. Mamie Bostwick. Dressed all in black, she commandeered the front desk in a room so still one could hear the pages turning. Her carriage was stern, her visage unsmiling, and the florescent lights made her appear sallow and frightening. She was my nemesis. Ever vigilant of the morals of Lima's children, she frequently challenged us on our selections.

"This book is a bit old for you, isn't it, missy?" Mrs. Bostwick said one day, regarding me with frosty disdain over her spectacles and holding the offending tome at arm's length. "I need to speak to your mother before I can permit you to check it out."

I backtracked into the stacks, found Mother, and tugged her to the front desk. Proud of my reading ability, Mother glanced at the title and gave the requisite permission. At the end of our visit that day, as I trooped back down the steep steps with my cache, I couldn't resist a victorious look over my shoulder in the general direction of Mrs. Bostwick.

Back home with our cargo, Mother settled in to read at her favorite spots. When she couldn't be in the backyard, she read in the living room on the east side of our old farmhouse, curled up in her plush armchair, with suntangles on the worn oriental carpet and dust motes dancing in the silent, still air.

By contrast, it didn't matter to me where I read. Wherever I could get a moment's peace and solitude from Debbie, Jennie and Ricky was deemed adequate. High in my home in the apple tree, with the dandelion lawn spread out below me, or nested among the white pines beyond the backyard. A large closet under the stairs was a favorite place, but I also read waiting for the ride to school, before class and at recess. I read in bed, at the kitchen table, and by the fly-specked windows in the attic. I read *Rebecca of Sunnybrook Farm*, *Little House on the Prairie*, *The Diary of Anne Frank*, and various encyclopedias (children's and Collier's). I read whatever I could get my hands on. And increasingly, I read my garden books, about nature, birds, butterflies, fish, weeds, rocks and soil. About growing vegetables and starting flowers. I asked for more, but there weren't many gardening books geared to children in the 1950s, and there wasn't much discretionary money in the Plimpton household.

In general, I coveted books. I scrounged everywhere for some to be my very own. I was given some of Nana's old books, a few hand-me-downs from wealthier cousins, and passalongs from school. One of the best hoards I ever found was out of the top floor of our house. The attic ran the length of the antiquated farmhouse, and was accessible by steep wooden stairs off my bedroom. The place was full of plunder: old trunks containing china dolls, antique Lincoln rockers, pictures in gilded frames, silver plated condiment servers. Tucked in under the eaves on the south side of the high-chambered room, across the splintery floor, I discovered three deserted boxes of books. Who had left them there? I didn't know, but it didn't matter. They were real hard-covered books! With fragile glassine pages and faded watercolor illustrations, covers coated as thick as lamb's fleece with dust. Full of tissue paper liners and bug spatters. Books in wooden boxes. Books no one seemed to want. And a copy of a 1924 book, *The Garden of a Commuter's Wife*, full of butterscotch pages about putting in a garden.

I was thrilled to the tips of my ten-year-old toes.

I lugged the books down the stairs several at a time, wedged them under my bed, and unbeknownst to my mother, wheedled a sturdy maple bookcase from my grandparents. That assumed a place of honor in the hall outside my bedroom. Carefully I placed the trove of books on the shelves and stood back to admire my handiwork. I was loaded. I owned 43 hardcover books. I know. I counted them so I could tell Sister Marie Ursula.

Task completed, I found Mother ironing in the kitchen, radio tuned to "The Edge of Night," the warm steam of the damping cloth under the iron hissing on the fabric-covered board. I watched as she wet her finger and lightly touched it to the hot surface of the iron. A plate of buttered saltine crackers lay on the enameled kitchen table, the snack we shared each day after school.

"Mother, you gotta come look at what I did!" She wiped her hands on her apron, turned off the iron and followed me up the stairs, where she stared in amazement at the crammed shelves.

"Where did you get all those?"

I had a moment's fear that she was going to lower the boom on me. "Remember the books I found in the attic?" I answered. "The ones you said must have been left by the Slatterys and that I might as well have? Here they are. I'm rich!"

And so it was that my wealth came to be measured in books. Today, as a professional gardener, it still is. My wealth is in books about wildflowers and perennials, about worms and butterflies. In books that instruct the gardener in coordinating tints and hues, and how to use ornamentation wisely. Books by Sydney Eddison and Ann Lovejoy. Books on how to build with stone and how to plan a vegetable garden. How to start seeds and build a fishpond. My bookshelves sag with gardening books; the tattered tomes of my childhood, and beautiful coffee-table books about roses and hydrangeas. Collections of essays by authors gone now. Compilations of perennials, annuals, the What-to-Do-This-Month-in-the-Garden books. The stories of plant lust and flower envy. The shambled, dog-eared reference books. I love them all. I know I have too many, but when the library leftover sales roll around each summer, I heed their siren song, and I'm there with my canvas bag, making a beeline to "Gardening." I'll never use all the books I own, and each year I vow to restrain myself in the future.

But who knows? I might just find another book on how to combat dandelions.

Those yellow weeds ultimately won the war in our backyard in Lima, and to this day I battle them at my Connecticut home. My techniques, however, have evolved from childish beheading. As a young adult I regularly sprinkled them with granular weed killer. In later years came spot weeding from a spray can. As I've become more aware of the dangers of chemicals, my present methodology is the best. In April, as the lawn greens up, I note the location of each dandelion plant. Since the ground is moist in early spring, that's when I attack. With either a narrow-gauge trowel or a handy-dandy dandelion puller given to me by a favorite horticulture student, Misti Pattison, I stealthily close in on the unwelcome visitor, plunge my tool into the ground, simultaneously tilt and yank, and voila! Out comes the interloper, taproot and all. I temporarily leave the weed draped on the lawn as I scout other marauders, and when I've completed the circuit, it's an easy matter to glance over the grass, gather up the now-wilted weeds and toss them into the compost.

Books, whether gardening tomes, classics, or contemporary novels, have been a constant throughout my life. They came with me when I arrived at college in suburban New York City. They moved with me to a commune in Pennsylvania; a primitive stone house in upstate New York; and a former bungalow colony in the Catskills. When I acquired a husband with a wandering career, they went with me to West Virginia, Indiana, California, New Jersey and at last, to Connecticut. But perhaps most significant is how my books link me securely to the past. They've jumped the tracks of history, and my memory races down the years as I recall the dandelion days with Mother, when thanks to her, my love of books and gardening bloomed, when we peacefully read in a long-ago, yellow-flowered backyard.

Dandelion (Taraxacum officinale)

Photo by Sue West

Description: Deep, tap-rooted biennial or herbaceous perennial native to temperate regions of the Northern Hemisphere in the Old World. Leaves form a basal rosette. Flowers are yellow to orange. Flower heads mature into spherical "clocks" (aka "wishies") which disperse in the wind.

Zones: 3 to 8.

Exposure: Sun.

Soil: Prefers rich soil but will grow almost anywhere.

Water: Not fussy.

Fertilizer: Please don't!

Pruning: Not necessary.

Potential Problems: Will take over if allowed to freely reseed. For organic removal, taproot must be removed.

Interesting Asides: The name "dandelion" is a corruption of the French *dent de lion*, referring to the corrugated leaves which are said to resemble the teeth of the lion. Dandelion wine is considered a delicacy in some cultures.

7

German Bearded Iris

Ralph and Elva Plimpton

Thou are the Iris, fair among the fairest,
Who, armed with golden rod
And winged with the celestial azure, bearest
The message of some God

—Henry Wadsworth Longfellow

My paternal grandfather didn't like me much. But then, he didn't like my brother and sisters either. He'd certainly never been fond of his older son, my father, and the deal was sealed in 1947 when Dad chose a Roman Catholic wife. Ralph Plimpton immediately, irrevocably and everlastingly detested Dorothy Kennett Plimpton.

Standing only 5 feet 2, with a bad comb-over and a nervous jigging leg, Grandpa was a strange duck. He had a fierce intelligence and abundant disdain for most of humanity, not just Catholics and children. He despised Jews, blacks, Asians and teachers equally. A farmer's son, Ralph finished his education at 8th grade, labored at various jobs, and became an itinerant preacher in his teens. Which is how he met my grandmother. A pretty, big-boned country gal, she worked as a maid at the House farm in Avon.

Nine months into Ralph and Elva's 1922 marriage, my dad was born at Elva's childhood home in Lima. Grandma might have loved her son, but since she was firmly affixed under Ralph's thumb, no one had a chance to find out. By the age of eight months, my father, a failure to thrive, had been relinquished to his maternal grandmother.

His parents moved three towns over and seldom visited. This was to be a pattern through the years of his growing up. Though his parents returned to Lima, Dad was never allowed to call them "Mother" and "Father," and was regularly given to relatives. A younger son, Frank, was kept. By the age of six, however, Dad was considered good enough to work for Ralph doing odd jobs, and of course was expected to hand over the pittance he made.

My mother, amateur psychologist that she was, always suspected that my dad's abrupt arrival had shortened Ralph's vagabond life, shackled him to a woman he considered his inferior, and generally soured him. But during my childhood in the 1950s, such theories were barely whispered, never discussed aloud.

Grandma and Grandpa Plimpton lived a mere three blocks from us, yet they never once set foot in our house. As a family we were allowed to visit them only on Christmas Eve. Lima was a small town; if at other times of the year I happened upon either of my grandparents, at Red Nichols' hardware store or the Marine Midland Bank, I was instructed to nod politely. They didn't always respond, but I tried.

In warm weather I'd sometimes pass their home in the elbow of Elm Street, on my way to Roundtree's Corner Store or up to visit my friend Ann Spencer. I would often stop there on the sidewalk, fascinated by the walnut trees in the yard, with their black bark and the green-husked fruits scattered on the skimpy lawn. In the spring I could catch the barest glimpse of Grandma's iris, which my dad referred to as flags. Old-fashioned peonies leaned by the front porch, weighed down with bloom in June, and pink roses rambled on the kitchen fence. All this I could see from the street. But if Ralph and Elva ever noticed their eldest grandchild studying their house, they never came out to greet me.

My mother, every bit a match for Ralph in intelligence and obstinacy, loathed them in return. But since she saw the pair so infrequently, my dad bore the brunt of her fury.

"Fred! How can you put up with this?" she'd say, rage gathering like a hurricane. "We have four children, THEIR grandchildren. Their only grandchildren! Wouldn't you think they'd want to see them? And wouldn't you think Elva could help out with the babysitting every now and again?"

"Now, honey, I'm never going to change them," my father would reply. "Ralph has always been as mean as an old goat. If I say anything, it'll just make it worse."

Mother, frustrated at my father's lack of action, furious at Ralph's contempt, and uncomprehending at Elva's spinelessness, nursed her resentment for years.

Until the day it turned to astonishment.

Abruptly, at age ten, I became interesting to Ralph. The Sisters of St. Joseph at St. Rose Parochial school were take-no-prisoners taskmasters, and I learned well. I was the youngest in my class, but only John Murphy got better marks. The *Lima Recorder* chronicled my continuous presence on the Honor Roll, and it had apparently come to Ralph's attention. He deigned to speak to my parents one day and asked if I might visit them upon occasion. Mother, suspicious of his intentions, but hoping for the possibility of Plimpton grandparents at last for us, agreed, but insisted Debbie come along too.

In the winter of 1960, my next-one-down sister and I saw Ralph and Elva at their home once a week. On the appointed evenings Deb and I, bundled up like cats on the way to the vet, would walk from our home on East Main Street to Maple Avenue and turn onto Elm, following the sidewalk on the north side of the street. We were greeted at the kitchen doorway of the Plimptons' brick colonial and ushered into their small, overstuffed front room with its gas fired heater and red glass chandelier. Dark heavy drapes hung at the windows; a stereopticon with pictures of long ago lay untouched on the marble-topped table. The smell of old dust and faded wallpaper permeated the air. Grandpa rocked in his small platform rocker, Little Friend the Chihuahua on his lap, while Grandma served us juice and cookies and made awkward chit-chat.

"What do you think of that there Elvis fellow?" she inquired with a smile one evening. "He sure moves around a lot!"

We had to admit that our parents didn't let us watch him. She nodded in approval.

Over time, the previous ten years of ignoring us melted away. Our grandparents were curious about their two eldest grandchildren, and gracious, and mostly kind.

Grandpa decided that Grandma should teach us crafts. The tick tock of cuckoo clocks entertained us as we first learned the fine art of fabricating putty jars. We'd never before (or since) seen one, but the process enthralled. Grandma schlepped out pasteboard cartons of small items: old keys, tiny metal license plates, marbles, rhinestones, pretty pebbles, miniature plastic flowers, and trinkets from their travels. Given sturdy ceramic jars, Debbie and I slathered on a thick layer of Atlas putty from a metal tube and pressed our chosen tidbits into the sides. One side one week, another the week following, turning the jar. Gradually the vessels became testimony to our individual taste and artistry. They were, however, fairly useless except to hold other small objects that could perhaps someday be made into putty jars.

Next up were lessons in chair caning. Grandpa had resolved by that time that I was to receive favored-grandchild status and learn the skill. Debbie, whom Ralph had admonished to stop biting her fingernails, be less shy, and speak up more clearly, was relegated to also-ran, and thereafter visited less often.

The seat-weaving came about because Grandma and Grandpa enjoyed collecting antiques, and they possessed many chairs whose cane seats needed replacing. It was Grandpa's idea to have Grandma teach me the dexterous art of caning chairs. My nimble young fingers manipulated the sharp splines and miniature pegs, while he jiggled his leg and told stories of Plimpton generations long gone. He pontificated on the genealogy work he'd done, showing me the onionskin paper dimpled with his heavy typewriting and strike-outs. He'd oddly focused not on 300 years of Plimptons in America, but on a tenuous relationship our family had with the firebrand preacher Cotton Mather.

However, my questions on the history elicited his approval. "I heard you were smart, Colleen," he said. "You are. That's all well and good at the Sister school. But here's what I want you to do when you get to the high school. You *show* them that the Plimptons are smart."

Winter wore on, and lessons in candle-making followed putty jars and caning. Grandpa supervised while Grandma taught me how to dip, layer, and season candle wax to make new tapers. Some of these we lit upon completion, and the soft burr of candlelight softened my grandparents' features.

As spring drew near and the days lengthened, Grandma and I ventured out to the yard, and I saw close up those plants, trees and flowers I'd admired from afar. My grandmother was fond of large flowered housedresses that emphasized her 30 extra pounds and the soft flab of her upper arms. Her pockets held clippings of Lenten roses, snips of herbs, an early spear of asparagus. Her wiry gray hair, bound by a net, was perpetually untidy and became more so as she wiped her brow in the spring warmth. She had a large, open face, with a warm smile for her grandchild, especially when Grandpa wasn't looking. Her eyes were pale, though, as if too many years of living had washed the blue away. On gardening, as in all subjects, she'd quickly demur that she knew not much about anything. Grandpa never disagreed.

In April, as the iris began to sprout sharp green leaves, Grandma dug some rhizomes, dumped them in a paper bag, and quickly, unceremoniously, handed them to me. "The old-timers say that flags are messengers, Colleen. I want you to have these."

Her message came through loud and clear.

My grandfather died of a stroke that June. But the brief time we two generations overlapped created relationships and lifelong interests. While it didn't improve upon how my parents and grandparents felt about each other, our visits had created a bond between Ralph and Elva and Debbie and me, one that I still feel 50 years later.

They never became doting grandparents. They still didn't babysit. There were no birthday gifts or phone calls or impromptu visits. But putty jars and candles and iris served another purpose. They helped me to forgive my grandparents their decision, until almost too late, to ignore their grandchildren. I learned the lesson that there was goodness in whatever they were willing to give.

That was one of the messages of the iris. Over the years I've discovered there were others, such as gratitude that from my grandmother, among others, I acquired an early love and knowledge of green growing things, and that from my grandfather I acquired an appreciation of antiques and a curiosity about my family history. And it would have pleased him to no end that in 1966 I was the Lima High School valedictorian.

They're all gone now, my grandparents, the iris bed and even my mother, who so hated her in-laws that she took the grudge to her grave. My grandfather, who spread such unhappiness, has been dead for 50 years, and still my father, old and frail at 87, has nothing good to say of him.

Grandma died in May of her 100th year, when the amelanchier bloomed white in the mountains of her beloved upstate New York. The added decades gave sufficient time to solidify a once-fragile relationship with a girl grandchild who learned to love flowers in part through wondrous visits to the house on Elm Street.

At the end of her life, when extreme old age had taken its toll on her flesh, when hugging her felt like embracing bird bones bound in wool, I thanked Grandma one last time for all she had done for me.

And I still grow iris.

Iris   Photo by Jerry Shike

Description: Perennial rhizomatous flowering plant; a traditional garden flower also known as "flag." Blooms in spring on long erect stems.

Favorites: 'Batik', 'Beverly Sills', 'Fringe Benefits'.

Zones: 3 to 9.

Exposure: Full sun. Leave rhizome tops exposed.

Soil: Not fussy, though rich, organic is best. Good drainage is essential.

Water: Sparingly.

Fertilizer: Iris are heavy feeders. Fertilize 2-3 times per year with bulb fertilizer. Sprinkle around plants, but be careful not to harm rhizome.

Pruning: Remove bloom stalk and dead blossoms after blooming. If desired, entire plant can be cut down to 6 inches at that time.

Potential problems: Iris borer. Look for notch marks on edge of leaves in spring, and failure to thrive in plants. If suspected, dig out tuber, examine for holes. The borer is large (3-4 inches), bright pink and segmented. To destroy, poke wire into hole. If bed is infested, it may be prudent to discard entire planting and start over. To prevent further infestation, be assiduous with cleanup in fall; borer overwinters in litter and in spring climbs up iris leaf, enters the leaf and begins to travel down to tuber. It may be destroyed by squeezing leaf between thumb and forefinger.

Interesting Asides: New iris breeding has produced plants which re-bloom, especially if deadheaded. Iris come in many colors, which is one reason they are associated with the rainbow. They also are the symbol of the mental health movement.

8

Lily of the Valley

Dorothy and Sylvalan (Fred) Plimpton

"Pleeease, Mother! Why *can't* I have them?"

The Saturday morning hubbub of the local IGA swirled around me. I was oblivious. I couldn't hear the chattering of the housewives in their belted dresses and low heels, the thwack of the butcher's knife on his maple board, or the rumble of the produce cart laden with lettuce, rhubarb and radishes. I ignored the other girls in their cotton frocks and sturdy oxfords, hanging onto their mom's grocery wagons, alternately bellyaching and laughing. The heady talk in that Irish Catholic slice of upstate New York of JFK's run for the presidency spun above my head.

I was focused on my own campaign.

Most 11-year old girls who accompanied their mothers to the grocery store in 1960 coveted the gimcracks that dropped from the gumball machine, or begged for frilly socks in cellophane packages, or whined for Sugar Smacks or Sugar Frosted Flakes.

Not me. What I wanted was the wooden flat of lily-of-the-valley pips that sat just outside the store in the early-spring sunshine, beside the gunnysacks of chicken feed, the hay rakes and the bee-hive supplies. The lily-sweet flowers were familiar to me from walks uptown, but I'd never seen them for sale, and the green leaves emerging from the dark dirt under the awning of the IGA promised the scented white flowers to come. My hands, grubby from the first-of-the-season Creamsicle I'd recently devoured, caressed the rough wooden crate holding the longed-for plants.

"Please, Mother, I'll take care of them. Cross my heart and hope to die."

Though not herself a gardener, Mother did not discourage my interest in all things horticultural. She gazed over my head for a long moment, then checked the billfold in her snap-clutch pocketbook, lifted a weary hand from the heavy grocery cart and waved me on. "Oh, go ahead, get them if you want. But they'll be your responsibility, you know. Not mine, not your sisters' and not your father's."

I grinned with pleasure and gave her a hug. "I know, and I'll take care of them, I promise. Thank you, Mother!"

I dragged the box into the store, proudly hoisted it onto the clerk's conveyor belt and, once it was paid for, traipsed my treasure to the car. My first perennials.

The smell of warm earth from the box balanced on my lap mixed with the organic scent of asparagus from the paper sack in the back seat and filled the English Ford as we drove the six miles home.

"How did 'lily-of-the-valley' get that funny name, Mother?" I asked. "What does it mean?"

"They've been around for a long, time, Colleen. My grandmother used to grow them; I remember her saying something about the saints. You'll have to look it up to make sure." Teacher that she was, this was a standard answer.

Our expansive lawn held several large lilacs, a ring of variegated hosta around the front porch, old roses out back, and spirea marching up from the creek. Most of these we'd inherited from the Slattery family, the previous homeowners. I admired and tended to them sporadically, but I'd long wanted my own flowers. Now that I had some, it was up to me to plant them. But where? I pondered as I looked out the window at others' flower beds whizzing by in East Avon and the outskirts of Lima.

When we got home, I rested my plants on the porch, consulted my rudimentary garden books, and learned that lilies-of-the-valley like shade and moisture. The east side of the house, up against the stone foundation of the cellar, seemed perfect. The bed would face the creek and be neighbor to the snowball bush and the porch hostas. It would be cool there, I figured. The cellar, that dark, musty place full of old stoneware crocks, leftover farm implements, and our coal bin, was always refreshingly chilly even on the hottest summer days. The various rooms with their nooks and crannies made good hiding places for games of hide and seek. Lilies-of-the-valley were old-fashioned plants, I reasoned, and they'd be happy close to an old-fashioned cellar.

I wished the gift of my new plants had included somebody showing me how and where to plant, but alas, I was on my own. I dug the bed with a rusty coal-scoop shovel, not designed for gardening, but the only shovel I could find. The soil was stony next to the foundation. It resisted my efforts. I wasn't sure how deep to dig, so I stopped after about two inches. I had no fertilizer nor soil amendments, and didn't know any was needed. Our place had been a dairy farm for a hundred years before us, so the clay soil was mercifully naturally amended with cow manure. I laid the roots of my silver-white bells in their new home.

The lily-of-the-valley bloomed that June, white and nodding and oh-so-fragrant. I couldn't believe they were mine. I harvested bouquets for Mother and then a tiny jar full for the nuns at school. I lay on the grass in front of the patch and inhaled the scent, marveling at how the bells dangled from impossibly delicate stems. I admired the green of the pointed leaves, and how the flowers, with their scalloped edges, were pure white with green centers. The incipient garden designer in me realized that an entire rectangular bed of just lily-of-the-valley was not exactly the way to go, but I was enthralled with my plants, and proud of my green thumb.

Weeding, however, wasn't my specialty. And I wasn't crazy about the earthworms who shared the soil. And so, after the flowers bloomed, the patch grew straggly and became a catch-all for discarded toys. My dad warned me to fix the bed, or he'd fix it himself.

This was the first year our family spent the summer at Blue Pond in an attempt to escape the annual Kennett horde that descended on us in the country late each June. In the exhilaration of a summer cottage and new friends, my flower garden was quickly forgotten. Dad came back to the house once a week or so to mow the lawn, and upon returning to the Pond, he'd remind me of the disheveled state of my flower bed. Busy with my exciting life among new friends, I continued to ignore him.

Summer passed in a delightful blur, and before we knew it, it was time to depart for home and school. We packed up the cottage, drove the 20 miles to Lima, pulled in the driveway and amid the squabbling, carried armloads of clothes, cookware and leftover food into the house.

It was the next day before I could get outside to make the garden circuit. How much had my favorite tree grown over the past ten weeks? How well had the hydrangea bloomed? Were there any more berries, or had the critters gotten them all?

I sauntered over to the east side of the house to check the creek level. On the way back, as I came near to my lilies-of-the-valley, adrenaline surged through me like water over a dam.

My garden was gone.

Not just gone to weeds, not just gone to seed, but *gone*. Mowed flat. My murdered plants had clearly been repeatedly rasped by lawnmower blades; short grass was growing up where bloom stalks had been. I knew at first glance that there would never be any more flowers from my first garden, my wooden crate of lily-of-the-valley. It was ruined.

I went tearing into the house, anger billowing. My father was repairing a leak under our kitchen sink. "Dad! Dad!" I shouted. "How *could* you?"

He glanced up from his work, hands covered with plumber's putty. "Colleen, I told you back in the spring when you let the lilies go after they bloomed that the bed was getting weedy."

"But, but..." I sputtered, metaphorical black robes flapping. "That was MY garden! You had no right!"

He wiped a sweaty arm across his forehead. "Now wait just a minute. You were pretty busy all summer with the kids at the Pond. I invited you to come along every time I came back to mow." He looked down at his hands, stained with grease. "You never did, so the flowers had to go. I'm sorry. But you have to take care of what you plant."

As angry as I was, the rightness of his statement seared itself into my brain. So much so that I never again neglected a garden bed, wherever I've gardened, whatever I've grown. Over the years I've learned to respect the needs of growing things, not to let other endeavors get in the way of my plants' requirements. Better yet, I've discovered that I find pleasure in tending to them. I've learned to mulch and to water and to weed. I've taught myself to identify predators and disease, and how to reckon with them. I've learned that the best fertilizer is the gardener's shadow.

And with all the knowledge comes that delightful suspension of care and worry when one is in the garden. The freedom to hear not the traffic, but the breeze whispering in the ferns, and the scritch of the wild turkeys as they hunt for insects below the white pine, and the tiny splash in the fishpond as the green frog leaps in at my footfalls. The freedom to not mourn what Nature has taken, but to revel in what has grown successfully. The freedom to feel pride in what I produce.

I learned to love caretaking the living things that depend on me.

Most importantly, I learned responsibility.

Photo from Wikipedia.com

Lily-of-the-Valley
(Convallaria majalis)

Description: Small, sweet-smelling, white-flowering perennial that blooms in spring.

Favorites: 'Rosea' is pink; 'Fortin's Giant', at 12 inches, is larger than the species.

Zones: 3 to 7.

Exposure: Partial shade.

Soil: Rich, organic.

Water: Appreciates extra moisture.

Fertilizer: A scattering of granular fertilizer in early spring, and an application of compost in the fall.

Pruning: Not needed, though some plants may need to be rogued out if they become invasive.

Potential Problems: If planted in too much sun or inadequate moisture, plants may go dormant. If allowed to go to seed, plant bears bright red berries which are poisonous to humans.

Interesting Asides: Some horticulturists believe lily-of-the-valley is an American native. The European name comes from devotion to the Blessed Virgin, as the pendant flowers are said to resemble the Virgin's tears.

9

Morning Glory

Carol Corlett

"How old are you?" the slight-built girl with the straight hair shouted from the next yard. My family and I, four kids and two parents, were filing single file, arms saddled with household goods, into our newly-constructed summer cabin on the shores of tiny Blue Pond, in Scottsville, New York. The sharp smell of raw wood combined with the interesting tang emanating from lumps of freshwater seaweed heaped by the water.

I hesitated, scuffed the beaten earth, turned pink, and considered an answer. What if she wasn't speaking to *me*? What if I'd misunderstood her?

"Eleven," I finally mumbled, and shuffled into the cabin with my load of clothes. When I came out, the girl had disappeared.

Maybe we were too strange a sight for her. We four kids *were* an odd assemblage that morning in 1960. I, the eldest child, a timid, bookish girl. My tall, beautiful sister, Debbie, one year younger. Next came Jennie, named after a Genesee beer jingle popular in the '50s, with a personality to match. Last was Ricky, the blonde, the baby, the boy. All of us marching lockstep from the car to the cabin in an unwavering wheeling, under the direction of our mother, the Director.

Not quite as poor as church mice, our family nonetheless could rival them. Dad was an office machine repairman, and Mother taught 7th grade at the local public school. Teachers were still mostly female then and still made mostly meager wages. We'd been living in our ramshackle old house in my dad's hometown, and though we kids loved the rural setting with its creek, woods, cow pasture and potato fields, my parents grew restive when Mother's folks descended from Rochester to stay each June. The old Victorian, big as it was, wasn't big enough for us all.

After ten years of summer togetherness, Mother had figured a way out. She raided her pension, our piggy banks and dime savings accounts, and hustled together $1200; enough to purchase a small building lot on a tiny lake a few towns west. She was determined to escape her parents.

The first June and July we camped on the lot sporadically and didn't manage to meet the neighbors. By midwinter, Mother had scrounged enough money to buy a log cabin kit, which my dad ineptly started constructing that spring. It was into this summer home that the parade of Plimptons was moving when Carol Corlett hollered at me.

Our cabin was composed of only three rooms and a primitive bath. It had no wallboard, no paint, and a muddy dented yard. Even I knew it was ugly. I decided to improve the look of things.

Where I got the idea, the initiative, or the seeds has been forgotten. But from somewhere I acquired a paper packet of morning glory seeds. I dug holes in the dirt surrounding our flimsy front porch and dropped them in, one by one.

To everyone's astonishment (including mine), they grew. They grew so much that they soon needed support, and my dad showed me how to affix string from the ground to the roof and help the seedlings climb. They agreeably did so, and twisted enthusiastically in on themselves, reaching for the sky.

And then they bloomed. And bloomed. Kids and parents alike marveled at my handiwork, asked me how I'd done it, asked me to teach them. Those morning glories were my first taste of success and identity as a gardener, and I loved the attention. A shy, solitary child in my hometown, the morning glories helped me to ease into friendship with the kids of the Pond. Over the years we didn't see our summer pals from September till the following June, but the memory of them lingers forevermore in the quiet recesses of my heart. Patty Morris. Mark and David Susser. Linda Atkins. The Jones family. Darcy and Doug Lester. And of course, Carol Corlett.

All that first summer a haze of blue morning glories shimmered on the side of our porch as we Plimpton kids stormed the cabin at noontimes, looking for a peanut-butter-and-jelly sandwich to fuel the remainder of the day. Their deep azure echoed the aptly named Blue Pond and were a backdrop to the activities of our tangle of friends as we swam in the deep waters, dove off splintery wooden docks, upended canoes, explored the inlet and the outlet, lit bonfires on the 4th of July, and discussed how best to tan.

We were outdoors kids, reveling in the freedom that comes with fealty to Mother Nature. We had no patience for *Mighty Mouse* and *Popeye* of the Saturday morning cartoons, nor even of that new dance craze, the Twist. We belonged outdoors. At Blue Pond *I* belonged, and I felt light and strong and ran with the others all that tumbled summer.

The morning glories offered fewer and fewer blooms as the days grew shorter. The scant flowers bore a tinge of purple in the cool mornings, and the first willow leaves turned yellow and drifted down onto the lawn. The asters and goldenrod bent under the weight of bees, their sharp dry smell a reminder that the remaining days of freedom were few, and that we kids would soon return to the schoolroom.

But a gardener had been born that summer, and a friendship begun.

We now live hundreds of miles apart, but I still see Carol Corlett Bartold once a year or so. Nowadays it's for lunch in some quiet restaurant instead of the dock at Blue Pond. But when we're together, we're teens again. We chortle over old times and share black and white pictures of ourselves as awkward youngsters. *Were we really that thin? Did we really dress like that?* And *Have you been to the Pond lately?* Or *Whatever happened Harry Richards?* We shake our heads in amazement at how the years have fled, the memories escaped.

We have changed.

And yet, our friendship endures. Women now, we are nonetheless still morning glories, still entwined, supporting each other, as women do, and still reaching for the sky.

Morning Glory (Ipomea tricolor)

Photo by Sue West

Description: Annual vine which blooms in shades of white, pink, red and blue. May grow 8 feet to 10 feet on its twining stem. Flowers open in early morning and fade by midday.

Favorites: 'Heavenly Blue', 'Scarlett O'Hara'.

Zones: Cannot tolerate frost; grows as annual zones 3 to 10.

Exposure: Full sun.

Soil: Ordinary, not excessively fertile.

Water: Sparingly.

Fertilizer: None needed.

Pruning: None needed unless vines encroach on other plantings.

Potential problems: Nick seeds prior to planting, or soak overnight to soften seed coat. Slugs may devour seedlings; if so, place each seedling in a copper collar; the metal acts as a repellent. Once the seedlings reach 1½ feet slugs no longer bother them. In certain locales morning glory and its relatives are deemed invasive.

10

Cauliflower

Frank Plimpton

"Gee whiz, Colleen, I never was much of a gardener. What do you want to know?"

Uncle Frank Plimpton, his once-strong body bent, his glorious white thick hair shaved to stubble by the cut-rate nursing home staff, his useless feet shuffling ceaselessly under the wheelchair, looked up just past my eyes with his characteristic half smile.

My dad and I were visiting his brother at the skilled nursing facility to which Frank had been discharged subsequent to yet another hospital stay. I'd asked him for his recollections of the sumptuous vegetable garden he grew in his back yard in Honeoye Falls, New York from the 1950s through the 1980s.

Finding Uncle Frank had taken some doing. Communication between the brothers had never been optimal, and the new, stringent privacy rules didn't help. Dad and I were delighted to finally sign in at the front door of the facility and realize that the quest had ended. He was here. We weren't too late.

We'd arrived right after the noon meal, and as we struggled down the interminable corridor, past TV's blaring from the too-warm rooms, past the shrunken bodies slumped in chairs outside their doors, the odor of the post-lunch diaper change followed us down the hall. We ignored it, though Dad shook his head in distaste as he began to worry anew.

"I hope Frank knows us. I wish we'd gotten here sooner. I hope he talks to us."

He needn't have fretted. As we turned into Room 211, Frank greeted us with grateful astonishment.

"Colleen! And who's this old guy you've brought along?"

And so the visit started.

"Now, Uncle Frank, I remember what a gardener you were," I said. "I remember you grew carrots and beans and potatoes, beets and tomatoes and parsnips. I remember how the garden took up your whole backyard, and I remember you taught me how to blanch cauliflower."

He glanced at me with renewed interest. "You remember that, huh? It was a long time ago."

It *was* a long time ago… 45 years, in fact, since I'd first laid eyes on Uncle Frank's vegetable garden behind his home on Maplewood Avenue in Honeoye Falls, New York. I was 14, and until that day in 1963 I'd had no idea his backyard held such extravagance.

Mother and I were on a rare visit to Uncle Frank and Aunt Vivian, and I'd been shooed to the backyard, where my uncle was tending his crops. If anyone had been looking out the multipaned windows of the kitchen into the garden where I stood spellbound that day, they'd have seen a skinny teenager with unruly brown hair, wearing hand-me-down denims and sporting green harlequin eyeglasses. A teenager more interested in agitating for a color TV to watch *The Beverly Hillbillies* and *Ponderosa* than in visiting relatives. But something about the backyard called to me.

At first I just stood there, amazed at the masses of corn, beets, spinach, tomatoes and celery, arrayed in rows seemingly as far as the eye could see. The orderly grass paths between the beds beckoned, and I followed. I stroked the silky skin of the tomatoes, smelled the basil, acquired a scarlet beet stain on my hand as I turned a leaf. I flicked a potato bug, admired the lacy outline of spent pea tendrils, measured myself against the statuesque sweet corn, and then glanced over where my uncle was bent over the cauliflower.

"You've got a lot of things growing here, Uncle Frank."

He looked at me as if I'd sprouted horns. "You interested in gardening?"

"Well, yeah," I admitted. "Some, anyway. But I've never seen such a big one."

"C'mon over here, I'll show you something."

I hesitated. While Aunt Vivian was as strong-willed as she was small, and often chatty, Uncle Frank was an odd man, an obliging, silent-Cal type who seldom spoke. At least, not to me. He and my dad always seemed to be on the outs, so I'd never spent much time with him. And I was creeped out by what I knew of his part-time job: hauling dead bodies from the hospital to the local funeral parlor.

But I was a good, obedient girl. I walked over to him, stood several feet away, and peered down into the row. Cauliflower was not a vegetable that appeared often on our dining room table. I'd never seen it in its natural state, and I was intrigued to observe that it grew in a compact nest of big green leaves.

"See here, this center part?" Uncle Frank pulled apart the leaves with a knotted hand (which lacked an index finger, I noted). "That's the egg. It'll grow into the head, which is what I'll pick in a few weeks."

I squinted into the center of the plant. What he was referring to was a cluster of white buds about two inches around.

Uncle Frank pulled a length of twine from the back pocket of his overalls.

"What are you going to do with that?"

"Watch."

I stared intently as he gently brought leaves on either side of the knobby, round head together over the top of the plant and tied them with the twine.

"Now the sun won't get at it, and it'll blanch."

"Blanch?"

"Means 'turn white,' 'cause it won't get no sun. Folks like the heads better that way."

I knew that cauliflower at the IGA produce counter was white, and that most vegetables were green, but I'd never stopped to wonder why.

"Or," he continued, turning to the next plant, "here's another way to keep it white. Just fold the big leaves over the egg, like a tent." He demonstrated, taking several outer leaves up and over the growing white head of the vegetable. "Tuck the ends under, so as to keep them in place, leave 'em there until the head's ready to pick, and you've got yourself a nice, round white head of cauliflower."

"What happens if you don't cover the heads?"

"Not much, really. They'll be greenish, that's all. Don't make me no never mind, but Vivian, she likes her cauliflower white. So I keep her happy."

"How do you know when the whole thing's ready to pick?"

"Thump it, like this." He tapped the small head with a knobby knuckle. "When it's ready, it'll sound full."

"And what do you do with it once it's cut?"

"I high-tail it into the kitchen, and Vivian'll steam it or cook it up into soup. Good either way."

A hummingbird whizzed by my left ear on its way to the honeysuckle draped over the side of the garage. Uncle Frank un-folded himself, straightened up, and pointed to another row.

"Let's go take a look at the tomatoes."

I trotted along beside him as he explained that something had been at the tomato leaves and he needed to inspect the planting carefully. We stood in front of the tomato patch, whose fruit was blushing pink. "Just stand here, and see what you see."

I did as I was told, and saw nothing.

"Lookee here." He pointed at a large green lump which lay on top of a vine. It was the same middle green as the stem and leaves, and lozenge-shaped, about six inches long.

As I watched, it moved.

I jumped back. "What *is* it?"

"Tomato hornworm. And it'll take a tomato plant down to skeleton quicker than you can say 'Cracker Jack.' " He pulled the worm off the plant, tossed it to the ground and stepped on it. "No more trouble from him."

We were headed to the strawberries when Mother, hands on her hips, called to me from the driveway. Too soon, too soon.

"Colleeeen! Time to go."

Aunt Vivian was nowhere to be seen.

Uncle Frank looked past me. "You better get along. Your mother isn't the patient type. But come round here more often, Colleen. I can maybe show you some more about gardening."

I badly wanted to come back, to learn more about vegetable gardening. I knew that he could teach me how to grow those sweet-tasting little tomatoes. Maybe he could help me figure out how to dig up a patch of our side yard and persuade my parents to let me plant a few vegetables. Maybe...

But even as I wished, I knew it was not to be. It'd be a cold day in down under before we'd be back. Mother had probably squabbled again with Aunt Vivian. The next time I'd see Uncle Frank would be the annual obligatory gathering at Grandma's. At Christmas time, when there'd be neither thought nor discussion of gardening.

As a child, I wasn't sure what the ongoing problem was between my parents and Frank and Vivian. My aunt and uncle never had children, and maybe that was one reason the two families had so little in common. During the infrequent times we saw them, they seemed simultaneously repelled and fascinated by the loud group of siblings that constituted my parents' brood.

And yet, when we were very small children, before disagreements drove a wedge between the brothers, there used to be visits to our home in Lima, only four miles, but a world away from the perceived sophistication of Honeoye Falls. Lima, one town south but in a different, more rural county, lacked the genteel atmosphere of its neighbor. I just knew that rich people lived in Honeoye Falls, but I wasn't sure if Uncle Frank and Aunt Vivian fit that category. They shared a pretty clapboard house on a residential, tree-lined street with Vivian's parents, John and Ada Zuber. The Zubers had been well-to-do dairy farmers, but produced no sons, and so in 1945 they sold the family farm and moved to town.

The Plimpton brothers' ongoing strife was a legacy, perhaps, from their angry, punitive father. Though only a year apart in age, the boys were never encouraged by their father, Ralph, to get along. Instead, they were forced to work at odd jobs during the Depression, sacrificing their education, and made to turn their wages over to "the old man."

The anger between the Plimpton families waxed and waned over the years. During that time there'd been an ongoing series of petty arguments concerning disposition of furniture, especially antiques, after Ralph died. Dad's kids were the only grandchildren, and Mother reasoned that family pieces should be left to us. Uncle Frank and Aunt Vivian thought differently, and Grandma acquiesced to the wishes of her handsome younger son, Frank. Mother resented this. Once again she felt she was the outsider, always the "city girl."

It didn't help that she mocked the way her brother and sister-in-law lavished affection on their miniature poodle, Sweetie. It didn't help that Mother was a college-educated schoolteacher, while Vivian didn't work outside her home. Frank worked at the local insulator company, and Grandma served up cafeteria fare at Lima High School. Bitter words were spoken on all sides. Frank and Vivian grew more and more distant.

Time, though, has a way of softening the edges of anger. As the brothers closed in on their ninth decade, their health began to fail. Mother died, Dad moved to assisted living, Uncle Frank moved to a skilled nursing facility, and Aunt Vivian attempted to keep going in the house on Maplewood Avenue. It became vital for Fred and Frank to see each other.

I'd sat demurely on the lumpy bed for two hours as my dad and his brother discussed long ago events and current health problems.

"Why are you here, Frank?" my dad asked. "What happened?"

"Not sure. I had to go to the hospital, that much I know. But when I got out, they brought me here. Vivian must know why."

"Can you walk?"

"Nah, I don't trust my legs anymore."

"Same here," my dad said. "That's why I've got this walker."

Talk veered to events recalled from boyhood.

"Do you remember who put the first bathroom in at the house?"

"Must have been Eddie Holmes, back in '35 or '36."

"OK, yeah, before that we had the 'little house behind the big house.' "

"You know, I got to thinking about Meredith Gibbs the other day. Remember he worked at his family's junkyard near the Masonic Temple?"

"What I remember was Louise hired him and his Model A to take us to the Hicks-Gary reunion in 1930. Ralph wouldn't go, and Louise had given up driving."

Only an occasional squeak, squeak of rubber-soled shoes in the hall intruded on the reminiscences of the two old brothers. Family lore and long ago events interested me, too, and I was happy my father and uncle were enjoying their time together. But I had an itch to scratch. I wanted more information about Uncle Frank's vegetable garden, tucked in my memory banks from decades ago.

"Remember how the old man yelled at us for the job we did weeding Lizzie Thompson's garden?"

"Oh, Lord, yes," my dad replied. "He was mad as a wet hen. He came up and dragged us right out of the baseball game at McKuen's. Said we left too much quack grass."

"You couldn't hardly get all the quack grass out of that garden, anyway."

As the brothers chatted, I'd jotted notes in my black Moleskine notebook. When the conversation segued to the Thompson garden, opportunity presented itself.

"Uncle Frank, can you tell me about *your* vegetable garden? For instance, why did you plant such a large one?"

Frank, a bemused look on his face, smiled towards me, not quite meeting my eyes.

"I don't rightly know. I guess it was because when Vivian and I got married and moved to her folks' house, there was all that room in the backyard. A double lot, and John, he couldn't do nothing with it, him with that bad leg and all."

"Why'd you garden, Uncle Frank? What got you started?"

My dad chuckled, but let Frank answer. "I'd have to say it was because of the old man. It was one thing I learned from him that was useful later on."

"What'd you do with all those vegetables?" Dad interjected. "I recall that was a *big* garden."

"Well, there was the four of us, and Ada canned. So we ate up most of what I grew. Later on, I guess I gave away a lot to the neighbors."

I shot a quick glance at Dad. That had been a trick question. I knew our family of six had never been gifted with any extra produce, much as we might have needed and enjoyed it.

Ah well, time to let bygones be bygones.

The light was fading and dinner trays clanged in the hall. Dad struggled to his feet, supported by his walker.

"We've got to get going, Frank. Colleen has to get me home, and she's got a long drive tomorrow."

"You'll come back and visit me again, won't you?" Frank pleaded. He sat slumped in his wheelchair, his face turned up at us. "I don't get much company anymore."

"Of course we will," my dad and I chorused.

"Debbie can bring me next time," Dad said.

"And I'll be by when I'm up this way," I volunteered.

There was a beat of silence while we listened to the rain running down the window.

"Colleen," Uncle Frank said, "It means a lot to me, you coming from Connecticut and all. And it means a lot that you remember my garden. There's not many left who do."

I took his cold hands in mine. "Uncle Frank, thank you for what you taught me in your garden. I've never forgotten that you took the time to show me, really show me, a vegetable garden. What I know about growing vegetables started with you."

His eyes filled with tears as we said goodbye.

My father and I inched our way towards the front door, under the buzzing florescent lights, passing stacks of plastic trays laden with gray peas, meager slices of beige meat and reconstituted mashed potatoes. We moved slowly past desiccated, vacant-eyed patients with frozen faces and shriveled limbs. I steered my dad in his walker to the front door and back to a world of whizzing cars, crying babies and hamburgers sizzling on barbeques.

As we walked toward freedom, I recalled Uncle Frank's words. How much it mattered to him that his garden was remembered. How valuable it was that I'd visited him and brought his garden to life once more.

I well knew I might never again see Frank Plimpton in this mortal life. He was so frail, so aged. The next visit might be at his gravesite in the old family cemetery in West Bloomfield.

But today, my words had made a difference. I'd repaid a debt too long outstanding.

I hadn't been too late.

Cauliflower (Brassica oleracea)

Photo by Sue West

Description: Cool-season vegetable; one of the cruciferous group.

Favorites: 'Snowball', 'Snow White'.

Zones: Temperate, zones 8 and cooler.

Exposure: Full sun. Can be started from seeds or sets. Prefers northern climates with warm days and cool nights.

Soil: Rich, organic, well drained. Set plants 18 to 24 inches apart for best head development. Pick when heads are full, before curds begin to separate.

Water: Plentiful; cauliflower will not head up with inadequate moisture.

Fertilizer: Broadcast and till in 10-10-10 prior to planting, and side-dress with nitrogen fertilizer when plants begin to head.

Pruning: Not needed.

Potential problems: Protect from cabbage worms with row covers, spray Bt. Practice crop rotation as with all brassicas.

Interesting Asides: Nutritious and packed with antioxidants, cauliflower is the same species as broccoli, and both were cultivated in Roman times. There are now green, orange and purple-headed types, as well as self-blanching cultivars.

11

Sugar Maple

Sylvalan (Fred) Plimpton

"Colleen won't talk to me lately," my dad said to my mother as he packed his Saturday tool chest on a cool April afternoon in 1964. "She won't even look at me when I try. 'Course, I never know what to say."

I heard Mother sigh from the stair landing where I quietly sat. On my way down the stairs I'd picked up the mention of my name and figured I'd better eavesdrop. "That's adolescence, Fred. She's pretty full of herself since she started high school, I grant you. But don't let her ignore you."

"It gets to me." Dad ran his hand over his balding head. "She's disrespectful, and as hard as I work for this family, I don't deserve that. I would have given anything if my folks had wanted to talk to me when I was 14."

"Maybe you could try spending more time with her. By the time you get home from work every day, she's off at cheerleading practice or Sodality and you two never get any time together, just the two of you. How about taking her along today when you look at the garage?"

"That's another thing, that darn garage! I told your father if he built it like that it wouldn't last the winter. And now that the frost is out of the ground, it's listing." Dad gazed into the middle distance and shook his head. "The whole north corner has come loose from its fittings. The thing's going to collapse, sure as shooting."

Mother waved an arm, her way of indicating frustration and incomprehension. "Another project gone wrong. He's a stubborn old man, and I can't begin to guess why he does the things he does."

Dad pulled on his coveralls. "There's no help for it anyway. He built the thing all wrong. I tried to tell him, but would he listen? Not to me. We're going to be the laughingstock of Lima."

In the early '60s in Lima, New York, where my dad was born and raised, such appearances mattered. Dad kept the lawn pristine at the old-fashioned farmhouse we rented from Grandpa and Nana Kennett. He tried to keep the house up, too, but pushback from Bill Kennett prevented most maintenance.

My maternal grandparents had purchased the Queen Anne, to be used as their country home, in 1930 for $1200. Even in the depths of the Depression, Bill, a mailman for the New York Central, had a steady job. Though his wages had been cut, food was plentiful on the large dining room table at Hawley Street in Rochester. Nana kept foster kids for Catholic Charities, bringing in a bit of money and complicating the Kennetts' life. Though Bessye had been raised in the city and Bill on a wheat farm in nearby Scottsville, she was the one who wanted a summer home. Real estate was cheap as economic hard times rolled on. The house in Lima, at the outskirts of a prosperous farm town, was available and ideal. They spent every summer there.

The problem was that Grandpa fancied himself a master carpenter, plumber, mason and roofer. The truth was he possessed none of those skills. And since he lived ten months of the year in Rochester and traveled to the Midwest regularly on his job, he wasn't available when domestic difficulties arose. He wouldn't allow my dad to make repairs, install modern appliances or even perform cosmetic changes. And when Bill did get around to home repairs, he did them halfway and grew testy when suggestions were made as to how things could be done better. He never used a 2x4 when a 2x2 was available, he wouldn't buy new galvanized nails when rusty ones were to be had for the taking from the dump, and he felt it senseless to let good, used (though discarded) lumber go to waste. And so the gracious, spacious house we lived in, and its new garage, were left to fall into wrack and ruin.

The garage, next to the ginkgo tree and situated above the swale beside the recently raised roadbed of Route 5 and 20, was Grandpa's current special project. Mother had begged for one for years. Our house possessed only a one-bay stall underneath the back porch, a musty place with a dirt floor and resident toads. The carriage house beside the elms was long gone. When a new garage finally topped the priority list, Grandpa, of course, decided to build it himself.

He chose a patch of property near the road, at the edge of the horse pasture where the violets grew in April and blackberries thickened in July. He clear-cut the surrounding woods, and since the tract was waterlogged in wet springs, filled it in and raised it up.

He'd worked out a deal with his cronies at Porcelain Insulator Company, and made numerous trips with his makeshift trailer to cart cinders and ashes to the construction site. The project commenced in the summer of 1962 and was quickly (too quickly) completed. My dad, a handyman since the tender age of ten, watched aghast as Bill refused to dig a proper foundation, slammed old boards together and used inadequate corner bracing.

Dad knew it was a goner.

I'd beat a hasty retreat as my parents finished their conversation, and now lay sprawled on my lavender ruffled bedspread, listening to the Saturday afternoon Hit Parade on WBBF. I was hoping to hear Leslie Gore's "You Don't Own Me," but "My Boy Lollipop" or the Beatles singing "Do You Want to Know a Secret?" would do fine as well.

My newly redecorated room delighted me, and I spent as much time there as possible. The previous year, to celebrate turning 13, Mother had allowed me to order wallpaper. The room overlooked the overgrown lilac on the west side of the house, and I was enamored of all things floral, so when we went to Red Nichols' hardware store I chose a flower-sprigged paper in hues of lavender, cream and green. I pasted the slippery stuff on the walls myself and couldn't believe my prowess. For Christmas I was given the bedspread of my dreams, a tiered dreamboat straight out of the Sears Roebuck catalogue, complete with dust ruffle and pillow shams. Since my room faced the side yard, not the front, the traffic from East Main Street was tolerable. And in May, when the lilac bloomed, it was heaven.

"Colleen, you in there?"

I knew my dad's knock, and chose not to answer. *How am I going to get out of this?* I muttered under my breath. I wasn't especially keen on discussing any of my latest shortcomings with him or anybody. Why couldn't they just leave me alone? Not that they spent much time with me, anyway. Mother taught 7th grade at Lima High School, had the four of us kids and plenty to do. Dad, it seemed, mostly ignored me, and I was just as glad, especially when I realized he couldn't discuss the English literature or French history I was learning in high school.

"C'mon, Colleen, I know you're in there."

I dragged myself off the bed and reluctantly pulled open the door. "What?" I said to the doorjamb.

"I need your help at the garage."

"The garage! I don't know anything about garages."

"I've got work to do on your grandfather's garage. You can carry my tools."

"What am I, your packhorse? How about Ricky or Jennie?"

"Don't give me any of your lip. You're the oldest. I expect you to help me."

Toting the tools! That was a new one. I was far from thrilled, but it *was* interesting to be needed not to set the table or babysit the bratty younger kids. So on a rare Saturday afternoon together, Dad and I went to inspect the wreckage of Grandpa's garage.

My father was measuring the separation of the floor joists with his wooden folding ruler, and I was outside, leaning over the edge of the raised quarter towards the horse pasture, when I saw it. A maple sapling. Four feet high, spindly and struggling off the northwest corner of the garage.

It had somehow survived Grandpa's sickle the previous summer. Not only survived, but it had grown tall and straight. Its smooth brown bark sported reddish twigs, and its splayed green leaves were flung out to catch what scanty sun shone in the dark corner between the listing garage and Routes 5 and 20.

"Daddy! Look at that tree. How come it's still there when Grandpa cut down everything else?" I leapt into the swale to get a closer look.

From the outside corner of the woebegone garage, Dad scrutinized the unfortunate scrawny tree. "I don't know, honey, he must not have noticed it. That's a sugar maple. Won't last long there, though. Too shady."

I touched the smooth bark. "Can we save it? Move it?" I felt like a Dickensian urchin peering into a bakery window. I wanted that tree.

Dad stood and straightened his back. "Colleen, I have enough to do today without transplanting a tree. And where would we put it? Anyway," he said, with a rictus of a smile. "Why would you want to spend any more time with me than necessary?"

He had me, and it took a second to recover my momentum. I decided to ignore his jibe, and thought quickly so as to regain an advantage. "Down in the backyard, between the creek and the clothesline. There's room there."

He gave the briefest of nods. "Good choice, it's sunny and flat. But it'll take time I don't have…"

"Please, Dad? I'll help."

He hesitated. "If we do it right now, and you help me with no backtalk."

I grinned. "You got yourself a deal!"

Dad reentered the sad garage and pulled a shovel out of the jumble of tools propped in the corner. "Let's get started." I dutifully followed him back to my prize.

"Here's how you move a tree, Colleen." He lifted the shovel. "You dig around the trunk; take a big hunk of dirt with the roots. On a tree this small, the roots won't be very big, but you have to be careful." He examined the top of the sapling. "This is healthy, see? It's growing at the tip. But it's going to need as much of its roots as possible in its new home."

We dug out a two-foot circle of soil with the sapling firmly in the middle and bundled it in burlap. Dad heaved it up over his shoulder and trekked down the cinder driveway. I followed, hypnotized at the sight of the traveling tree. My self-appointed job was to scoop up every clod of dirt dislodged from the root ball. I was pretty sure my tiny prize would need the scraps. We walked carefully by the apple and elm trees, down the clothesline hill until we arrived at the flat lawn beyond the metal T-shaped poles.

"Here?" Daddy plunked the tree down on the grass. "Do you think it'll be happy here?"

I looked past the spot, eastward to the creek, resounding with the roar of snow-melt, south past the spirea, and north to the East Main Street traffic thundering over the bridge. Despite the racket, the air was full of the smell of spring. "It's a little noisy, but yep, I think this is a good new home for our tree."

Dad started to dig a hole and after a few minutes, handed the shovel over to me. "Your turn."

I dug. For about two minutes.

"This is *work!*"

"Told you. You never listen though, do you?" This was supplemented by a grin.

Since it was no time for surliness, I decided to make nice. "What does it mean, Dad, that our tree is a 'sugar maple'?"

"A long time ago, before stores had white sugar to sell, maple syrup was one of the only sweeteners around. Remember going to

Dansville last fall to the Harvest Festival? Remember the maple sugar candy in the shape of leaves?"

I nodded.

"Where that candy originally comes from is the sap of a tree like this. Full grown, though. A group of maple sugar trees is called a 'sugar bush,' and that was a valuable commodity to farmers a hundred years ago. The Iroquois taught the early settlers about sugaring." He scanned the tree line south of our yard and pointed. "Sap starts running in the late winter. The old-timers would go up College Street and look towards those Bristol hills, starting in February. When there was a wash of red on the swamp maples, they knew the time was coming. Then they'd tap the trees with a wooden or metal spigot and put a bucket under the tap. Next day they'd gather the sap and start boiling it down." He leaned on the shovel, remembering. "Takes a bunch of sap to make syrup, though."

For once, I was enthralled with something my dad had to say. I hung on every word.

"Season doesn't last long. About six weeks. It takes cold nights and days above freezing, so once spring really starts, sugaring's over." Dad glanced at me. "You know, some of those old Plimpton farmers Ralph used to talk about probably sugared, too."

I stared at my teeny tree. "Then we could, too, someday. But doesn't tapping it hurt the tree?"

"Nah. Not if it's old enough. There's a lot of sap runs up and down the trunk in the spring, and it doesn't do any harm if some is taken out. Just not too much."

I gingerly broke off a leaf and tasted the stem. "This isn't sweet!"

"Well, no, because first, this sugar maple isn't big enough to put out much sap. And second, like I said, it's too late in the year for the sap to run."

Scudding lambswool clouds skimmed over the yard as Dad and I worked. He looked to the sky. "You know, this is the ideal time to move any growing thing. Best to do it in the cool of the day, after the sun has passed, and early in the season, before they know they've been moved. But I don't like the wind coming up—it'll rock the tree, and it's not anchored in the ground yet. We don't have a choice today. It's getting late, but we might have to stake him tomorrow."

The lesson continued. "Now scrape the dirt up, like this." Dad shoveled a well of soil around the sapling. "It'll keep the water in when it rains. That's real important, keeping enough water on a newly transplanted tree." He pointed to the rain barrel under the downspout at the southeast corner of the house. "See the coffee can over there? Go fill it up and pour it in here."

I did as I was told. No complaining.

The sun was fast sliding towards town. Peepers were calling from the marsh, and the breeze began to freshen as Dad patted the ground around the tree with his shovel. We were done. He stood up straight, squared his shoulders, glanced at me and headed for the back porch. "Let's go in. I'm sure your mother wants us for dinner." He patted my shoulder. "You did a good job, Colleen. Now take care of your new tree."

We left our shovel in the cellar, trudged up the back stairs through the sun porch and into the kitchen, which was full of the familiar sounds of sibling bickering. Mismatched silverware clanged as Debbie plopped it on the enameled table. Jennie carefully set out the Melamine plates.

"The fork goes on the left," she said to her big sister. "You always do it wrong."

"Can I help it if I'm left-handed?"

The dryer thumped its afternoon's last load of clothes. Potato chunks and thick pork chops spattered in the cast-iron skillet.

Mother shouted into the living room. "Ricky, turn off that TV! It's time for dinner!"

Dad and I lined up alongside the sink to wash our hands. Mother turned from the stove, spatula in hand, and took a look at our stained hands. "What on earth were you two doing? You couldn't have gotten that dirty at the garage."

Dad and I exchanged significant glances. He motioned towards Mother, and I tugged her to the window and pointed. "Look, that's what we did!"

She took in the tiny tree now nestled between the creek and the clothesline. "Just what we need, another tree." She stopped, eyeing us both. "You and your dad planted that?"

We nodded in unison. "We saved a sugar maple tree, Mother." I beamed. "Dad showed me how. It's my tree now."

And there it stands to this very day, a testament to reconciliation. My dad and I would have many more set-to's before I finally matured. But transplanting a tree together was a good start.

I think of that long-ago Saturday each time I move a tree in my yard. The white-tailed deer have decimated our woods here in suburban Connecticut. In many places there's nothing between the Christmas ferns on the forest floor and the 80-year old canopy of tulip poplar, hickory and oak. It's therefore incumbent upon me as gardener and steward of my small patch of earth to reforest where I can. That means guarding seedlings which birds or squirrels inadvertently plant in the garden, growing them on for a couple of years and moving them to the woods' edges. Just as Dad demonstrated, I carefully judge the tree's transplantability, scope out the root spread, find precisely the correct new home, and excavate a hole prior to moving the tree. The cavity gets amended with a bucket of homemade compost and thoroughly watered from my rain barrel, as does the tree, before the shovel touches the earth. I scrutinize my trees, large and small, year round. But I only transplant in the early spring, before they know they've been moved.

Of course, subsequent applications of deer repellent are crucial. Weekly sprays of rotten-egg-based liquid and monthly broadcast applications of Milorganite keep most new trees safe until they can grow out of the deer's reach.

I proudly assess my trees' growth each year: the red cedar junipers, the swamp maples, the walnuts, the white oak. I take care of my trees, just as I was bid to do almost 50 years ago with my very own sugar maple.

And so it goes. Out of the roots of time and the seeds of precious hours my father spent with his sulky teenager daughter long ago, my forest grows.

Sugar Maple (Acer saccaratum)   Photo by Sue West

Description: Deciduous hardwood tree, also known as Canadian maple. Will grow to 80 feet at maturity. Known for its stature, blazing orange autumn leaves, and sap, which is boiled to produce maple syrup.

Favorites: 'Bonfire', 'Green Mountain'.

Zones: 3 to 8.

Exposure: Full sun preferred; will grow in less.

Soil: Grows in clay, loam, or sand. Does not do well in wet soil.

Water: Moderate drought tolerance; water well first season.

Fertilizer: None needed.

Pruning: Not essential; sugar maples naturally assume a rounded shape.

Potential problems: Browsing deer have destroyed much new growth in many areas.

Interesting Asides: Attractive as homes and food to birds, squirrels and other mammals. Makes a good shade/lawn tree, but not a roadside planting where salt is used in the winter as it is not salt-tolerant. Maple sugaring was a vital economic venture of early American settlers, the skill taught to them by Native Americans. Maple sugar was used as sweetener in the absence of cane or beet sugar, and maple syrup is still one of the most significant crops in New England. In 2009, almost 2 million gallons were produced.

12

Easter Lily

Carlos Huerta

St. Rose of Lima Roman Catholic Church, that august building, echoed with the steps of exiting parishioners on a Sunday morning in the spring of 1966. Fellow churchgoers greeted one another, the women's white gloves upraised, children softly giggling, men quietly discussing the Dodgers' Sandy Koufax and the war in Vietnam. The air inside the vaulted, statue-ringed sanctuary was still redolent of incense. The hymns from the choir lingered, and I could still taste the communion wafer on my tongue.

Sister Ann Michelle, my former 8th grade teacher, approached me with a smile as I walked into the sunshine. Her long black robes swept the stone floor, the starched wimple drawn tight under her chin, headpiece pressed into her forehead, coif modestly covering her chest. "Colleen, I hate to see anything go to waste. We have some orphan potted plants left over from Easter." She rattled the rosary beads dangling at her waist. "Would you like any of them?"

"Sister, what would I do with them?"

"I know you like plants. I was hoping you could put one or two of them in your yard." She patted my arm. "Why don't you meet me at the side door of the convent? You can see what we have."

I agreed, and went off to tell my parents to go on without me, that I'd walk home.

The bedraggled collection of potted hyacinths, daffodils and lilies weren't enticing. Easter was several weeks gone, and though the pots, covered in colorful foil, had been watered, the flowers were faded and wilting.

But something about the single lily plant impelled me… drooping, brown, spent blooms notwithstanding, the elongated green leaves tattered and forlorn, the sweet odor of redemption and Easter remained. The clay pot with its crinkly covering was solid in my hands.

"This one, Sister. I'd like to take the lily."

"You're welcome to it, Colleen, and a good choice it is." Sister pulled her hand from the deep recesses of her habit and made the sign of the cross over the plant and me. "The lily is a favored flower of the Blessed Virgin, you know. God bless you, and take good care of your gift."

I bid good-bye to Sister, crammed my mantilla into the plastic clutch purse tucked under my left arm, hefted the pot in the crook of my right elbow, and started for home.

I didn't mind walking. Though it was almost a mile, the day was fine and I was used to trekking back and forth to town. We'd always walked to school, whether to St. Rose Parochial, or later the half-mile to Lima High. The walks took us past Lima's turn-of-the-century Victorian houses replete with gingerbread, scallops and curlicues, and Arts and Crafts bungalows with shingled sides and spacious front porches. We walked to the library, to Schwartz's Drug Store, to the bank, to the post office, and sometimes to church. The sidewalks paralleled Main Street and led under the sheltering branches of the horse chestnut trees.

Wrens and robins sang with gusto that Sunday morning. A squirrel bounded from a sugar maple, chittering its way across a lawn. There was an intoxicating freshness in the air as I carried my new plant, full of promise, homewards.

At our house, in the hollow of East Main Street where Spring Creek crossed the road, I deposited the forlorn thing on our wide wooden front porch, beside Grandpa's platform rocker. And there it sat. For weeks. Despite Sister Ann Michelle's confidence, I didn't know how or where to plant it. No one I knew had ever planted an Easter lily. And I was too busy to think of whom to ask for advice.

A high school senior that year, I would soon be off to college, and I was shedding my old life as a dry fir sheds needles. Among the transitions was the relationship with my boyfriend. I'd been going with Bill for a year, since we'd met at a SUNY Geneseo program for college-bound kids from rural Livingston County. He'd graduated from Mt. Morris High the previous year and matriculated at Yale. But he'd left after a semester and was uncertain of his future, and where I might fit into it.

Though after years of writing poor poetry in the woods behind our house, I fancied myself at heart a solitary philosopher, my after-school job waitressing at Pete's Sandwich Shoppe in tiny downtown Lima kept me interacting with the public. People came and went at Pete's. One never knew who would come through the heavy glass doors.

The stranger was compact, dark, with square shoulders, white teeth and a dazzling smile. His black hair was curly and his eyes bottomless brown. And he didn't look like anyone I'd ever seen in Lima, New York. I mentally put two and two together... he had to be my friend Paloma's older half-brother, freshly arrived in town. Since Paloma herself was relatively new to Lima, he was that oddity, that rarity, a person unknown to us all.

"Hi, I'm Carlos." He held out his hand. Not skilled in the art of handshaking, I stood immobilized on the tile floor of the Sandwich Shoppe.

He smiled. "I'm Paloma's brother, and I don't bite."

I pulled my right hand out of my apron pocket. *No time like the present to learn to shake hands,* I thought to myself. *Might be something I need to know in college.*

"That's better." His voice was soft and resonant. "I saw you at the basketball game and thought we could get acquainted. My sister tells me you'd be interesting to talk to. I already know you're a good cheerleader."

I liked him immediately, and not just because he was 23, from California and seemingly curious about me. Carlos was on an extended visit to Lima, so we had time to strike up a friendship, which at first mostly involved long discussions. We discovered we shared an interest in green growing things, the siren song of nature, and the fleeting state of happiness.

In the living room at my home, or on my breaks at work, surrounded by the pungent smell of catsup and the grease of French fries, with Simon and Garfunkel's "The Sounds of Silence" playing in the background and the sizzle of frying burgers in the air, Carlos and I meandered into dialogues about the meaning of life. I'd never met a man who spoke so deeply, so eloquently about the natural world, love, life. Starved for such conversation, I took to it like a sunflower tracing the arc of the day.

Having stepped over it one too many times on my front porch, Carlos decided several weeks into our relationship that the time had come to plant the Easter lily. We selected a sunny spot on the west side of the house, under my bedroom window and adjacent to the purple lilac.

The chosen day shone with a clear wipe of blue sky. Crickets chirred in the grass. We removed the foil sleeve and tipped the plant out of its pot. It was bone dry, and the roots, white and tangled, circled around themselves at the bottom.

"Not good," Carlos said. "It's been in the pot too long. But we'll give it a chance."

We dug a hole in the fill dirt beside the stone wall.

"Do you have any fertilizer? This soil's not so great, and the plant must be hungry after all that time in the pot."

"Fertilizer? Nope."

"How about mulch?"

"Not so's you'd notice."

It didn't take long to settle the pathetic thing into the hole. "When it blooms, if it blooms," Carlos said, looking up, "you'll be able smell it when you get ready for bed. Easter lilies are most fragrant in the evening."

Carlos and I graduated to long car rides, where we'd periodically stop to listen to the peepers and the rustle of rain on willow leaves. Increasingly, there was an audible quality to our listening, an intense value to our conversations.

As spring progressed we spent more and more time together, but weren't sure where the relationship was going. On one of our drives we stopped at Mendon Ponds Park and sat in the car, discussing the horrors of war, the book *Born Free*, and whether color TV would negatively impact people's imaginations. A silence fell. Then he turned to face me, tipped up my chin, and looked into my eyes.

"What do you feel for me, Colleen?"

"I can't answer that, Carlos." I squirmed in my seat. I knew I cared for him, but was he asking for more?

"Let's go for a walk, OK?" he said.

We climbed out of the car. I stopped and closed my eyes to collect myself. He tucked my hand into the crook of his arm, and we wandered down a path towards the lake where I'd played as a child. We sat on the sandy beach, tossing pebbles into the water, watching the ever-expanding rings in the moonlight.

"Life is complex, isn't it?" he said.

I nodded.

"It's all right, you know, if you aren't sure of your emotions about us. I have to believe there's a plan for each of us, even if it's not being together."

We stayed until rain threatened, and then headed back to the car. He leaned against the car, laughing gently at me, while I helped a toad off the path and into the woods. A light drizzle obscured the underbrush.

"You're so pretty, and so curious about the trees and animals and flowers."

I smiled.

"I'll remember this night, Colleen. For always. No matter what happens."

We looked at each other very steadily for a moment. Then he kissed me on the forehead and we got back into the car.

My family was tolerant of the relationship with Carlos, perhaps because Mother thought highly of Paloma. And because she trusted me. She still hoped Bill would pull himself together and return to Yale, but saw no harm in my friendship with the older brother of a classmate. My dad was more worried about the size of my miniskirt than the shade of my boyfriend's skin.

Some of my work friends, however, thought I'd lost my mind. I'd thrown over a Yalie (albeit a lapsed one) for an older man who might as well be a foreigner. In the convoluted calculus of adolescence, there was bound to be finger-wagging. The girls convened for an intercession one day after our shift.

"But, Colleen, he's so *dark*."

"And he comes from *California*. You know what that place is like!"

"What kind of a future could you possibly have with the likes of *him*?"

"What about Bill?"

I listened, and bit my lip, feeling fragile and mortified. Was I doing the right thing? My foot jiggled in anger, but I held my tongue, put my Coke bottle back on the table with hands that were almost steady, and laughed a short, brittle laugh.

It didn't matter. I cared about Carlos. My life was my life and mine alone, and I would do as I pleased.

And I told them so.

The Easter lily we planted didn't survive, and neither did our relationship. The lily never regained vigor and faded into the soil within a few weeks. My relationship with Carlos languished and finally ended over the summer, when our family moved to Blue Pond.

As I look down the corridor of the decades, I wish Carlos Huerta the best, wherever life took him, whatever his path. The memory of our talks, the first I'd ever really had about life and love and nature, still resonate. They set the stage for many discussions in college and beyond. Carlos taught me that men, too, could be sensitive, that it was OK to discuss peace and flowers, mellow music, and spring rain. He taught me that it's OK to care about another person who looks different, despite what friends may say, think or do.

I never forgot.

It was 43 years and hundreds of miles before I attempted to grow another Easter lily. In the spring of 2007 the minister at our Methodist Church in Bethel, Connecticut, stopped me after service. The air inside the sanctuary was tranquil, and the hymns from the choir lingered. Downstairs, the social hall of our small, white clapboard building hummed with parishioners who chatted and laughed and drank weak Methodist coffee.

Reverend Vicky Fleming caught up with me between conversations about organic insecticides and leaf blight on impatiens. "Colleen," she said, "we have some orphan plants left over from Easter. I hate to see anything go to waste. Can you use any of them?"

I hesitated.

"I know you like plants; I was hoping you could put one or two of them in your yard." She patted my arm. "Why don't you meet me in the vestibule; you can see what we have."

Once again, the bedraggled collection of potted hyacinths, daffodils and lilies weren't enticing. Easter was several weeks gone, and though the pots, covered in colorful foil, had been watered, the flowers were faded and wilting.

But something about the single lily plant impelled me... drooping, brown, spent blooms notwithstanding, the elongated green leaves tattered and forlorn, the sweet odor of redemption and Easter remained. The plastic pot with its crinkly covering was solid in my hands.

It needed saving. I lugged it home and planted it, alone this time, but still not knowing what to expect. However, decades of experience had taught me the basics. I selected a sunny spot, dug a good hole, amended it with compost, loosened the lily's roots and tenderly placed it. I mulched, deer repelled and protected, but was horrified when the lily seemed to promptly die, just as my other lily had many years ago.

Sometimes plants, just like people, surprise us. The next spring my lily boasted a basal rosette of green leaves, and then sprouted a stem that grew tall and strong. The second week in July it bloomed white and smooth and perfumed, between the ruby-red peony and the cast iron pot of pansies. The lily's orange anthers were long and weighted with pollen. Its petals were velvety smooth. It held court for weeks in the center of the Mailbox Garden.

And then the memories flooded back, tumbling through the hatch of time. Carlos. Senior year of high school. A disheveled Easter lily. A man who looked different. Friendship that didn't turn to love.

And I had to wonder. Did Carlos and I simply give up too soon when the lily plant went dormant, as, unbeknownst to us, it was supposed to? Probably. By the next year there was no one to watch over it. Carlos had returned to California and out of my life. I'd gone off to college, and my family had moved from my childhood home.

I never went back to see if our lily grew and bloomed.

As teens we try out different loves and lifestyles. If we're fortunate, we learn through these experiences to further explore what is meaningful to us, and to stand up for what we believe. Carlos, though different, opened my eyes to the beauty of nature and the necessity for some to remark on it. I learned that knowledge, that sharing, was worth alienating some of my friends.

Deep into my middle age, in a time of diversity and difficulty for our society, I close my eyes and reach for the far corners of my mind, my scrapbook of memories.

For times not remembered, for things that you did, Carlos, I remember.

Easter Lily (Lilium longiflorum)   Photo by Sue West

Plant Description: Bulbous herbaceous perennial, grows to 3 feet tall and 9 inches wide.

Favorites: 'Nellie White'. 'Elegant Lady' is a pink-tinged cultivar.

Zones: 3 to 9.

Exposure: Full sun. If planting a potted plant, be aware that the original stem will die back, to return the following year. If planting bulbs, place 3 inches deep.

Soil: Organic, moderately moist, well-drained. Provide a mulch, either living or organic, to retain soil moisture and protect the plant in winter.

Water: Average. Water during drought and at time of transplant.

Fertilizer: Add granular fertilizer such as Plant-tone at planting.

Pruning: None needed. Spent stem of first year potted plants may be clipped. Plant will produce "daughter" bulblets, offsets of the mother plant. These may be left in place or transplanted.

Potential problems: Do not allow plant to remain in standing water. Lily beetle, a bright red insect. It does no damage, but its nymph, a tiny slug-like creature which carries its excrement on its back, can defoliate a lily in days. If seen, spray entire plant with insecticidal soap at regular intervals.

Interesting Asides: The Easter lily remains the traditional, time-honored flower of Easter. Symbolic of a resurrection, Easter lilies rise from earthy graves as scaly bulbs and bloom into majestic flowers that embody the splendor, grace and tranquility of the season.

13

Compost

J.I. Rodale

"Sit down and be quiet!" I said in my sternest teacher voice, employed despite the fact that I was merely a lowly substitute, a walk-in, walk-out, on-again, off-again teacher in the 11th grade science class on a warm autumn day in 1972. In my narrow-wale blue print corduroy skirt and peasant blouse, I hardly looked different from the students in their bellbottom jeans and vests, miniskirts and psychedelic-colored tops. But perhaps they heard something in my tone. They returned to their seats and listened.

It'd been my teacher boyfriend Peter who'd persuaded me to try subbing, though my heart wasn't in it. Mother was an educator, and I'd vowed I wouldn't follow that career. There were other options. After all, the Equal Rights Amendment had been recently passed by Congress and sent to the states for certain ratification (where, of course, it failed); *Ms.* magazine had just debuted, and opportunities were bound to open for women. I didn't know exactly what I'd do, but I was sure I'd build a career in something besides teaching, social work or nursing.

God knows I'd been searching. My degree in anthropology from Fordham University was two years old, and already I'd worked as a benefit checker for Morrisania City Hospital in New York, as a chair caner in a rural Pennsylvania communal-living arrangement, and as a cocktail waitress. At age 23, it was time for me to try something more mainstream.

"Look, Colleen, you need a job, a real job," Peter advised. "And subbing's a good way to bring in some money while you decide what you might want to do when you grow up."

It turned out to be suspiciously easy to earn $20 per day as a substitute teacher. All one needed was a pointer and a pulse. When the school district started calling *me*, a young, inexperienced unknown, I should have realized they were desperate.

And so it was that over the course of the next several months I held things down to a dull roar in various classrooms in a suburban Rockland County high school. Not only in history classrooms spread thick with the smell of Wrigley Spearmint gum, chalk dust and the perfume of adolescent hormones, but also in study halls, where the sounds of rustling homework, ticking wall clocks and principal's footfalls mingled with the occasional whizz of a paper airplane. Often, however, there were interruptions by the kids:

"Miss Plimpton, I can't find my assignment!"

"Don't be such a spaz, Doreen," the gangly boy in the corner of the room retorted. "It's probably back at your crib."

"Miss Plimpton, James took my seat!"

"Miss Plimpton, do you live in Stony Point?"

"Dream on, John, like she's gonna tell *you!*"

A substitute teacher, I observed, is an object of both curiosity and ridicule. She's an unbaggaged shoulder to lean on and sometimes a plank to stand on. She puts up with the occasional diffident handwriting and obscure lesson plan from the regular teacher, as well as the intermittent frosty shoulder from full-time educators in their (formerly) smoke-filled lounge. A substitute changes professorial colors like a chameleon as she charges each day into a new classroom. Will it be a science day? How about English literature, or, glory be, a long-term assignment?

It takes guts to be a successful substitute teacher. I didn't have guts. What I had was distress. I needed to make a decision on what to do with my life. Preferably before I was ready to retire.

"Peter, how is subbing helping me decide on a career?" I wailed one day in October after a particularly difficult day. "All I know is I can't do this forever!"

"Well, that cuts your choices down somewhat."

He was right, and, truth be told, the real petunia in the onion patch was that I didn't feel the tug, the rewards, the gratification that a good teacher should. By January, it was time to shift gears and renew the search.

I'd just emerged from the '60s, when we were all enthralled with living communally, going back to the land, and growing our own food. I recalled the Kuder Preference Test I'd taken as a high school freshman. Hadn't it decreed that'd I'd make a good forest ranger? That was pretty close to agriculture, which was beginning to call me. I hadn't planted a thing in years, but the urge remained. At 23, anything is possible.

Peter's family in Pennsylvania was knowledgeable about growing vegetables, and we decided to experiment with making jam from the Concord grapes that scrambled over the arbor behind our small rented home on the Hudson River. The venture was an utter failure; no amount of pectin and sugar could make the mixture stand up. But this whetted our appetite for horticultural information.

Off the shelf came two Rodale books, J.I. Rodale's *The Complete Book of Composting* and *The Encyclopedia of Organic Gardening*. These became my essential reading at school. Once attendance was taken, if I'd distributed a test or gotten the kids immersed in quiet study as prescribed by the regular teacher, I was free to lose myself in the study of the soil.

Dense in my hand, the *Encyclopedia* was crammed with 700 pages of A to Z on how to be an organic gardener. *Composting* carried on for 1000 pages of data on making rich dark compost, which I learned was paramount to organic gardening.

Never had I experienced such books. During the previous years I'd become familiar with *The Whole Earth Catalogue*, *The Mother Earth News*, and *The Have-More Plan*, but Rodale's books were different. I read them cover to cover; from *Abelia* to *Zucchini* and from *The History of Composting* to *Compost and the Law*, while my students were occupied. I toted the tomes back and forth between school and home. I made lists on scraps of discarded paper and old envelopes. I mooned over what vegetables I'd grow. I wrote letters to my mother, who didn't care a fig for gardening but who loved me, about what I'd grow when I got some land. Beets and rutabagas. Carrots and turnips. Tomatoes, of course, but *heritage* tomatoes. Spinach. Swiss chard. And so much more.

I loved the idea of composting. The concept of producing something from nothing especially appealed to me. Even if I couldn't figure out how to build my life, I was surely capable of building compost and growing vegetables. Not that I had a clue, on a substitute teacher's salary and no future, when and where I'd be able to purchase property upon which to grow these wonders. Further upstate New York? I knew there was plenty of land there, but gosh, that's where I came from. Did I truly want to go back?

I had to decide. When it turned out that Peter and I didn't love each other enough to make a permanent commitment, we parted ways, and opportunity was born.

Free again, but as broke as ever, I moved to a bungalow colony in Orange County and acquired a roommate, Nancy. In the summer of 1973 I decided to put my book knowledge about composting into practice.

Our ragtag colony was composed of vacationing Brooklynites, aging hippies who'd never left the vicinity of the nearby Woodstock Music and Art Festival, and a smattering of young people who couldn't afford more spacious digs.

"Nancy," I said, shortly after we moved in, "I want to try composting. I read a great how-to book. It should be simple."

"Where are we going to make compost? We can't use any of the lawn, that's for sure."

"We'll compost in a garbage can, one of those big jobbies. J.I. Rodale says that'll work fine. We'll just appropriate a spare one from behind the office."

And so a bargain on the Great Compost Experiment was struck. We stole the garbage can in the dead of night and set about filling it with banana peels, soggy cereal, assorted kitchen leftovers and apple cores. Unfortunately, I forgot the part in the Rodale book where he mentioned the need for both "green" and "brown" material. Ours was all green, all splendid nitrogen sources. No buffers, like withered leaves, soil or twigs. Nope. Our mixture was rich, and we were convinced that it'd make up to fine, fine compost. What we were going to do with the finished black gold, lacking a garden, has been lost to memory.

The experiment was cut short a week later when, upstate visiting my parents, I received a frantic call from Nancy.

"Colleen! Have you looked at our compost lately?"

"Well, no. I'm here in Lima."

"Our next door neighbor, you know the lady with all the kids? She complained about a nasty smell. I sniffed around, and the can of compost *stinks*. And it's moving."

"Moving?"

"As in boiling with maggots."

"Uh oh."

"So here's what I had to do. Don't hate me, but I hauled the whole mess out into the woods and dumped it."

"My compost!"

"I'm sorry, I know you had plans for it, but keeping our apartment is more important, don't you think?"

Thus ended my first trial in producing something from nothing.

The next attempt didn't come until a decade later. By then I'd married an itinerant IBM'er and we lived in the highlands of New Jersey. It was the mid-1980s and I'd become thoroughly perturbed at the sheer waste of tossing kitchen and garden leftovers to the landfill. Having read more articles about the science of composting, and having learned from the bungalow colony attempt, I once again thought, *It can't be that hard!* I figured this time I'd investigate buying some bells and whistles to hasten success. Ads for various types of tumblers and containers were studied, but the expense seemed ridiculous. A simple pile on the ground, however, seemed lackadaisical. Soooo, I persuaded my bemused husband to build me a three-bin contraption.

"You want me to build three wooden bins so you can make *dirt?*"

"Yep. One container for raw material, one to turn the cooking compost into, and one for the finished product."

Jerry did as I requested. The arrangement was placed at the top of our hill, and I started conveying organic booty up the slope and into bin one.

Within *days* of properly layering my first contributions of garden weeds, old spinach salad and spent soil, my hand felt the warmth of the composting action as I bent close to check its pulse. I fell instantly in love with the whole process. The fecundity, the pleasure of procreation grabbed me hard and has never let go.

Though my limbs got a daily workout from hauling garden leavings and household remainders, it was worth it. My piles increased exponentially, and I soon outgrew the three-bin system. In fact, the thought of having a larger, level corner for composting was one of the few bright spots when a corporate move loomed.

"I don't care much about what house we buy, Jerry," I said in the midst of getting-ready-to-move anxiety. "But I need a place to compost." I warmed to my topic. "It has to be a level spot, fairly close to the house, but not too close. And shady. And with access to water. A supply of old leaves wouldn't be bad, either. "

Bless him, he just smiled and nodded. "We'll find it."

Our new home, complete with potential compost site, was soon found, and a 30-gallon garbage can full of finished compost was ceremoniously carted in the back of my pickup from New Jersey to Connecticut. Little did I know that I also carted a few errant Johnny jump-up seeds. (Or maybe a bazillion.)

I was able to greatly expand operations. Leavened by my out-of-state compost, and aided by the knowledge of how the wonderful stuff can improve one's soil, I quickly amassed larger and larger quantities of raw material. I raided my upstate New York sister's stash of ripe horse and chicken manure. From neighbors I begged old, imploded Halloween jack-o-lanterns. I rustled bags of autumn leaves off the street. I purchased a *diesel* pitchfork and bent with pleasure to my weekly task of turning the steaming mass. Oh, the joy, the scent of half-done compost! The deep tobacco brown, the texture, of the crumbly soil-to-be. The thrill of spreading the richness on my garden beds. The surprises it yields; scuffed Legos, gigantic worms, and one magical time, a tarnished silver dollar.

I built my soil while I built my life. I got a master's degree in social work and worked with the mentally ill. My husband and I raised three children. I grew fabulous flowers and a few vegetables in rich, compost-amended soil.

And so it is that I am out at my compost corner every day from March to November, taking its temperature, fingering its composition, diagnosing its issues. Does it need more green material? Are there too many sticks? What about water?

I am now a certifiably crazed compost creator, producing about ten cubic yards a season. My manufacturing facility looms large at the southeast edge of the backyard. Lately, in addition to the old standbys, I have several new sources of raw material. An agreement with Molten Java, the local funky coffee shop, allows me to stop by twice a week with my empty bucket and exchange it for one filled with lovely, sodden coffee grounds. The greengrocer at my local market allows me to cart off all the corn shucks I can carry. My husband's woodshop keeps me supplied with huge amounts of sawdust. I drag home 40-gallon bags of shredded paper, heaving them along city streets under the amazed eyes of passersby. Friends, eager to be rid of the autumn leaves littering their lawns, actually drop off bags of treasure. I even compost in our frozen Connecticut winters, using a garbage can system on the back deck.

I'm now 38 years past my subbing days. My kids are grown and gone. But still I follow the precepts of J.I. Rodale. This spring I started my 90th compost heap. I nurture my piles, selecting just the right environment for them. Not too sunny a locale or they'll dry up. Not too wet either, or they'll ferment. And they live right on the ground, no compost boxes or bins or tumblers for me. I want them in contact with Mother Earth.

I see parallels among substitute teaching, raising kids, and composting. To wit:

Just like children, compost piles need nourishing food. A mixture of green material, like grass clippings and kitchen waste, and brown material, like autumn leaves and twigs.

Compost piles sometimes require discipline. When they're rowdy and outgrow their boundaries, I find useful things for them to do, like become potting soil, or garden mulch, or an additive to a planting hole.

When at times they fail to thrive at their job of turning garbage into gold, I take their temperature and, like any good parent or teacher, diagnose their issues.

Sometimes they need more fiber, so I feed them pine cones.

Sometimes they're thirsty, so I give them water.

Sometimes they're hungry, so I add nitrogen.

Sometimes they don't have enough friends, namely the worms, soil insects and microorganisms that are essential in the manufacture of compost. So I give them some horse manure.

Just like with my children and my former students, I try to be patient with my compost piles. I learned that it takes several months, even in warm weather, for organic matter to develop from a heap of refuse to usable soil additive.

And I learned that as with children, compost piles need to be handled gently.

And so it goes. My students and my children, like my life and my compost piles, have matured into useful, beautiful adults.

Nurtured by compost, the garden path of life stretches onward.

Photo by Sue West

Compost

Favorites: Basic compost recipe is composed of approximately 40% greens (i.e. kitchen waste, herbivorous manures, garden left-overs, and commercial coffee grounds) to 60% browns (fallen leaves, twigs, sawdust, shredded paper, etc.).

Zones: All.

Exposure: Partly shaded site is ideal; too much sun and the contents dry out. Too much shade and it won't cook properly.

Soil: Add ordinary garden soil as a starter; a shovelful will contribute billions of essential microorganisms to the mixture.

Water: Good compost should have the texture of a wrung-out sponge. Mother Nature generally assures that, but if She doesn't, add water.

Fertilizer: Not necessary, but if things aren't cooking, a handful of fertilizer or sugar will get the process going.

Pruning: Draw down the pile as it nears maturity. When raw material is becoming unrecognizable, it's time to start using.

Potential problems: Too much green material and the pile will smell and become home to maggots. Too much brown material and things won't cook properly. If scavenging animals are a problem, bury fresh additions deep in the center of the heap. Contrary to urban myth, a proper compost pile is too hot for animals to live in it.

Interesting Asides: Mother Nature, of course, has been composting from time immemorial. That's what happens each year on the forest floor, as the leaves fall from the trees and gradually become rich soil, which in turn feeds the woodland. A gardener's compost is simply a more rapid version of this process.

14

Arborvitae

Debbie Seelos

"Debbie!" The voice catapulted across the floral-sprigged hall-way of the gracious old house on a hot July afternoon in 1985. "Debbie, where's my pants?"

My sister Debbie and I, surrounded by female relatives in various states of undress, were preparing for our younger sister Jennie's wedding. She was to be married that day at the fieldstone country home of her in-laws-to-be, on a lawn overlooking rolling upstate New York fields and farms. A faint breeze through the open windows carried the summer-sweet smell of newly shorn hay. Cicadas hummed among the Queen Anne's lace and chicory at the edge of the woods. A bullfrog harrumphed in the distance, his reverie interrupted by the noise of our bustle and anticipation.

"What do you mean, where are your pants?" Debbie said to her husband. "Aren't they on the hanger with your dress shirt?"

"Nope."

"Frank, I have about a thousand things to do in the next few hours to pull off this wedding." Her voice skittered a trifle higher. "Your pants must still be in the car. Go out and look."

In his shorts, Frank retreated to the gravel driveway, clogged with sundry vehicles. A minivan, a rented Chevy pickup truck and assorted cars were all jam-packed full with wedding necessities. Tables and chairs on loan from the Livonia Fire Department. An armada of toys to keep the little ones occupied. Pots of flowers tenderly shipped from Debbie's garden. Pink cotton bridesmaid's dresses. The wedding cake.

But no dress pants.

Frank once again consulted his wife. "It's too late to go back home and get your pants, Frank," she said. "I don't know where they are. Just borrow a pair!"

This he did, and Debbie, dressed and now busy with arranging bouquets of the yarrow, cornflowers, tiny roses and ivy she'd grown for the reception tables, sighed and returned to her work. She draped the three-tiered wedding cake with wild sweet peas and placed a miniature cup of clustered pink roses into the center of the sweet buttercream icing. She checked the men's boutonnieres, created that morning out of bachelor's buttons and sprays of baby's breath. Her three-year old daughter, Brooke, was to be the flower girl. Brooke and Debbie filled a white wicker basket with extra rose petals while Brooke was instructed in the art of walking down the aisle, scattering the floral confetti as she proceeded. Debbie checked the bride's headpiece, woven out of cornflowers as blue as Jennie's eyes. She nuzzled the flowers in the bridal bouquet, the grouping of ivy and arborvitae, of tiny pink roses and of wild sweet peas with a scent reminiscent of honey and orange blossoms.

Our baby sister, Jennie, was finally getting married. Rounding the bend of 31, she'd already lived several lives: as an on-again off-again college student, as a carnie, and as a peripatetic dental hygienist. She'd decided, in short order, to go to dental school, get married, and start a family.

When Jennie had asked our sister the previous spring to do the flowers for her July wedding the following year, Debbie decided to grow them. Until then, despite a sunny, level yard, she'd only fiddled with a few landscape shrubs and simple annuals, nothing more. The serene yard at her home in Livonia, New York, was punctuated by the swing set, above-ground swimming pool and a few saplings. The neighborhood of new homes, carved out of bean fields a decade before and monitored by aging, century-old sugar maples, still overlooked the farmer's fields. Other young families lived close by, and Debbie's kids could walk to school.

The wedding request provided inspiration, impetus, and, as it turned out, an opening door to a lifetime of gardening. Without an excess of knowledge, but a year to fulfill the appeal, she purchased plants: sweet William, foxglove, and pinks. These grew well in soil that had for a hundred years prior to hosting houses had been a cow pasture, with accordingly rich soil.

But they all bloomed the following May, long before the wedding. The problem was clear even to a novice gardener. Enter Helen Seelos, skilled plantswoman and Debbie's mother-in-law.

"Tsk, tsk." She surveyed the barren bed. "These aren't going to give you what you want for Jennie's wedding. About all we can do now is plant wildflowers. And soon."

"But where?" Debbie asked.

"Here." Helen pointed to the southeast side of the small raised ranch. Debbie set to work, removing a wide swath of sod, then digging up the patch to a spade's depth. She broadcast fertilizer, raked it in and scattered several packets of wildflower seeds. The expanse was watered well and prayed over.

Success! Within several warm spring days up sprang seedlings of cornflowers, poppies, coreopsis, yarrow, flax, wallflower, and daisies. Enough, Debbie and Helen figured, to make a wedding.

At my visit a few weeks prior to the ceremony, I stared thunderstruck at Debbie's formerly nondescript yard. A sea of flowers drowsed in the sun. A haze of blue and pink encircled the red maple tree in the front yard. Salvia, snapdragons and hesperis preened from the corner of the driveway. It'd been a contentious spring in the world; a crazed Unabomber was still on the loose, the IRA was raging in Belfast, and the FDA had just announced a diagnostic test for the new and frightening disease of AIDS. But in my sister's garden, all was in peaceful preparation for a life step, a coming together, a family wedding.

My sister had grown all those flowers! How, I wanted to know? I fancied myself a gardener, yet my yard, compared to hers, was nothing to proclaim. Upon returning to my New Jersey home, I stood in the weedy driveway and surveyed my yard, full of scruffy foundation shrubs, patchy grass, and too many monotonous pink and white annuals. Fibrous begonias lined the rock walls of the side garden, and petunias lazed over the sides of our landscape-timbered front beds. A few impatiens graced the shady backyard. That was about it. Nary a perennial in sight, much less wildflowers. My fingers ruffled the petunias. *Not much, are you guys?*

The die was cast; I had to try harder. One more inning in the game of catch-up I'd been playing my entire life.

She was the pretty one, the blonde, and for the five years before Jennie's birth, Debbie was the baby. One year younger, she seemed to be everything that I, the dark, small older child, could never be. Sweet tempered, with a ready smile, she won the hearts of all whom she favored with her clear blue-eyed gaze.

I was jealous from the get-go. Imbedded deep in family lore is the harrowing tale Mother told of a train trip from Rochester, New York, where she'd been teaching, to Illinois to join our dad, who'd moved ahead of us to attend Bradley University in Peoria. The plan was that Mother would make the trip with us, and Dad would meet his three girls at the station in Chicago.

At 1½, I made the trip miserable for Mother and three-month-old Debbie. Not only would I not sleep on the 20-hour journey, but I insisted on wandering off down the aisle and would be handed back to Mother by concerned older women in white gloves and small hats.

"I found her climbing over the seats by the water fountain," a lady would say.

Or, returned by the conductor: "Lady, you have to keep this youngster in your seat! We can't be responsible for lost kids."

My mother, temporarily overwhelmed at the rigors of traveling with two small children, financially fearful after leaving her career to join our father, and apprehensive at the new Midwestern life she'd soon be starting, only nodded.

It didn't help that I'd broken every baby bottle of the Karo syrup and evaporated milk formula my mother had prepared for the interloper. The first one hit the floor by Buffalo. Mother had a stash, so she simply collected the shards and scavenged in her suitcase for a replacement. By Cleveland, however, something else had set me off, and a second bottle bit the dust.

"Colleen! You bad girl! Your sister needs those. Now don't you dare touch the last one."

I couldn't resist. As we pulled into Chicago's Union Station, I threw the last baby bottle onto the floor.

Not much ever vanquished my mother, but that episode came close. With Debbie screaming from hunger, me pulling at her skirts with hands sticky with Zwieback, and both of us children in need of a diaper change, Mother was out of money, stamina, and patience. She wearily carried my sister and me to the side exit of Union Station where our dad would be waiting in his 1950 Chevy coupe to take us home to Peoria.

He was nowhere to be seen.

Mother waited 15 minutes, then 20, searching the crowd, despair growing within her. At half an hour she backtracked into the station in search of a telephone. As she gazed up a long marble staircase towards the public phone kiosk, a young serviceman spoke up.

"Is there anything I can do, ma'am?"

Mother, exhausted and close to tears, gratefully pointed at me and said, "You can lift that one and carry her up the stairs." He did.

When the phone rang unanswered at our home, Mother called the next-door neighbor, Betty Donner.

"Betty! Have you seen Fred? I'm here at the station in Chicago with the girls, and he's not here to pick us up. Is anything wrong?"

"Dorothy, he's right here at my kitchen table, drinking coffee."

The letter Mother had sent to my father informing him of our arrival date and time was languishing unread in the mailbox. My dad hadn't gotten the mail, but he made it to Chicago in record time. He scooped us all up, drove to a grocery store where he purchased another bottle of formula, put me in the front seat, and Mother with Debbie in the back, and off we went to Peoria.

Mother never again allowed herself to be the lone traveling parent.

Child development experts opine that acute sibling rivalry is more apt to occur if children are close together and of the same gender. *Eureka!* My parents were good Roman Catholics, to whom birth control was anathema, and anyway, World War II was over. It was time to make babies! I had barely a year of Mother's time to myself before Debbie was born. At first we all three seldom saw my dad, who, urged by my mother, moved three states west to study watchmaking, courtesy of the GI Bill.

I tormented Debbie during our childhood. I hid her toys. I dragged her downstairs by her heels. I fibbed to and about her. I directed unfair punishment her way. As the older child, my physical strength outmaneuvered hers for a number of years, and since I didn't possess her quiet personality, I also ran roughshod over her verbally whenever given the chance. No wonder she resorted to playing with her imaginary friends, Patty, Dinky and Molly.

Our childhood was made more complicated by the arrival of the next two children, Jennie and Ricky. By the age of ten I'd been forced to relinquish my corporeal advantage, but still I tried to best them in academics. A détente was called when Debbie, a bright girl, won a scholarship to Nazareth Academy in Rochester, and we were therefore not forced to compete at Lima High School. However, I seethed when Debbie was chosen Livingston County Fire Queen in 1965. She rode regally in the convertibles during that summer's Fireman's Parades while I stood on the sidelines.

Not surprisingly, we developed into very different adults. She remained a devout Roman Catholic, studied nursing, stayed in upper New York State and married her high school sweetheart. I threw religion to the winds, became a social worker, moved to New York City, and married an older, divorced Midwesterner with two children.

As we both settled into our respective lives, however, and our children were born, one thing we had in common was a rising interest in gardening. Despite that, I continued to compete, sometimes consciously, sometimes unconsciously. Whose child was the better student? Whose new house was more appealing? Whose daughter was prettier? Which of us was the more dedicated volunteer? Whose town retained more charm? On and on. I'm not sure Debbie was aware of the competition, but it was exceedingly real to me.

But despite my envy of her wedding flowers, the rivalry didn't flourish in the garden. I'd seen firsthand Debbie's skills, and I knew we could learn from each other. Over the years we exchanged plants; salvia 'May Night' to my home, rose campion and verbena bonariensis to hers, daylilies both ways. Information flowed, too. She taught me how to grow tomatoes, and I instructed her in the ways of composting.

Still, our war continued in other areas. Would her children get into better colleges and more prestigious graduate schools than mine? Who would be the first mother-in-law, the first to become a grandma?

The absurdity came to halt after our mother died.

Our father, who'd taught us early lessons in the garden of life, who'd walked each of us down the aisle, our father after Mother's death was old, alone, and frail. He needed us. Not sisters who fought and competed and argued. He needed us to pull together and help him, at the age of 84, plan the rest of his life.

We did.

Our task now is not growing a field of flowers in joyful preparation for a wedding. It's easing our father's days in his final stage of life. Coming together over flowers and gardening, we've been successful. Frank helps, too. He's matured; he might not have been able to find his pants at a long-ago wedding, but he now manages Dad's money, hauls laundry, and accompanies Debbie on the many visits to Dad's new home in a gracious, caring assisted living facility. The same residence, in fact, where Dad's mother, Elva Plimpton, lived until the age of 99.

My father now resides comfortably in a small, plant-filled apartment where he proudly shows off his sturdy red geraniums grown in the Earth Box I bought him and which Debbie and Frank helped set up. Though he lives in Honeoye Falls now, the view out his south-facing window skims over cornfields and woods to encompass a distant vista of his hometown, Lima. Dad gestures with a flourish to the Christmas cactus, abloom again, gentled along by my sister; a plant I couldn't grow if my life depended on it. He's a plantsman, always has been, though he gardens now only on his windowsill and terrace. Debbie and I, his firstborns, have become the family gardeners. It's a huge responsibility, and one that brooks no such nonsense as sibling rivalry.

Instead, we have become like Jennie's long ago wedding bouquet. In the language of flowers, roses represent love, baby's breath stands for joy, and arborvitae denotes lifelong friendship. This bouquet is one we now, at long last, share, Debbie and I. It marks the milestones of life, over and over, the weddings, births, deaths and births again.

Forever and ever in the garden.

Photo by Sue West

Arborvitae (Thuja occidentalis)

Description: Upright evergreen tree or shrub in the cypress family. Its scale-like leaves form flattened sprays. Often used as a hedge.

Favorites: 'Steeplechase', 'Green Giant', 'Bowling Ball'.

Zones: 2 to 7.

Exposure: Sun/part shade. The less sun, the more open the form.

Soil: Prefers organic, moist soil, but will grow in poorer conditions.

Water: Tolerates damp soils; grows naturally in swampy areas. Conversely, is somewhat drought tolerant.

Fertilizer: Incorporate compost at planting time; top-dress annually with acid fertilizer such as Holly-tone.

Pruning: For shape, or after winter damage. Allow to assume its natural form.

Potential problems: Whitefly can be destructive. Spray with dormant oil in early spring, or with insecticidal soap if they appear later in the season. Space plants adequately to prevent dieback between specimens.

Interesting Asides: Known in ancient lore as a *Tree of Life*, for the supposed medicinal value of its bark, sap and fan-shaped needles. The essential oils are still used as in soaps, cleansers and disinfectants, though the presence of neurotoxic compounds make it dangerous to ingest. Often used as a privacy hedge or windbreak. The wood is a favorite for structural elements of birchbark canoes. New cultivars range in size from dwarf to towering.

15

White Tail Deer

My beige linen suit was a trifle wrinkled as I pulled into my driveway, back from the lovely ladies' luncheon I'd just attended. Before I got out I brushed the madeline crumbs off my lap and scanned the garden. My plan was to get in some outside work while the kids were still at the babysitter's. But the allure of the warm July afternoon bled away as my eyes found the daylilies.

Something seemed amiss. In fact, something was *missing*. It took a moment for my brain to register exactly what was wrong.

"Noooo!"

The daylily bed had been ravaged. The flowers, borne on tall wands, the ones I'd looked forward to for the past 11 months and 20 days, were stripped. The daylily blossoms, chosen from the Gilbert H. Wild, Bluestone Perennials and Wayside Gardens catalogues with such care, such attention to size, height, bloom time, shade, and sturdiness, were gone. No more delicately-rippled petals of 'Apricot Ruffles', nor saturated deep yellow of 'September Gold'. Forget about green-throated, shell-pink 'Fairy Tale Pink', and the sweet old-fashioned scent of 'Hyperion'.

They were gone, all gone. Chomped down. Eaten. Devoured. Oh, a few straggly stalks were left, their raggedy stems pointing heavenward. And there were a few skipped shoots. But hundreds of other daylily buds and all the flowers had simply disappeared. Vanished.

The deer had struck.

When I'd moved to New Jersey from California two years prior, our realtor had warned me about white-tailed deer.

"They're beautiful, Colleen, and I have clients who can't wait to get home from the city and see them on the hill. But if you're going to garden, you'll have to either put up a fence or restrict yourself to dill and daffodils." She looked at the meager plantings surrounding our almost-new house and shook her head. "Around here they eat everything else."

I promptly ignored her warnings. After all, it couldn't possibly be *that* bad.

Busy with the move and two small children, I didn't plant much the first year. But by the spring of 1987 I unearthed a few spare moments and stuck some colorful 'Accent' impatiens into big plastic tubs flanking our front door. They shone in the shady, damp nook, and their presence cheered my comings and goings. The pink, lavender, white and orange mixture brightened our dark sidewalk. As the season wore on, the kids and I were intrigued at the round green pods that ripened on the plants. Chock full of seed, they popped when touched, exploding all over the front walk.

We enjoyed the performance every day, taking turns with our "popping seeds." Until the morning we stepped out to discover the pots of pretty flowers sheared off at tub-top.

"Jerry!" I called to my husband, who was pulling stone in the nearby woods for a planned rock wall. "Did you accidently lop off my flowers when you pruned the shrubs?"

"And risk your wrath? Of course not."

"Well, something happened. They're gone."

He and I bent over the wretched pots, closely examining the evidence. Our glances met. "You don't suppose...?"

"Deer? Nah. I've never seen them this close to the house. They wouldn't dare."

The following morning I was straightening up the living room when a movement outside caught my eye. I approached the window, and there, a few feet away from my amazed eyes, stood two large does, placidly dining on my yews. The pared-down pots of impatiens stood behind them, even more demolished.

I grabbed Kyle from his playpen and stood with him in my arms, both of us mesmerized, watching the large, gentle herbivores lunch on our foundation plantings. They grazed on the yew, moved on to hosta, and for dessert ate the remaining leaves of a straggly, chlorotic rhododendron.

The deer had found our yard.

And thus began my personal Deer War. After the impatiens and daylily debacle, I discovered that I did indeed garden in deer country. What is deer country, you may ask? It's not on any map, but nonetheless spreads over much of the Northeast and parts of the Midwest and South. It's everywhere that deer have overstepped their boundaries and dine too frequently on gardeners' hopes and dreams.

This territory contains a variety of habitats: many of the tasty shrubs, flowers, vegetables and trees that unwary gardeners try to nurture; new-growth forest, abandoned fields, meadows, and the special place where all this comes together, known as the edge. Which is where deer especially like to hang out.

Deer are browsers. Ever alert to predators, they'll eat a bit, raise their heads to do a safety check, and if the coast is clear, continue to feast. They'll consume a crabapple twig, then move on to the maple saplings. They'll munch on the hollies and saunter over to the sweet peas. Unless there's a herd at the banquet, they seldom finish off a garden bed at a sitting. Edges, however, provide perfect deer turf; a combination of sun and shade, variety of foodstuffs, safe travel lanes and handy-dandy escape routes.

My introduction to the power of the edge came the day I stepped onto my back porch and heard an odd, soft grunt off by the woods. My attention was drawn to the rear of the perennial border, where a mama deer nipped my *Amelanchier laevis* 'Snow Queen'. Behind her, tucked into the underbrush of spicebush, tangled Virginia creeper and statuesque Solomon's Seal, was curled her spotted fawn.

I watched, transfixed, for a moment. Then I shouted, "Shoo!"

Mama swished her white tail, lifted her ears, and bounded off into the sparse woods, over the deer trail which has undoubtedly been there for the past hundred years, since farming had petered out on my stony, infertile hill. The fawn rose on stork-like legs and scampered after her.

Despite their instinctive caution, there are few deer predators remaining to be fearful of. Humans have extirpated the wolves and puma. A pack of the resurgent coyotes will perhaps take down a fawn or an impaired adult, and the occasional rare bobcat is capable of killing deer, but between them, coyotes and bobcats cannot make much of a dent in the deer population. In the meantime, we've simultaneously squeezed the deer out of the forest by building on their land, and supplied them with a tasty, easy buffet full of succulent, well-watered, well-fertilized shrubs, trees and flowers, setting up a bound-to-happen culture clash.

Add to that the recent furor over tick-borne illnesses such as Lyme disease, ehrlichiosis and Rocky Mountain Spotted Fever, plus ever-increasing deer-car collisions, and we have a crisis brewing. It's not just about gardeners protecting precious plantings. It's about the health of the ecosystem, including the forest, the wildlife, and ourselves.

Given the approximated deer density of 61 per square mile where I garden (anything above 10 to 20 impacts natural plant communities negatively), I've found over the years that it's impossible to be much of a gardener in the Northeast without a methodology to combat these worthy creatures. I'm still in awe at their beauty and grace, sheer size and gentleness. But I knew in 1987 that, if I was to garden, a plan would be required. My initial strategy involved using our new personal computer to research the riddle. Despair reigned in the primitive chat rooms. Gardeners threw up their hands in cyberspace. Nobody, it seemed, had a clue what to do.

So I visited the local nursery. They sympathized and tried to sell me juniper. I hated juniper.

I talked to gardening friends. They'd already lost their hosta, lilies and roses and had no answers for me.

As the damage progressed, I no longer stood in wonder when the creatures visited. Instead, I swore, I stomped my feet. When I saw deer parading into the yard I ran outside like a madwoman, waving my arms and screaming. To no avail. All I succeeded in doing was scaring my children. The deer had discovered that my yard tasted good and added it to their traveling buffet.

As I finally found after diligent searching and the loss of many plants, there *were* solutions out there, but for one reason or another they weren't for me.

We couldn't afford a fence after the cataclysmic stock market crash in October of '87, and I doubted my neighborhood association would let me construct one, anyway.

I didn't have enough time to wind narrow-gauge wire around the stems of susceptible trees and shrubs, as one magazine article bid me. And I was afraid I'd stick myself. Then too, I worried about the deer. I didn't want to hurt them; I just wanted to exclude them from my yard.

Hanging bars of soap on individual trees and shrubs was a lot of expensive work, and threading a piece of thin metal through the thick bar proved difficult. So I laid the pieces on the ground and fretted about soil contamination. Anyway, their presence didn't seem to deter much traffic.

I didn't want a big dog. It appeared our son was allergic, so that was out.

The one time I tried netting foundation shrubs I got so entangled in the black plastic stuff that I had to cut my way out, thus rendering the sheeting useless and embarrassing myself to no end. I wasn't skilled at trussing shrubs with burlap either, and the resulting entombed plants looked unnatural and ugly all winter.

The scattering of human hair I'd snagged from the barber looked bizarre in the yard. Then again, I wasn't able to get a regular supply, and it seemingly was too clean to be a deterrent.

I tried bitter-tasting pellets (to the deer, the package said), planted with new material. Didn't make much of a difference as far as I could see.

Things were getting to the garment-rending stage. My friendly neighborhood deer were chowing down on stuff they weren't supposed to enjoy: lilac, grape hyacinth, sedum, willow, redbud. A pacifist, I wasn't about to start supporting hunting, but still... It was time to circle the wagons.

All the failed efforts had left me with two choices. Either I could pare my plantings down to the few that I'd been told the deer surely wouldn't eat (at least for one season, but who knew about the next year, or the next herd?). Those plantings included herbs, which deer don't like due to pungent flavors and nubby textures. However, we didn't have enough sun to grow herbs. Hellebore was recommended, but it cost too much. The others were likewise rejected. The reasons were varied. Plants such as barberry were invasive; forsythia and its ilk were too common; and some flowers such as bergenia I couldn't grow successfully to save my soul.

That left repellents, which made sense to me. As a beginning gardener, I didn't want to be circumscribed in my experiments. I wanted to grow fancy hosta on my shaded plot. I wanted to try the new roses. After coming from California, where the weather isn't suitable for tulips, I had to have some in New Jersey.

I knew any useful repellent would have to be reapplied frequently, but I also knew the best gardeners are those who are out in their gardens frequently. I believed the old adage "The best fertilizer is the gardener's shadow." So I opted for repellents.

Over the next several seasons I tried most of the affordable ones, and noted the results in my garden diary. Some concoctions had a pleasant-smelling base of cloves and cinnamon that the deer must have appreciated as an appetizer, for all the good it did saving my flowers. Some potions had a nasty, bitter smell. And the container admonished the buyer to not let the substance fall on kitchen counters or hands. A few were built on predator urine, and the knowledge of how the urine must have been collected repulsed me. Some mixtures were based on animal blood, and I didn't want to even *think* about that.

I finally hit upon my own mixture: a thick blend of eggs, water, liquid hot-pepper sauce, and Wilt-Pruf. The concoction smells vile when first applied, especially after a few days of fermenting. But it's easily slopped onto garden plants, doesn't burn, is organic, inexpensive and simple to prepare, store and use. Once it dries, it's undetectable to the human nose. The only drawback was the comments from my family. A typical scenario:

"Oh, Mom!" My daughter stomped into the house holding her nose. "Why'd you have to go and stink up the yard when I'm having friends over?"

Or:

"Mom! Did you have to have deer repellent on the yard when we're gonna play ball? We'll get it all over us!"

Nothing is 100% foolproof, of course, and those in the know say a starving deer will eat anything. Even with my magic elixir I still lose the occasional azalea branch or red cedar seedling. But with judicious use of this mixture I discovered I could grow tulips, hosta, roses and daylilies. And I do.

The stuff proved to be enormously popular. I freely gave away the recipe, answered questions on where to purchase Wilt-Pruf, how to mix, where to store. I posted it in my newspaper column. I shooed away suggestions that I should license, sell or patent it. I didn't want any gardener to go through what I'd been through in saving my garden.

Over the years I've become a mellower, more philosophical gardener, though I still battle deer. And they remain an enormous problem for the ecosystem. In the scourged woods beyond my home there's not much left under the ceiling of 80-year old tulip poplars, beeches and pignut hickories. The deer have devoured everything else. Yet, they are sentient beings, too.

On a skiing trip years ago, minivan stuffed to the gills with children and equipment, a deer rushed out of the forest and careened into the side of our vehicle with a sudden, enormous crash. Jerry maintained control of the car, and the deer leapt off into the underbrush. Stunned, we pulled over and examined the point of impact. There, wedged into the metal striping, was a tuft of deer fur. I plucked it out and held it in my ungloved palm. It was coarser than I'd imagined, and heavier. The piece of gray-brown pelt was coated with a thick, waxy substance, and I realized what I had in my hand was a small portion of a deer's winter coat. They, too, had to prepare for winter.

And I knew the truth. Deer are living creatures, belonging to the forest and fields, rivers and meadows, just as we human beings do and are. It's not their fault that we've altered the environment to the point of disaster for them. It's not their fault that we've thrown Nature out of whack by banishing natural predators and building on every square inch of land possible. It's not their fault that many of them die of starvation in ugly winters, or that so many perish in collisions with their only real enemy, the automobile.

Yes, there needs to be a solution to deer overpopulation. But that's not in my particular purview. I can't consider the lovely creatures "rats with hooves." I can't countenance bow hunting on my property. I can't think about poisoning or shooting them.

As I grow in the gardening arts, I increasingly esteem other entities in the web of life. I understand more fully that we all have a place in the universe. It's not simply human beings who mentor. We are all creatures of this earth: mammal and mollusk, reptile, bird, insect and amphibian. It's possible we gardeners can learn from the other denizens of the earth, and that this knowledge can expand and disperse over the years, like ripples on the surface of a lake.

Sometimes at dawn or dusk I hear the thunder of hooves, and from my family room window I watch the antlered bucks, the yearlings and does, loping down the logging road just beyond my property line, on their way to the pond. I stare in amazement and awe.

But I don't invite them in.

Deer Repellent

Photo by Sue West

2 gallons water

4 beaten eggs

Enough Wilt-Pruf (an anti-desiccant available at Agway) to make the mixture milky (about ¼ cup)

Enough liquid hot-pepper sauce to make mixture pink/orange (about ¼ cup)

Occasional Additives: ½ cup pureed garlic and/or some commercial deer repellent

Mix all ingredients. Store in leak-proof container. When ready to apply, pour liquid (it will be thick) into a plastic pitcher, then into dishwashing detergent squeeze bottles. Squirt on plants. Do not apply in full sun on hot days.

May be used year-round, but store where liquid won't freeze. Mixture is foul-smelling, but once it dries most people cannot detect the odor. Deer, however, stay away! The secret is to apply

REGULARLY (once per week in active growing season, once every 3-4 weeks in winter, once every few days on budding tulips and daylilies), especially in early spring when deer are establishing territories and early fall when they are setting winter feeding patterns.

Maintain a handy supply. I keep a 2-gallon container made up at all times, and as it's used, I make more. I then stuff a 5-gallon bucket with 5 or 6 full bottles, and keep this at the ready in my unheated garage. It's easy to grab the container and dose the garden.

16

Toads

Yikes!

The fist-sized clod of earth exploded out of the ground inches from my nose, arcing over the frozen-in-place, upturned garden pitchfork, and landed, *splat!* a foot away from my astounded face.

Commandeering my brain, which had disappeared into fight-or-flight mode, I surveyed the possibilities. Was I being attacked by an earth-dwelling monster? Had I happened upon a suburban land mine? Or was it merely a jumping, dun-colored snake? (In times of stress it's amazing how primitive our brains really are).

The balmy haze lying over our Kinnelon, New Jersey, home filtered the summer sunshine as if through layers of cheesecloth while a squat, warty creature sat calmly regarding me with unblinking hazel eyes. And once my heart started beating normally, I realized the creature must be none other than *Bufo americanus*—the common American toad. My troweling had interrupted his daytime snooze in the warm, moist mulch of my New Jersey garden on a summer afternoon in 1988.

"Jerry!" I called to my husband, who was laying brick in the front walk. "Guess what just happened?!"

He set aside his chisel and wiped his hands on the sides of his Harley Davidson T-shirt. "What?"

"A toad jumped out of the garden right at me! I didn't know we even had toads, and I've never seen one so close up!" I gestured toward the slope where I'd been attempting to plant a clump of 'Ruffled Apricot' daylilies. "And such a big one! He scared the beje-sus out of me!"

"Do you think it's still there?" he asked, following my glance up the hill. "I bet the kids would love to see a toad."

He went to check on the visiting amphibian's status while I sprinted to the nearby sandbox and hustled our two kids away from their Tonka trucks and Barbie dolls. "There's a surprise on the hill. I want you to be very quiet, and look, but don't touch."

Courtney, age four, stared at the lumpy little creature still sitting next to my discarded pitchfork. "Mommy! A brown froggie! Where's his pond?"

"It's a toad, Courtney. And toads don't live in water like frogs do. They hatch out of an egg in the water, but then they live on dry land. This one was taking a nap when I found him."

Kyle, at two, was mesmerized by the strange sight. He squatted down on his haunches, blonde curls bobbing over his face, peered intently and put out a tentative, chubby finger to touch the toad before I stopped him.

"Let me pick him up, Kyle."

I gently scooped up our guest and carefully opened my fingers to show the kids.

He peed in my hand.

"Can we keep him for a pet?" Courtney asked.

"He's a wild creature, Court, and he wouldn't be happy in a cage. His mommy and daddy and brothers and sisters would miss him. He'll be better off living here in the yard. We should be glad he's chosen our garden to live in, though. That means we have food for him, and places he can make a house in."

"Like where, Mommy?"

"Toads live in corners, where the sun doesn't hurt their sensitive skin. See the rock wall that Daddy built? I bet our Mr. Toad has a snug bed in there somewhere. But we could also put a flower pot on its side in the garden and see if some toads come to live there."

"Oh, let's do that! But what will he eat?"

"Worms, probably, and grasshoppers and other bugs. We'll look it up in our nature book. OK, honey?"

Reluctantly Jerry and I drew the children away from their toad encounter. Our amphibian visitor, no longer under scrutiny, hopped away into the woods. I was exhilarated to have been visited by a creature J.I. Rodale in *The Encyclopedia of Organic Gardening* highly recommended as a primo pest patroller.

More toads soon came to live in our garden. I found them in the ajuga by the flower bed, on the patio behind the hose, and one adventurous soul evidently lived in a large crack between the flagstone pavers. We'd see him emerge daily, scrambling up and onto the sunny courtyard. Later on there were tiny toads who'd hatched just that spring, and medium-sized toads who'd been around for a while, evidently living in the woods. And several large guys, two inches across, who rather dominated the southwest corner of the hillside patch of phlox.

My family and I happily welcomed each of them as part of the marvelous diversity in our organic garden. At first I simply respected their presence, which validated my poison-free environment. After Courtney and I did a bit of research, however, I learned that toads were actually my ally in the ongoing struggle against that mollusk of gardening evil, the common slug. Turns out that a toad's favorite meal is a fat slug, and his second favorite meal is a nice dish of slug eggs. A toad thus provided for will happily live, procreate, and hibernate in a garden where such delicacies abound. Good for my slug-devastated hostas and good for the ecosystem.

The following spring Court and I paid a visit to the Cooperative Extension Service in Morristown, part of the Rutgers University/New Jersey Agriculture Experiment Station. I'd heard that the volunteer horticulturalists at Extension Offices answered all manner of questions concerning the garden: weed identification, bug classification, the name and etiology of obscure flowers. Didn't matter—if they didn't have the answer at the ready, they'd look it up and get back to inquirers. I'd wanted to check them out, and our tiny visitors provided the perfect excuse.

They were chock-a-block with information about toads. After hearing our description, the plump lady with a corona of white hair smiled and said to Courtney, "Sounds like you have American toads in your yard, young lady. What color did you say they are?"

"Brown, I think."

"American toads can be brown, rusty or tan. Are they about yay big?" She held her thumb and forefinger a few inches apart.

"The big ones are. But there's itty-bitty baby ones, too. And they're all bumpy. But Mommy says they won't hurt me."

"Your mom is right, they won't hurt you. Some silly people think toads cause warts!"

"One peed in Mommy's hand!"

"That's because he was a little afraid of her; she's a lot bigger than a toad. I'm sure she washed her hands after that, right?" She glanced at me, then back to Courtney. "A toad's pee is really like a poison that protects him from bigger, meaner creatures."

To me she said, "You must garden organically, right? Toads aren't likely to live where there's chemicals. They're a real asset to the natural garden, though. Did you know a single toad can eat 10 to 20 thousand pests a year?"

We learned a lot about toads that trip, and more after looking at the take-home material. We discovered that toads prefer to live under logs, in leaf litter, anywhere damp, as their skin must be kept moist. We learned that their prey is captured with a long, sticky tongue—and essentially anything that will fit into their mouths is considered prey. Toads will even use their arms to stuff in oversize victims.

We found out from our reading and also from evening excursions in the yard that *Bufo americanus* is most active at night. Our study told us that to protect themselves from larger predators who find them delectable, they have several defenses, primarily the foul-smelling and awful-tasting secretion from their paratoidal glands, which can sicken and even kill mammals. A toad can choose to either play dead or puff himself up to appear larger and thus more daunting to those who would dine on him. A successful toad can live 30 years, and there have been cases of them living for decades in conservatories, hibernating in the potted plants each winter, emerging dirt-covered and hungry come spring. Courtney and I speculated that the large guest in our patio pavers spent the bitter months in the relative warmth and security of that sheltered corner.

The discovery of the toads validated my decision to garden organically, and the quest for knowledge about them became a shared learning experience between mother and daughter.

I mourned my toads when we moved to Connecticut. Would the next homeowner return to using chemicals? Would that harm the toads, or would they simply move too? I never knew, but it quickly became apparent that our New England yard had its fair share of these special small amphibians.

New toadlets stared appearing in my garden about the 4th of July, hitchhiking up the hill from the farm pond below. They arrived just when I was despairing over an onslaught of slugs, which were destroying my hosta and epimedium, carefully carried from New Jersey. So pleased was I to see them that whenever I found a baby toad, I'd cautiously pick him or her up and transport it to a part of my garden being plagued with slugs. Sometimes in distress he'd wet my cupped hands, so I'd try to soothe him with words as we moved up the path.

"I'm thrilled to see you, little guy, and I think you're gonna like it here. But if living under the hosta leaves isn't suitable, I've got lots of other areas you'd love."

In addition to gardening organically, I've tried, over the years, other ways to make our yard amphibian-comfortable. To further entice *Bufo* to take out a mortgage at the Plimpton garden, I provide some rather luxurious toad homes in the form of turned-over, halved crockery pots sited at various points. I really don't know if there are residents in those terra-cotta dwellings, but in any event, my garden seems to be winning the War of the Slugs, and for that I am grateful.

When clement weather arrives it's always an occasion when I happen upon a good-sized specimen in one of my garden beds. I just know that I must have welcomed him in years ago, and now here he is—enjoying a successful, middle-class toad life in my yard.

Just recently, as I was pitchforking compost, drizzle settling onto my skin like a layer of silk, a moving speck of dirt caught my attention. Bending close, I saw it was a tiny new toad, not larger than my pinkie fingernail. It must have been a long journey from his birthplace to the relative riches of the compost enclosure. I murmured my welcome to him, and advised him to move on over to my hosta patch. It would be safer there, and certainly better for my plants. Then I paused to marvel anew at the great reciprocating wheel of all living things and at the goodness of Mother Nature.

Garden toads provided an introduction to a service that I continue to use wherever I live, that of the state cooperative extension agents. Toads gave me an ongoing dialogue with my daughter, who cared not much for other aspects of gardening but was interested in the small creatures inhabiting the land. Garden toads have reinforced my wish to garden in concert with what's best for the Earth.

Are there other gifts, other lessons from the toads?

Yes.

The summer I first became acquainted with *Bufo americanus*, our country was still resonating with President Reagan's "Morning in America" message. And a popular tune danced its way into everybody's head. "Don't Worry, Be Happy," Bobby McFerrin sang.

For me, struggling with my husband's multiple career moves and raising two small children, while trying to scratch an increasing itch to garden when there was no spare time, was easier said than done. Relaxing and simply being happy became an art form. Until I stopped to consider a toad's life.

The annual July appearance of these amphibians in nature's never-ending cycle indicates that once again, the tasks of spring and early summer are complete, and it's time to pause and enter a period of contemplation, of satisfaction. Soon the toad will settle into his new home, eat and grow fat, snooze in the afternoon, and prepare for the hardships of winter.

So too with we humans. Midsummer is the time to sit on the screen porch and savor the voluptuous reward of field and garden, to revel in a job well done. Or to kick back from the office and spend a lazy two weeks at the beach, reading a best-seller and building castles in the sand. Or go to the fairgrounds, admire the blue-ribboned produce and cheer at the tractor pull. The weeks of July and August offer a respite in which to attend a craft show or view an outdoor art event.

It's the time to listen to the cicadas of hot August nights, or the music of a free concert on the town green. Feel the soothing sway of a hammock in the shade. Breathe in the aroma of the tall garden phlox. Watch the shortening days of August and drink in the welcome rains. Taste a sumptuous tomato fresh from the garden. Scan the night sky for meteor showers. Watch a drive-in movie from the comfort of your car. Feel the grass under your toes as you walk barefoot across your lawn. Observe the butterflies waft from the Joe Pye weed to the black-eyed Susans.

Work is part of life, of course, and we all, large or small, have jobs to do. Some of us understand our task early in life. Complete school, marry, raise a family. For others, the work is a process, an evolution. A ministry to be fulfilled, perhaps, or music to be made, or care to be given. What all these life tasks have in common with the toads is that they have junctions, periodic turns, where it is crucial to reflect upon where we've been and where we're going.

But it's easy to get lost in the weeds and work of life's garden. It's easy to miss the moments of satisfaction, to get caught up in the needs of the workplace and ignore family, friends, nature. It's easy to lose our way, becoming slaves to the never-ending demands of the "to do" list.

Watch for the markers that signal the pauses. They are the intermezzos of the seasons, like the toads of midsummer. Seek them out. They're not hard to find.

You just have to look past your pitchfork.

Photo by Jerry Shike

American toad (Bufo americanus)

Description: A common species of toad found throughout the Eastern United States and Canada. Toads have been known to live decades, and a noxious skin secretion keeps potential predators such as dogs at bay. But they do have some enemies, most notably certain snakes; and automobiles, bicycles, and human feet.

Favorites: Different types of toads are native to distinct parts of the U.S. American and Eastern spadefoot toads are found predominately on the East Coast. Southern toad lives south of the Mason-Dixon line, and Western spadefoot and Plains spadefoot toads live in their eponymous areas.

Exposure: Toads live in places that are fairly light, humid and out of the wind, such as a rock garden or an old stone wall.

Water: A plant saucer or ground-level bird bath will provide water.

Soil: They prefer moist and organic soils, which offer an abundance of food. And organic mulch such as Sweet Peet or Agrimix provides burrowing material.

Fertilizer (Food): Will clean up slugs, flies, grubs, wood lice, cutworms, grasshoppers and anything else that's slower and smaller than them. They may eat 50 to 100 insects per night, and are referred to as "Bats of the Earth."

Potential problems: For the gardener, few or none. Toads will not feed on garden plants.

Interesting Asides: The gardener can make a toad feel at home by providing turned-over crockery or digging a shallow depression and loosely covering it with boards. These creatures are capable of playing dead in the presence of an enemy. Contrary to the old wives' tale, handling a toad does not cause warts.

Lungwort

Kathleen Tabor

"Not again, Jerry!" My shoulders slumped as I sat in the family room across from my husband on a crisp November day in 1991.

"Honey, it's too good an offer to pass up."

"That's what you always say. What would this be, the sixth time IBM's moved us?"

He enumerated on his fingers. "New York, West Virginia, Indiana, California, New Jersey, now Connecticut. Yeah, that makes six."

To me, the news was almost as bad as if we'd been one of the thousands of unfortunate inhabitants of faraway Oakland, California, whose hillside homes had been destroyed in a firestorm that autumn. I'd never wanted to move around the country as an IBM wife. My preference would have been to plant an oak tree in our first backyard and watch it grow old as we did. But that was not to be. Prior to meeting me, my husband had already moved four times in his IBM career, and the first 15 years of our marriage were spent being uprooted every few years. In each place I planted a flower garden, and in each locale I learned more about horticulture. By the time we got to New Jersey, I'd amassed quite a bit of knowledge, and had grown quite a large garden. A corporate promotion meant I'd have to leave it behind. Again.

I protested. I cried, I cajoled, I bargained. I wallowed in my sorrow. It did no good.

"Look, Colleen," Jerry pointed out in subsequent discussions. "I'm 27 years into my career; too old to change companies, too young to retire, and anyway, what other kind of job could I get? You need to see this as an opportunity for us, and for the family."

He was right. Jobs like the one he was being offered didn't grow on trees. And he, the breadwinner, wanted it. So… move we must. But still I grieved. Would we *ever* settle down?

Over a glass of unsweetened ice tea in her comfortable kitchen, I sought solace in the company of my friend Kathleen. "It's not like you're going across country, Colleen," she pointed out. "Not like last year, when you thought it'd be Atlanta. Connecticut isn't that far away. We can still see each other."

I nodded, head down, tears stinging my eyes. I'd moved many times before and knew how these things went. There would be a flurry of calls and back-and-forth visits with former neighbors the first few months, maybe even the first year. Then we'd all roost into our own routines. New friends would be made. The fractures produced by leaving previous friendships would be filled. Life would go on.

But I was losing so much. It was during our several years in New Jersey that I'd begun to acquire a reputation as a plantswoman. Rebecca Hetherington, the Mother's Support Group organizer in our community of Smoke Rise, had been the first to say something, noting the 'King Alfred' and 'Actea' daffodils I'd planted on our driveway slope. I basked in the compliment, decided to expand my reach, and asked my family for a flowering crabapple for Mother's Day.

Since our home stood near the community entrance, whatever I grew got noticed. The copper-red coleus along the stone wall one year, the row of emerald-green arborvitae sheltering our turnaround, the undulating nasturtiums and gawky forsythia guarding the back drive. Friends like Kathleen Tabor, Judi Feinberg, and Lori Dandrea began to seek my advice on various aspects of their yards. At first I hesitated. Surely I didn't know *that* much about gardening?

But apparently I did.

To bolster my neighborly counsel, I clipped and collected the weekly gardening column from our daily paper, the *Newark Star-Ledger*. I started a habit of garden diary writing, and found myself identifying flowers, diagnosing problems and offering basic design ideas. I designated a living-room shelf for nature and horticulture books. Deer were an ever-increasing threat, so with trial and error and gleanings from my readings, I concocted an evil-smelling-yet-effective repellent and urged my friends to try the formula.

As I visited others' gardens, I admired plants that I didn't yet grow or with which I was unfamiliar: rose of Sharon, kerria, hydrangea. I noted in my garden diaries, among other horticultural musings, the plants I wanted to attempt someday.

The requests multiplied:

"Colleen, could you come take a look at the tree in my front yard? It's dropping its leaves and I don't know why."

"Can you tell me what happened to my impatiens? And what should I do now?"

"Why are my crocus bulbs scattered all over the place instead of where I planted them?"

"The top of my mugo pine lost its needles. How come?"

One of the first gardens formally visited was Kathleen's. She needed an assessment of a scruffy perennial whose attractive, spotted foliage was withering. I touched a hairy, puckered leaf. Limp. Not familiar with the plant, at first glance I didn't know what to advise. The poor suffering specimen was tucked in under towering Norway spruces, as Kathleen knew it preferred shade. I dug the tip of my trusty trowel into the soil around it. Dry as dust. I rubbed the grit between my fingers.

"I'll look the problem up for you, but one thing is for sure. This plant isn't getting enough water. What did you say it's called?"

She pulled the identifying tag from beside the afflicted plant. "Lungwort. 'Mrs. Moon,' to be specific."

I looked up Madame Moon and found her to be desirous of shade, yes, but also of copious amounts of water, which she was most assuredly not getting. To Kathleen's credit, once she knew the treatment, she watered the plant more generously and it quickly revived. In gratitude she dug up a clump and gave it to me.

In the intervening decades, I've never again been without 'Mrs. Moon'. She came with me on my eventual move to Connecticut, and happily spread out from the shady bed I prepared for her. She's hopped into the Shade Garden and traveled to upstate New York on my lap in a wad of wet paper toweling to live with my sister, Debbie Seelos. She's been donated to innumerable plant sales and to many an admiring fan. She blooms pink and blue in early April, among the first of the perennials. Her silver-spotted leaves brighten the rhododendron border and twist among the azaleas. Her dainty flowers make a pretty bouquet on the bathroom sink. About the only thing she doesn't do is cure tuberculosis.

Lungwort, you see, is one of the many old-fashioned plants thought to have had medicinal value by our forebears. Since she bears spotted leaves, and diseased human lungs are often speckled, it was assumed she would heal lung conditions such as pneumonia, asthma and coughs. Alas, it isn't so.

My introduction to wild pansy was also in New Jersey, by way of Meta McDowell. In Meta's driveway cracks it grew with abandon in colors of yellow and purple and white. Seeing my amazement at the tiny plant's fortitude, Meta plucked a spray one June morning and handed it to me. It exuded a sweet, old-fashioned scent, like cloves.

"Taste it," she suggested.

I must have looked surprised, because she added, "Yes, it's edible. And it looks pretty in salads, by the way. It's called Johnny jump-up because it crops up where you least expect it. Plant it, Colleen, and you'll have it forever." (She was right.)

Spring came, and with it our inevitable move to Connecticut. Debate on the goals of the first Gulf War was still raging, but Jerry and I had reached a domestic détente. We settled into our new abode. The kids went to school, Jerry went to work, and I joined both a book club and the Garden Club. I busied myself the first few years with children and civic activities and with drawing up plans for various named gardens in our sloping property. There'd be the Main Garden, of course, and the Mailbox Garden, and the Patio Garden…

What began in New Jersey flourished in Connecticut when the calls began again, from my new garden friends this time. The back and forth among gardeners started; the helping, the advice-giving, the sharing. With all this came more garden gifts, more passalong plants.

Before charming, pretty Ann Tibbatts, with her lovely manners and giving heart, relocated upstate, she gave me a cottage cheese container of pungent *Perilla frutescens*, beefsteak plant. A stout burgundy-purple, perilla doesn't always behave itself in the ornamental garden. It likes to seed promiscuously hither and yon. But its lacy leaves and three-foot stems make a statement, and its foliage tastes like a combination of anise and mint. I think of Ann whenever I note how beautifully perilla contrasts with the white of *Phlox paniculata* 'David' and the pink of cleome. I thank her again when my Taiwanese friend Chia-Li Sung gathers its leaves and passes it along as a gift for a Japanese family who calls it *shiso* and uses it in making pickled plums.

And then there's Judy Dauphin, who's sung in the Methodist Church choir for 40 years, and gardens on her small in-town plot. When she offered me a start of obedient plant, I took it because I needed a late dash of magenta in the east end of the Mailbox Garden, but also because I needed practice pronouncing its name. Fy-o-stee'-ja. (I have since decided it's easier to simply call it obedient plant.) It now dominates the corner by the compost, and has insinuated its assertive self between the pavers. Obedient indeed! It's time to pass some of it along.

The lamb's ears in the Patio Garden came from my neighbor and fellow book club member, Cheri Levine. She'd planted it by her mailbox, and I admired it as I passed by on my daily trips to town. The next year a seedling showed up under her hemlocks, ten feet away. I asked, she granted, and now the moonglow-soft leaves of *Stachys byzantina* act as an intermezzo, separating the warring colors of coneflower and daylily next to the hammock.

Dorothy DeNigris, my busy neighbor who's a school nurse in nearby Danbury, primarily gardens in containers surrounding her spectacular swimming pool, but her small perennial bed possessed several plants I longed for. She gifted me with *Lysimachia nummularia* 'Aurea', golden creeping Jenny, and when that prostrate enchantress lights up the ground under the hosta, I'm indebted anew. A campanula, also from Dorothy, used to romp in my backyard garden and present me with armloads of pendulous, cherry-pink blooms until the resident groundhog under the gazebo found it. The transplanted flower is now much happier in the front yard garden, immune from the reach of the beast, and arching gracefully over my fishpond.

Dorothy also gave me toad lily, which I'd never grown before and evidently couldn't learn how to care for. With its warty flowers, handsome clean foliage, and late bloom, it's supposed to be a standout in the dappled garden, and I reasoned it'd be satisfied in my narrow shade bed between the house and the woods. Sadly, too much shadow and too many slugs did it in. I moved the tattered remnants into more sun in the same garden, and sprinkled organic slug control when I thought of it. For a couple of years I saw signs of the poor thing struggling along against insurmountable odds, but it finally croaked, and to this day I feel guilty.

On a sprightly June day a bright fuchsia color attracted my attention as I strode up my hairdresser's driveway. Kathy Griffin had been trimming and taming my disorderly curly locks at her home salon for two years, but I'd never before noticed the short, deep-pink flowers carried atop a basal rosette of gray-green leaves that sparkled under her front windows. I had to know the plant's name.

"Sorry, Colleen, I've had it a while, but I just don't know what it is," Kathy said. "Help yourself to some, though, and if you figure out what it is, please let me know."

I gently lifted several clusters, noting the gummy stems. I went home, grabbed my digital camera, returned to Kathy's, and took a few pictures of the largest plants.

Later I searched both the computer and my memory banks. In its basal rosette, though not in its flower, the plant was reminiscent of rose campion, which I'd grown since my sister Jennie gave me a handful from her yesteryear garden on Irving Avenue in Granville, New York. But aha! Mentioned in the rose campion entry was a reference to German Catchfly, complete with a description of its sticky stems. The designation fit, and with the plant identified, I placed the transplants into my Mailbox Garden, where they amazingly proceeded to bloom later the same season. I know I'll have to watch this enthusiastic grower before it takes over that particular garden like the gooseneck lysimachia and the *Monarda didyma* 'Marshall's Delight', which came before. But forever more, German Catchfly will bring to mind my favorite hairdresser: sweet, trim Kathy Griffin and her charming garden that delights the eye from afar.

Other gardeners over the decades have also shared their passion for plants. Before I knew I really was a gardener, while still in my early 20s, I had a chance encounter with Laurence Pringle, a successful author whose children's books focus on natural history, animals, and science. He hailed from the same corner of upstate New York as did I, and on a visit to his cottage hidden deep in the woods of suburban Rockland County, I admired a clump of dried flowers that smelled like fresh air with a hint of vanilla and sage. The stems were suffused with soft downy wool, and white, papery bracts surrounded the yellow centers.

"Pearly Everlasting," he said. "It grows in the Adirondacks, and butterflies like it."

Several weeks later he arrived at my crowded rental house with a handful of Pearly Everlasting just for me. I was touched that he remembered, and years later, when I finally settled into my garden in Connecticut, I recalled his gift. Pearly Everlasting was one of the first plants I bought, attracted by not only the memory of a fellow upstater, but also by the swarms of American Painted Lady butterflies it brought. And though my connection to Larry Pringle was but a moment in time, I've never been without the charming native wildflower to which he introduced me.

From a floral basket given by my friend Darla as a cheer-me-up when I was ill, a carpet of variegated ivy drapes between the Shade Garden and the Patio Garden, a legacy from a sprig that lived one year in a container on the shady side of the patio. I never expected the piece to haul itself over the side of the terra-cotta planter and establish itself in an inhospitable patch of mulch and fieldstone. But it did. And each April, when it revives from our Zone 5 winters, I mourn anew my friend Darla, dead of a broken heart at 40.

Suzanne Galante is one of those rare home gardeners who specializes in propagation. She delights in making more of whatever she has. She sees the possibilities in the forlorn, underwatered plants at the big box stores, or grocery store leftovers, or neighbors' mal-planted perennials. Suzanne starts seeds, air layers, and grafts. She divides mercilessly, takes cuttings and swaps specimens. As a consequence, her one-acre garden is overflowing with towering shrubs, trees, vegetables, and perennials. Her arbor drapes with purple wisteria, and her walkway is lined with self-sown lilies, pink mallow and maroon daylilies.

As a fellow member of the Bethel Garden Club, one wet spring I assisted Suzanne in taming the public garden near the Teen Center. We dug weeds, wheelbarrowed mulch, transplanted hefty shrubs and wiped our brows in the rain. As we finished our stint, she asked me if I'd like some of the browallia she'd started from seed. There's only one answer when a gardener is posited with such a question:

"Sure! I'll take however much you want to give me. Is it hardened off? What exposure does it like? What shade of blue will it bloom?"

Five six-packs of browallia seedlings went home with me that day, and I learned through experimentation they preferred my hot and sunny Front Walk Garden. On the way down the sidewalk to the car, as I brush against their blousy, soft leaves, gaze into their azure blooms, and listen to the whisk of butterfly wings as the swallowtails land on the tiny flowers, I smile at Suzanne's abundant generosity.

There are so many gardeners' plants accepted and given that the memories crowd one another. Alice Mayer, who introduced me to calamint. A distant cousin-in-law who sent me heritage iris from the family farm. My husband's mother, Bernice Shike, who in 1986 insisted I take a shoot of a lilac that had been given by *her* mother-in-law in 1936. Anne Binnie, who gave me my first liatris, which blooms amusingly from the top down and drives the butterflies wild.

All these, and more, make my garden what it is.

My front yard is appealing, orderly, and clearly the domain of an individual who knows something about plants. But most of the work went into the backyard. The steep slope had been useless for a children's swing set or a swimming pool. The first week we lived in Connecticut Courtney gave up on the backyard when she tried to ride her bike down it and ended up doing a header into the woods. I subsequently established a small vegetable patch and plant nursery in the center of the lawn, but the rest of the yard was simply mowed and ignored.

Years later, as a young teen, Kyle decided he needed more skateboarding turf than the driveway provided, and that the lower edge of the backyard would be perfect for a half pipe. After much father-and-son labor, expense, and several smashed thumbs, Kyle used the apparatus for his ollies, kickflips and grinds for a total of about 17 minutes, until he passed his driver's test. Skateboarding was supplanted by cool cruising to Molten Java, band meets and bookstores.

The half pipe fell into disrepair, and I quickly claimed the spot for my own purposes. Now, as visitors round my garage and catch their first glimpse of the backyard, surprise is evident in their faces. The downslope, two major swaths divided by a grass path, stretches 50 by 100 feet north to south. Awash with pinks and purples, greens and grays and the occasional red, full of stature and form, and defined by a magnificent Victorian gazebo where the halfpipe used to live, the garden speaks for itself. It's replete with passalong plants of every type. A huge, red-hued rhubarb, given by Kathleen, which sends forth a ginormous ivory bloom each spring, baffling visitors and anchoring the garden. Tens of hosta from Paul Young, in all shades of green, chartreuse, gold, and blue. Sedum from Rose Fogelman and red maple from Leona Fraser. And so many more. Between my front, side and backyard gardens I grow perhaps a thousand different annuals, perennials, shrubs, trees, biennials, herbs, and vegetables on the acre given to me in this particular way-station of life.

I've now been in my Connecticut garden 18 grateful years. My husband has long since retired from IBM. I planted that oak tree.

Perhaps my grandchildren will see it grow to maturity. I have my memories, and my plants.

And, in the flowering of their gifts, I have my friends, both here and gone. Kathleen Tabor, despite my fears, has remained my friend. Jerry and I are godparents to her second son, Benjamin, and the families manage to communicate, converse and connect on a regular basis. E-mail has allowed me to remain acquainted with many of my plant-loving friends from New Jersey and elsewhere across the country.

Moving, it turns out, is not the end of the world. Sometimes all that's needed for peace of heart is a dose of perspective and soupcon of love.

Lungwort (Pulmonaria saccharata)   Photo by Jerry Shike

Description: Herbaceous perennial in the borage family. Bears springtime nodding blue and pink flowers.

Favorites: 'Mrs. Moon', 'Roy Davidson'.

Zones: 2 to 9.

Exposure: Shade.

Soil: Moist, organic.

Water: Generous amounts; plant will enter dormancy if dry.

Fertilizer: If grown in organic soil, none needed.

Pruning: Pull/cut older leaves if they get ratty. New ones will emerge.

Potential problems: Slugs may dine on leaves, and lungwort is likely to spread by runner and seed, but is easy to pull out. Mildew may visit.

Interesting Asides: Like many heritage plants, such as boneset and feverfew, lungwort's common name is derived from the Middle Ages perceived belief that a plant which resembles a part of the human body should be beneficial in treating that portion of the anatomy.

18

Turtlehead

Judy Feinberg

Controlled chaos reigned on the beach. Toddlers wailed for their mommies, kids shouted and played tag or begged to go swimming, a girl squabbled with her brother. I alternately smiled and sobbed while Courtney and Kyle exclaimed over their gifts. The smell of Coppertone mingled with the brisk scent of the lake and the bouquet of fresh-brewed coffee. The going away party was sad, exhilarating and exhausting, all at once.

It was our last morning in the lovely community of Smoke Rise. We'd lived there seven years, and I'd already cried my heart out at the necessity of leaving. But my husband's IBM job had been transferred, and I had no more tears. Resigned, I led the kids and myself through the sorrowful steps of separation, which is always painful, whether it involves leaving a house or leaving a spouse.

The goodbye gathering of kids and moms, arranged by my friend Kathleen, was the picnic on the beach. The moving van would arrive in our driveway the following morning, so this was the last swim, the final sandcastle, the ultimate minnow chase. It was farewell to the lifeguards who'd taught Courtney to swim and goodbye to the slide in the shallow water that had taught Kyle courage. It was adieu to my Mother's Support Group and a valedictory to a life I'd come to love.

We shared cupcakes and coffee, tears and talk there at the picnic tables in the playground surrounded by beach grasses and flowers. Most of the gifts were for the kids, small things to remember their New Jersey friends by. Teenage Mutant Ninja Turtle action figures and a Cabbage Patch doll. Water toys and Legos. Baby-sitters Club books. And the ceremonial gift: two fluffy white beach towels emblazoned with the names of the kids they'd grown up with, gone to kindergarten with, been in play groups with. Leah, Ben, Larry, Brad, Evan, Colin, Megan, and so many more.

I swiped at my tears, joyful for the memories, sad at the leaving.

As we were packing up, Judy Feinberg held out a small package. "This one's for you, Colleen," she said, dark blunt-cut hair framing her pretty face. "It's so you, I had to get it."

A tint of blush peeped through as I unwrapped the white tissue paper around the soft parcel. I held up a cotton T-shirt in a perfect shade of pink.

"It's beautiful, Judy, my favorite color."

"Read the print on the shirt. Read it out loud, if you want."

"Wildflowers of North America." I brushed the smooth fabric. "Oh, the pictures are lovely!"

And they were. Muted, silk-screened drawings of coreopsis, aster, foxglove and daylily. Of Joe Pye weed and lady's slipper, turtlehead and chicory. A flower for each month of the year.

"I remember you and Courtney searching the roadside for wildflowers at the school bus stop," she said, "with your *Reader's Digest Guide to Wildlife*. I wanted to give you something to remember both Smoke Rise and us." She gestured to her children: Bryan, who was in Courtney's class; Eric, a few weeks older than Kyle; and Cyndi, her baby.

"You know me well," was all I could say.

The moving van arrived bright and early the next morning, and after a 30-hour ordeal of insufficient staff, lost goods and mislaid hotel reservations, it unloaded at our new home in Connecticut. The T-shirt was unpacked and placed with other clothing, forgotten for a time.

Within a few days the kids were off to their new school, my husband off to his new job, and I faced either an expanse of ungardened lawn or a house full of boxes. A Hobson's choice.

Out came Judy's gift; on went the old garden sneakers. I choked back sobs as I unwrapped plants I'd gently carried from New Jersey and considered where to put them in the new yard. Turtlehead was one of the first. The late-blooming, pink blossoming perennial had been growing on a damp slope at our former home, and I knew it to be deer resistant and shade-loving. I dug a hole behind the back deck, dumped in some transported compost, and plopped in the turtlehead. Then I stood back, admiring my handiwork. The sturdy, 18-inch perennial would soon flower, I knew, welcoming us to our new home. *Good placement, Colleen. It'll get morning sun and it's close to the outdoor faucet in case it needs more water. It'll be the first perennial to bloom for you in Connecticut.*

And so, with Judy's going-away present, I cultivated new ground. Her gift was the first instance of my setting aside perfectly good wardrobe pieces for hard use outdoors, but it wasn't the last. As cultivation of my patch of Mother Earth expanded, many other clothing items have been dedicated to the same use over the years, to the extent that my stash of garden clothes now exceeds other wardrobe categories. As I wear out exercise attire, splash bleach on a favorite blouse, or snag a good pair of shorts on the fence, into the outdoor stockpile it goes. My garden tees now boast pictures of moose from northern vacations, logos of long-ago cruises, and slogans from now-defunct gyms. My sweatshirts range from the beloved purple *Telluride* one that stretches to my knees but which I can't quite abide discarding, to ones of washed-out unidentifiable colors, to those bearing crests from my children's colleges.

To accompany the shirts and sweatshirts, my chosen apparel in balmy months is generally used-up shorts. In the shoulder seasons of spring and summer, however, I wear overalls, the kind with the pockets and loops and metal clasps to hold them up. The kind poor folk wore in the Depression and Midwest grain farmers still wear today.

The first pair of overalls I owned was courtesy of my daughter and a winter vacation in Lake Placid, New York. That lovely Adirondack village, home to two winter Olympics, features many apparel shops that assist the weary in forgetting their foibles on the ski slopes.

The air was sharp with frost as Courtney and I strolled down the snow-packed main street on a February day in 1996. From the frozen lake just beyond came the calls of ice skaters and families enjoying dogsled rides. Ice sculptures decorated all corners of the town.

"C'mon, Mom, let's check this out."

This was a Gap outlet. We entered the crowded store, the air fogged with shoppers swarming around overflowing tables and racks. Like most teens, Courtney ranked high in recreational shopping, and she soon convinced me to try on a pair of pale-blue overalls, a garment which I never before would have been caught dead in.

They fit.

Once home, however, it became apparent that they didn't fit my lifestyle. I couldn't wear them to work, to church, or to club meetings. Into the garden duds bin they went. In March I discovered that they provided warmth in the cool days of our New England spring, coverage when I bent over, and practicality, since the loops and pockets were generously spaced for hanging tools and storing tags, tissues and gloves. As I transplanted a stand of Joe Pye weed in the shade garden that April, I found the denim fabric also provided protection against the rough stems of that purple-blooming, butterfly-attracting stalwart garden perennial.

Eventually I also purchased shoes meant only for the garden. I was helped along in this decision by my husband.

"Colleen, what are your wet sneakers doing on the kitchen counter?" he said one autumn, his voice bounding over that of David Duchovny and *X-Files*.

"They got dirty in the garden, so I rinsed them off. Why, what's wrong?"

"It's not sanitary, that's what's wrong. There's grit all over the countertop, and it's a terrible example to the kids." He motioned toward the sink. "And the grass and weeds clog the drain; I don't want to have to plunge it again. I can think of a few more reasons, if you've got time."

I didn't.

The perfect pair of garden shoes beckoned to me in March at the Boston Flower Show. My next-door neighbor, Sharon, and I had opted to remain longer at the show rather than spend the remainder of the day shopping at Faneuil Hall, where our tour bus headed with the rest of the group. I couldn't fathom why anyone would want to shop at Boston's most popular tourist attraction rather than usher in an early spring inside the scented, hushed convention hall, so Sharon and I stayed behind. We'd have to catch up with the bus later, but we weren't worried.

The shoes were forest green, comfort lined, and composed of a sturdy rubberized material; they were lightweight and rinsable with the garden hose. Unfortunately, at the time I was already lugging a Martha Washington geranium that I just *had* to have, a plastic-enshrouded copy of Ann Lovejoy's most recent book, *Further along the Garden Path*, and a huge blue watering can. I bought the shoes anyway.

Hugging our purchases, we at last reluctantly exited the Flower Show, found the entrance to the mass transit system, and climbed the staircase to the train. The gigantic map of the "T" was daunting whether I looked at it head on, sideways, or compared it to the crumpled paper map we'd secured. I felt a jumble of anxiety and helplessness as I shifted my garden treasures and girded my loins for the trip. For heaven's sake, why had we decided to go it alone?

"Don't worry, Colleen, between us we can figure this out," Sharon said, her young voice brimming with confidence.

A few missteps and an hour later, we'd taken an intriguing tour of South Boston and were playing race the clock with the tour timetable. We did eventually make it to Faneuil Hall, and with a churning mix of relief and exasperation, we hopped on board, swag and standing intact.

The shoes proved to be just the ticket in the garden. I no longer cared if I slogged through coffee grounds in the compost. It didn't matter if I stepped in chicken manure, trudged through mud or inadvertently crushed a banana slug. I hosed my green beauties off after each garden adventure, and no longer did soggy sneakers adorn the kitchen counter.

My husband was happy. I was happy.

A spatter of rain doesn't stop a dedicated gardener. If the iberis needed transplanting or the woodland phlox needed deadheading, I'd venture out in my trusty dark green rain slicker, the one with the marker stain on the sleeve and veteran, crumpled Kleenex in the pocket. It's a relic from the single attempt Kyle made at going to camp. He was 13 and on the cusp of a dreadful adolescence. We'd hoped the wilderness camp would pique his interest in something other than grunge music and skateboarding. It was 2000, a millennial year and a leap year. The world had lived in fear of Y2K for months, while all we feared was that Kyle would hate our choice of camp. I outfitted him with the requisite woolen cap, metal meal utensils, warm pants, and waterproof rain gear, and sent him off. But unbeknownst to us, he'd been infected with Lyme disease before his departure, and the whole week was a misery. He never again went to camp.

That was the bad news. The good news was, I inherited his slicker. It fits me fine, and each time I drape it over my shoulders, I feel close to the troubled adolescent who was my boy that terrible summer.

I'm fairly sure I didn't wear gloves as a young gardener. But I do now, and can no longer remember when or why I first donned them. It probably had something to do with sandpaper skin after a day spent double-digging the iris patch. I had torn fingernails and dirt in the crevices of my hands that even Lava soap wouldn't wash out. And just maybe it had something to do with the presence in my life of two gardening friends who are repulsed by earthworms.

I'd tested various methods of keeping my hands clean before switching to gloves, but rubbing my nails over a bar of soap left determined residue long after gardening, and Vaseline applied before a work session left my grip too slick for effective labor.

So gloves it was. I found that a sensible amount of Bag Balm applied prior to slipping them on kept my hands spa-soft, and that the gloves safeguarded me from all manner of garden gremlins. In short, I love my gloves, but I have to admit that they've awakened the sleeping beast of acquisition. I have waaay too many pairs. I'm drawn to the glove display like the bee to a buddleia, and so over the years I've tried many varieties.

Here are my favorites:

For early spring when all is muddy, and for wet work year round, I choose a heavy gauge pair with plastic coating on the fingers and back of the hands, such as Mudd gloves. These provide protection, enabling me to reach into the fish pond and pull out debris without freezing my digits. I can gather handfuls of soggy compost for spring repotting and not get stiff, chilled fingers. The gloves do become a trifle warm in the hottest days of the season, however, and so are replaced by lighter weight pairs.

Delicate work such as deadheading coreopsis, pulling sorrel and separating seedlings of heuchera call for Foxgloves. These are lightweight yet strong, with a touch of stretchiness, and come in gorgeous colors such as fuchsia, cherry red and hollyhock pink. They reach high up on the forearms and are composed of a featherweight yarn, so the sense of touch isn't blunted. Detail work is easy with Foxgloves.

181

I first saw West County gloves at a Garden Writers of America symposium. These assemblies of plant nerds and garden communicators are a cornucopia of plant sellers, book merchants, and garden vendors of all types. One of the purveyors the year we met in Pennsylvania's Delaware Valley had a new glove line, and all comers were invited to try on a pair. If we liked what we felt of the heavy duty fabric, with Velcro fastening at the wrists, reinforced fingertips and two-tone palette, we were welcome to complete a postcard with our size and color preference. My very own free pair arrived at my doorstep the following spring. I use them when pulling weeds and separating daylilies, to firm my grip when employing the lawn mowing beast, and for general garden use.

My gloves go on as an essential part of my gardening uniform, and I wouldn't feel dressed without them. Since I garden each day except in the depths of our New England winter, I'm a serious user of gloves, and I have several criteria for mine. They must be at least minimally attractive, machine washable, and durable. I expect them to last at least two years, and I do rotate them. However, no matter what type of gloves I wear, no matter what the season, I continue to wear out the middle fingers of the left hand. A small price to pay for protection, comfort and warmth.

Not only do I protect my hands, but my face as well, since my skin becomes more sun sensitive as the decades inexorably advance. I've known since I was a girl the necessity of protecting my Celtic complexion (this despite a wanton few teenage years of competitive tanning). Therefore, there's been many a hat in my collection of gardening clothes. Straw hats, baseball caps, floppy hats. New hats, old hats, pretty hats, ugly hats. Anything to keep the darn sun off my face and neck. Nothing worked well, and in desperation one autumn I even tried a Halloween mask. It didn't provide enough visibility, however, and I was embarrassed to be seen in the front yard as Richard Nixon. It didn't stay on long enough for its effectiveness to be judged.

I hit upon the chapeau solution quite by accident. Kyle had moved to Australia, where he worked at an eco-nursery, propagating and transplanting forbs, sedges and grasses. In preparation for visiting him at the height of a southern hemisphere summer, I perused travel clothing catalogues and located a wide beige sunhat. With its broad brim and back flap that tucked up with a Velcro patch, I figured it would surely beat back the semi-tropical sun. When I arrived at the Melbourne airport and stepped into the midst of a blazing Australian December, I plopped on the hat.

My son, age 19, regarded me with astonished, embarrassed amusement.

"Mom," he said, "you might just as well slap a great big 'T' for Tourist right in the middle of your forehead."

I gave him a cloud-splitting smile. I didn't care what I looked like. The hat did the job, in Australia and later in my garden. It's indestructible, crushable, washable, and inexpensive. When I transplant daylilies in the heat of the summer sun, their sweet smell wafting upwards as recompense for the hot, dirty work, I'm protected from the sun. When I deadhead the hydrangea and plant tree seedlings, I'm safeguarded. When I water annuals at church or prune the crabapples, I'm shielded. The hat's inner sweatband absorbs perspiration, the visor can be adjusted depending on the angle of the sun, and the tan color hides a multitude of sins. No more masks for me!

If the pictures in the antique gardening books are to be believed, long ago lady gardeners wore flowing dresses, elbow-length white gloves, floppy hats with flowered bands, and of course, pearls. My attire could not be more different, but I doubt they loved their gardens any more than I love mine.

My accumulation of well-worn, cherished gardening togs lives just inside my closet, clean from the wash, a heaping mixture of comfort and nostalgia. My stockpiles of gloves, hats, and Bag Balm live on top of the retired file cabinet at the entrance to the garage, where I can find them, but where their presence drives my spouse mad with their clutter. My garden shoes live wherever I kick them off. The articles of clothing represent years of work, and carry a residue of knowledge and expertise. The pieces do wear out eventually, but I hate to give them up. The United Methodist Women tag sale each spring and fall is closet-assessing time, and it's then that I take stock of my collection.

Invariably, my shirts are ratty and worn; the shorts and overalls are ripped in unfortunate, strategic places. They've all seen better days. Should I replace them? After all, there are now catalogues full of gardening clothing. Some showcase color-coordinated pants with padded knees, or bandanas impregnated with a special concoction that chills the gardener's brow; aprons that lug the gardener's prized possessions and shirts that proclaim in multicolored embroidery the gardener's favorite plants.

But my plain, time-worn gardening clothes all have memories woven into their fabric. Judy Feinberg's gift of a wildflowers T-shirt. My next door neighbor and our Boston adventure. Kyle and his camping slicker. The Lake Placid overalls my daughter shanghaied me into purchasing. All these and more. How could I give them up?

As I walk back in memory, I realize the truth. I don't have to relinquish them. My recollections, my garden clothes, my flowers, they're all threaded together. I haven't seen Judi Feinberg in18 years, and her wildflowers T-shirt has long since gone to the great rag bag in the sky. My neighbor has moved away. My daughter is grown and lives in Beijing. But they, and all the others connected with what I wear in the garden, just like the flowers I grow, are still in the garden with me.

They always will be.

Turtlehead (Chelone oblique)

Photo by Jerry Shike

Description: Native, herbaceous perennial which prefers moist locations. In favorable conditions will grow from 1 to 3 feet high and 1 to 3 feet wide. Range extends from Georgia to Newfoundland and Mississippi to Manitoba.

Favorites: 'Hot Lips'

Zones: 4 to 9.

Exposure: Part shade.

Soil: Damp, organic. Add compost. Grows well streamside, where it helps control erosion.

Water: Appreciates above-average amounts. The common name may remind the grower of its water needs.

Fertilizer: None needed if grown in organic, rich soil.

Pruning: Not indicated.

Potential problems: Can be attractive to deer, but is rarely disfigured by disease.

Interesting Asides: Greek mythology holds that a nymph named Chelone insulted the gods and was turned into a turtle. A member of the Figwort family; an extract of this   perennial wildflower was used for birth control by the Abenaki Indians. It's also been used as a de-wormer and as an anti-itch salve. Turtlehead's handsome form bears bitter leaves and so is unpalatable to many critters. Multiplies rapidly in moist, shady environments. Related to snapdragons, its flowers resemble the head of a turtle. Bees and butterflies love it. Turtlehead is the only plant the Baltimore checkerspot butterfly lays its eggs on. Also known as fish mouth, bitter herb and shell flower.

19

Aster

Mary Maloney

On Friday morning, the 4th of September, 1992, a hint of her-alded New England autumn hung in the air. The Atlas moving van edged out of the raw asphalt driveway adjoining our new home in Connecticut. The kids had been trundled off to their first day at school. My husband had departed at 6:30 to do battle in his new office. The contents of our New Jersey household had been depo-sited in the center-hall colonial we were to call home for the fore-seeable future. A veteran of multiple IBM moves, I knew those boxes would not miraculously unpack themselves.

I hesitated, then shrugged.

The work would mostly fall to me, but it would have to pa-tiently await my efforts. So, alone at last after an emotional several weeks spent saying goodbye to dear friends and a much-loved com-munity, I seized the moment, hopped in my pickup truck and went to town. Time to check out the new grocery store.

I was a half mile from my destination when the tag sale sign beckoned. I slowed, tempted. There are few times in life when one NEEDS garage sale castoffs, I reasoned, but on the heels of a move might be one.

It was as good an excuse as any.

The driveway was chock-full of other voyeurs, so I parked on the street. As I perused an accumulation of vases, a flash of deep purple caught my gardener's eye, peeking through a tilted picket fence around the corner of the backyard.

"Nice, isn't it?" The homeowner, a sun-seamed woman deep into her 60s, drew near. "That's aster 'Purple Dome', one of my favorites. And it's just coming into bloom." Apparently she could spot that I was a gardener just by the gleam in my eye.

"Come on, take a look. This stuff can take care of itself," she announced with a wave at the array of items. "I'm Mary Maloney, and I'd rather talk gardening anyhow."

She led me to the backyard. I felt a tinge of jealousy at the mature French lilacs, the statuesque viburnums, the well-developed flower beds. *Oh, to have the luxury of years in the same garden!*

Mary turned at my gasp, a smile wreathing her careworn face. "When I saw you spot those asters, I knew you'd appreciate this. Just wish it looked better."

I murmured. The entire backyard, though derelict, was soaked in floral form and texture. Clearly, at some time in the past, love had been lavished here.

She gestured towards the house. "My husband's an invalid. Got a bad heart. I'm his caretaker, so I don't get out here as much as I used to. Looks like it, too."

I bent over the rich purple of the aster. Yellow solidago vied for attention. Round-budded Japanese anemone swayed on arched stems. An array of fibrous begonias trimmed the plot. The sharp hay-smell of new-mown grass rose as a small garter snake darted past us over the edge of the bed, his tongue flicking.

"Shoo!" She flapped her apron at the creature.

"I just moved to Bethel," I said. "Yesterday. Yours is the first garden I've seen in New England. It's a beaut."

"In that case, honey, you need a welcome-to-town gift." Mary grabbed a rusted trowel discarded in a topsy-turvy dog dish and dug out a section of 'Purple Dome'. She trotted up the drive to grab a plastic grocery bag from the stash by the money box, and proceeded to drop a slice of aster into my outstretched hands. Then she looked around. "You know what goes real well with that?" My newfound gardening ally surveyed the chaos in the flower bed. "Montauk daisy, that's what. I know I've got some somewhere."

I waited, drinking in the happy buzz of shoppers in the driveway. I was no longer so alone.

Never having heard of the chrysanthemum known as Montauk daisy, I appreciated the lesson in late blooming color that Mary launched into. Ten minutes later she finished up with, "And oh, one more thing." From the bed she extracted an elongated bluish-green trailing succulent. Its white milky sap seeped onto my wrist. "This is a euphorbia, donkey-tail spurge. Interesting shade, don't you think? It'll bloom chartreuse in the spring, the same as the daffodils. You *are* going to put in some daffodils, right? There's nothing that'll make your new place seem more like home."

I nodded. "Of course."

Delightfully burdened with goodies, I thanked her profusely and beat a retreat to the garage sale, where I purchased a few items I didn't need. Grocery story forgotten, I hurried home to tuck in my first Connecticut plants.

She was right about the aster. It bloomed a long time that fall, and it contrasted nicely with the pure white of the daisy.

She was also right about the euphorbia. When the 'King Alfreds' and 'Ice Follies' presented their regal heads the following April, and for many Aprils thereafter, they sang with the bracts of the euphorbia marginata.

I should've stopped at Mary Maloney's home to thank her on one of the many occasions I subsequently saw her "Garage Sale" sign displayed. I always meant to tell her how much the spur-of-the-moment gardening conversation and gifts meant to a young gardener, a newcomer to her town. I always meant to let her know how well the plants had done for me, how colorful they were in waning autumn days; how I thought of her and her garden each year when her plants sprang yet again out of the earth.

I didn't. And now I never will.

The obituary in yesterday's paper says Mary Maloney died last Sunday. Listed as survivors are her husband and many friends in Bethel, Connecticut. No children.

To the best of my knowledge I hadn't laid eyes on Mary in 15 years, and most likely wouldn't have recognized her if I had. But I, and my garden, am forever in her debt.

Mary Maloney lives on in my garden. Not just because my patch of earth is still graced by Montauk daisy, aster 'Purple Dome', and donkey tail spurge. Not just because vases of white daisies and purple asters decorate my church altar each September. And not just because I use the chartreuse of the spurge and the chrome yellow of the daffodils to teach tints and hues, shades and tones to my students.

Mary is with me still because her presence is part and parcel of the thousands of plants I have given away in my years in Bethel. She's there amidst the campanula and coneflower seedlings I keep under the Norway spruce, with which I gift the casual admiring passerby. Her essence goes with the hosta divisions in plastic grocery bags I hand to my bemused postman; it's in the freebies presented to tour-goers, or the tokens awarded to students who complete their composting class in my yard. Mary is near in the plants carefully selected and potted as houseguest favors to friends; the babies given whimsically to book club members, to other gardeners, and to fellow patrons at the annual library gardening series. Mary is there when the Brazilian women who clean my house wonder over the felted gray leaves of *Salvia argentea* when they find several by their car when they load vacuums and dust mops. Mary is there in the plants dug up and donated each year to the Garden Club; the plants which go to my sisters, coddled on my lap during the long drive to their homes. And she is there in the clump of purple aster I planted on my mother's grave.

She is everywhere I am as a gardener.

Photo by Sue West

Aster

Plant Description: Herbaceous perennial that comes in a wide color range. Native to several areas around the world. Depending on cultivar, can grow from several inches to several feet tall. Known for spectacular autumn display.

Favorites: 'Purple Dome', 'Alma Potschke'.

Zones: 4 to 8.

Exposure: Full sun, though will grow in less.

Soil: Rich, organic.

Water: Adequate amounts.

Fertilizer: Annual application only, if grown in good soil.

Pruning: Cut by a third to a half in late June to keep stems from flopping.

In the Vase: Wonderful cut flowers; combine with *Sedum spectabile* 'Autumn Joy' and boltonia.

Potential Problems: Lower leaves often mildew. Place smaller plantings in front to disguise. Eaten by deer at times.

Interesting Facts: "Aster" is Latin for "star," after the star-shaped blossoms. Some larvae of Lepidoptera butterfly feed on aster. Potted plants are increasingly being used as late-season annuals; sold along with chrysanthemums.

20

Croton

Eddie Rosario

Eyes luminous with fever, eight-year-old Eddie placed his small, sweaty hand in mine and looked up from his gurney in the emergency room. The clamor of medical equipment and the wails of pain down the corridor made it difficult to hear as he whispered, "My teacher says I'm the smartest boy in her third grade. And someday, I'm going to be a policeman."

I'd known him exactly 24 hours.

He'd been the last boy off the Fresh Air Fund bus the previous hot July day. We hadn't realized our visitor had come to us with strep throat, so the first day was consumed with figuring out what was wrong and getting treatment for him. Luckily the local hospital took Medicaid, and antibiotics quickly dealt with his illness.

We were on our way to a long-term relationship.

Our daughter, Courtney, was ten and our son, Kyle, was eight that summer of 1995. Months earlier we'd decided as a family to apply to be Fresh Air Fund hosts. We'd read that FAF, founded in the 19th century, had a continuing goal of providing a summer vacation in the countryside for inner city children ages 6 to 14, among green grass, clean lakes and healthy air. Applicant families, interviewed thoroughly by their local Friendly Visitor coordinator, were expected to welcome a visiting child into their home and help him or her experience a typical middle class kid's summer. We wanted to be a part of that.

Successfully vetted by the Fresh Air folks, spring turned into summer and we found ourselves standing in a library parking lot in a neighboring town. Two hours late, the big Coach bus finally pulled alongside, and families who were obviously familiar with the process crowded the vehicle, looking for "their" child. Our family waited as each boy or girl alighted; all shapes, sizes, and colors. Some kids with cheerful smiles were joyously reuniting with families who'd hosted them in prior years; others were more tentative, meeting families new to them. Child after child descended those bus steps. None of them was our Eddie.

We were wondering if we'd gotten our wires crossed when finally the local FAF coordinator appeared on the top step, holding the hand of a solemn, handsome boy with big brown eyes. He had a white tag around his neck proclaiming him to be Edward. We welcomed him with smiles and soft hello's, and despite the illness which became apparent over the next hours, it was love at first sight.

He was open-mouthed as we pulled into our driveway. The kids piled out, and Eddie turned to me in astonishment.

"Is this really where you live?" he said. "Who else lives here?"

"No one else, just us," I replied, my hand on his shoulder. "And we're glad you'll be spending part of the summer with us."

Courtney and Kyle's individual bedrooms amazed him, as did the three (count 'em, *three!*) bathrooms. And the wonders continued. Garden hoses and lawnmowers fascinated him. He delighted in lying on the green expanse of lawn, fingers entwined in the blades of grass. He couldn't get enough of hamburgers fresh from the grill or Jerry's homemade ice tea. He was awestruck at the playhouse in the side yard, and the first time we went to town, he was dumbfounded upon our return to find the playhouse still standing—no one had stolen it! He took pleasure in the pots of pretty flowers on the patio, the ruffled coleus, handsome croton and delicate impatiens. He loved the woods behind our home, though at first hesitant to enter them, sure that dangerous wild creatures dwelt there.

During the initial two-week visit, a quiet, easy-to-smile, intelligent boy emerged. His foster mother, who was also his maternal aunt, called to relate that Eddie was her deceased sister's son, and he had a younger brother, Joshua, who was ill and had remained in their previous foster home. The boys had been in several homes subsequent to having been neglected, abused and finally abandoned by their unmarried, cocaine-addicted parents. Eddie's aunt told me that her sister had died the previous year. A hospitalized HIV patient, she'd lit a cigarette while in an oxygen tent and was severely burned. It took her 19 days to die. Eddie's father also was ill and currently homeless. Mercifully, the scourge of HIV had not infected Eddie.

He never showed an ounce of homesickness and, once cured of his strep, joined our summer life with gusto. He played with our kids and the neighbor kids. He romped on the swing set, ate cookies, helped in the yard, watched TV, and did all the other summer things that Bethel, Connecticut afforded. Our children got along great. Courtney ordered him around just as she did her younger brother, and Kyle and Eddie schemed to get even.

As the end of the two weeks drew closer, however, he grew very quiet. In a pattern we were to see over the years, he didn't want to go back to the Bronx. No way, no how. He didn't cry (he never cried)—he didn't ask to stay. He just got very quiet.

Over the next ten years Eddie came to us every July and often visited at Christmas, when the house was filled with poinsettias, and Easter, when the daffodils were in bloom. In a further churning of his life, his name changed twice, and he moved three times. But he continued to be a cheerful boy who was happy to be with his Connecticut family.

In turn, he opened our eyes to a different culture. We learned Puerto Rican songs, a smattering of Spanish and even a few steps of salsa. He introduced us to adobo seasoning and urged us to try more spice in our food. We listened to his stories about gunfire at night in city streets. We heard about the time Eddie was four and his mother failed to return to their apartment. In a quest to find a peanut butter sandwich for his hungry younger brother, he'd gone knocking on strangers' doors. We heard about the subsequent shuffle to foster homes, some good, some bad.

At the outset of each of Eddie's visits with us—winter, spring, summer or fall—he would pause in our driveway as he emerged from the car, sniff the clean air and stand silent for a moment in the peace and quiet of the country.

A bright boy, and in the same grade as Kyle, Eddie was nonetheless educationally behind. The New York City public school system was failing him, there wasn't enough emphasis on education in his family, and often there was a lack of money for adequate supplies. There wasn't much structure or encouragement to read, to do homework, to think about the future. His foster family mostly loved Eddie, but like many financially shaky and chaotic families, just surviving each day was exhausting. Our family helped when possible and appropriate. We sent books to the family. We provided Eddie with a summer tutor. We bought clothes and school supplies. We talked to him about the future, including college.

Most of all, we loved him. For at least a month each summer he was our boy, our bonus, and he was treated exactly like our other children. He got an allowance each Friday, was expected to do his share of the household chores, and was corrected when necessary.

When he was in 5th grade we asked his foster mom if we could pay for parochial school—if college was to be a reality, he'd need a college preparatory education. She said no, that she would not allow for one child what she could not do for all her kids. The matter was dropped. But perhaps it planted a seed, because several years later, when it came time to choose a high school, she insisted Eddie take the placement test for a Catholic high school. He was accepted, and financing was found.

As a teenager he increasingly helped me in the garden. He battled the antiquated lawnmower and transported gravel, mulch and soil as I built patios and berms. He accompanied me to the local nurseries when I purchased huge pots of hosta, and with his strong young arms, helped me plant them. Each summer there was garden work, and he did it willingly.

He was 13 when his younger brother died of HIV. His biological father died when Eddie was a high school senior. His aunt and uncle formally adopted him at age 15, but it became clear that the family had issues. Eddie was the oldest child, and several of the others were not doing well. One boy was sent to a group home. A teenage daughter looked and acted much older than her years. Another baby was born. The parents always worked—the mother was employed by the city, and the dad held various jobs. But there was never enough money, and there were lots of arguments. Those were the years when it seemed Eddie's dream of becoming a police officer would be unattainable.

But with help and his diligence, he won a college scholarship.

And failed out the first semester.

We persuaded him to try a local community college, then another one. Neither was a good fit, and he dropped out. He entered a period where he didn't work and didn't go to school. He lived with his deceased father's wife and did little except sleep until noon and play video games all night.

We talked, cajoled, pleaded. We prayed.

But college was not to be.

Instead, the lessons of a Connecticut yard came in handy. Eddie found meaningful work in horticulture. He now lives in Florida with a woman he cares for deeply and is the supervisor of the garden department at a Fort Lauderdale Home Depot. He's proud of his plant knowledge. He enjoys working with people. He's an understanding, empathic, and effective leader. He's got a 401(k) and savings in the bank.

The dream of becoming a police officer, however, has been deferred, at least for now. I asked him about that dream in a recent phone call.

"Colleen," he said, "I like what I'm doing. I like people, and plants. I like the fact that I can advise customers what kind of croton to buy and how to repair their lawn." Confidence rumbled in his deep voice. "I might think about policing once I decide where I'm going to live permanently. But for now, I'm happy."

The tears that sprang to my eyes were inexplicably pleasurable.

My Eddie, my boy from the Bronx, looks forward to the future with hope, faith and love. And so it happens that *this* particular cycle of addiction, poverty, neglect and abuse comes, with the help of green growing things, to an end.

Croton (Codaeum variegatum)

Description: Native to the tropics, where they are often used as hedges, crotons are easily cold-damaged and thus are often used elsewhere as houseplants. A member of the euphorbia family, it comes in many shapes and colors: yellow, orange-red, green, and purple-red. Variegated croton is the most popular form. New leaves are green and change color as they age.

Favorites: 'Petra', 'Gold Dust'.

Zones: 9-11.

Exposure: Color develops best in shifting sunlight.

Soil: Rich. Amend with compost or muck.

Water: Plentiful, but allow soil to dry out between waterings.

Fertilizer: Monthly, balanced.

Pruning: Not generally indicated if grown as a houseplant. In tropical or ideal conservatory conditions, however, pruning may be desirable, as most of the waxy, wavy leaves are borne at the top of the plant.

Potential problems: Scale, mites, thrips and root-rot diseases are possible.

Interesting Asides: In the wild, crotons are a small shrub and can reach a height of 6 feet. In the past decade they've become increasingly popular as houseplants, grown primarily for their brightly colored foliage. Other types of croton are being explored for potential as biofuel. The name "croton" comes from the city of Croton in the "toe" of the Italian peninsula, which was a Greek colony from 700 B.C. and known for the number of Olympic athletes it sent to the ancient games.

21

Abutilon

Ellen Brotherton

The perfunctory phone call of the previous week gave no clue as to how striking Ellen Brotherton would be in person. She'd phoned to introduce herself as the supervisor at my new job with the State of Connecticut. In person she turned out to be a sophisticated, self-confident 30-something blonde dressed in a flowing skirt with an aquamarine silk-screened scarf draped around her neck. She had perfect nails, a warm smile, trim figure, tumbling curls, and a cultured voice. Dressed in my sensible shoes and navy-blue suit, I quavered inwardly as she steered me around the office on my first day, introducing me to co-workers whose names I was sure I'd never remember.

What the heck have you gotten yourself into, Colleen? What made you think you could do this job?

It was the '90s, and the state of Connecticut was taking a stab at managed care. A clinical social worker, I'd been recruited from the private sector to assemble a system of utilization management for the expensive and extensive services given to the seriously mentally ill.

"Working for the state can be confusing, Colleen," Ellen said, elegantly crossing her ankles at her desk during my orientation. "Let me help you get acquainted with its arcane ways." We sat in her office in the recently-vacated Fairfield Hills State Psychiatric Hospital, where the smell of years of patients' cigarettes, sweat, and sorrow still permeated the walls. Once an isolation chamber, the room now held her desk, a wooden straight chair for visitors, a barred window, and twelve years' worth of papers Ellen had transferred from job to job as she'd advanced through the state system.

"You'll need time to get to know the lay of the land," she said. "While we're eager to hear your ideas for managing care, we need to talk every day to make sure you're on track. Please ask me any questions while we shape your role."

As the weeks passed, the inevitable tensions with the new project ebbed. In our time together, Ellen and I found common ground on many fronts. We were both Methodists and social workers from middle-class families. We shared an appreciation of New York City, a mounting despair over the lack of funding for our patient population, and a head-shaking disappointment at the peccadilloes of Bill Clinton's presidency.

We were also both gardeners. In the early stages of my new job, when I needed focus and clarity, I'd often visit a well-known local nursery during lunch hour, and sometimes my boss would accompany me. Long a gardener, my interest in all things horticultural was burgeoning. Ellen and I had many discussions which included not only best practices for the treatment of intractable schizophrenia, but best practices for hosta, how to tame a mulberry bush grown into an untidy tree, and what to do with a chlorotic lilac.

One mild day in March she asked, "Have you ever been to the Farmer's Market in Hartford?"

"I've heard of Farmer's Markets, but never been to one. What's it like?"

"An open-air space where growers come on the weekend. They sell all sorts of plants: trees, shrubs, perennials, hanging baskets, annuals, you name it. I go every year. Great prices, I promise you."

She had me at the combination of "plants" and "great prices."

"Sounds terrific. Can I tag along?"

"I usually go the Saturday of Mother's Day weekend. But it opens at the crack of dawn, which is when the best buys are. Hartford's a long way from Danbury; how early can you get up?"

"Well..."

"How about this?" she asked. "You come to my house the night before the market, and we'll get up early the next morning and hit the road."

With a smidgen of trepidation, I agreed. This was my boss, after all, and I felt obligated to respect professional boundaries. But there seemed no other practical way, and I badly wanted to see such a wonder as a market that sold perennials directly from the grower.

"OK," Ellen said in her customary straightforward manner. "Here's your homework. Since you have a minivan, you get to drive. You'll need a wagon of sorts to move your stuff around at the market. And bring cash, lots of cash in small bills. The growers don't take checks and they won't take credit cards."

The van and the cash were no problem, but my mind searched for a suitable cart. Courtney, Kyle and Eddie were past the little red wagon stage. Maybe the neighbors... In the end I called my friend Cheri Levine and secured a pledge of her kids' Radio Flyer.

The great day finally arrived. After work I followed Ellen to her burnished jewel box of a home in Southington. Vintage '30s, it was dressed with scalloped cedar trim, a front porch and tidy sidewalk. Indoors it featured hardwood floors, polished *objets d'art* shining behind glass-fronted cabinets, and two much-loved tabby cats who rubbed a greeting on our shins. In her miniature, stylish kitchen Ellen prepared our vegetarian dinner.

We went to the mall that evening, Ellen offering me much-needed sartorial advice in the dressing room at Nordstrom. It soon became apparent that her skill set included not only managerial expertise, but a sense of what would look good on me. "And look for the sales," she said, examining the price tags. "Even Nordstrom has sales."

At her call the following morning in the still hour that is neither night nor day, I arose from under an old-fashioned coverlet and lavender-scented sheets. As per Ellen's instructions, I dressed in warm, no-frills clothes which would allow freedom of movement and ease of extracting my cash.

Our first stop was Dunkin' Donuts. Next, Ellen directed as I, unfamiliar with Hartford and its environs, drove down local roads, then the interstate, and finally off an exit where cars were backed up to the gates of the market. We inched along.

"There! There's a good spot." She pointed to a speck of bare pavement just beyond the entrance.

"I don't think I can get it in there, Ellen."

"Of course you can!" she replied.

And I could. With her guidance I steered the van into the impossibly tiny parking spot so close to the action. We hopped out, checking our cash supplies, one hand grasping our coffees and the other pulling our wagons.

It was not quite dawn. Tall lampposts illuminated people clustered everywhere, unloading wagons of potted plants, small trees, rhododendron, flats of impatiens and begonias, and hanging baskets. People arriving, people leaving, some thumbing empty wallets, some calling to wayward kids and spouses.

"Look what I found!"

"I gotta come back next week!"

"C'mon, honey. Let's get breakfast!"

As we converged on the selling aisles, the mingled smell of donuts, heliotrope, viburnum, and stock filled the air. Idling panel trucks, their sides emblazoned with horticultural business names, lined the main row. Growers, bundled against the chill, offloaded their wares with a thump.

Shouts of glee abounded as shoppers discovered goodies. Shopkeepers called to the throngs. "Get yer best azaleas here! Right here!"

Many feet trod the gravel byways. Gloved hands clapped together for warmth. Carts clanged, water hoses hissed. I stood still, taking it all in, eager to begin, but bowled over by the bounty.

Ellen beamed like a Boy Scout. "What'd I promise you? Isn't this amazing?"

I blinked the blurriness out of my eyes and could only nod, overwhelmed by the presence of all manner of plants. Annuals, hanging baskets, vines on tuteurs, labeled shrubs, pots of bulbs ablaze with feisty oranges, glaucous blues and bubblegum pinks, all begging for new homes. A vendor stood alongside rows and rows of perennials packed in cardboard boxes: hellebores, ferns, dianthus. Stacks and trays of color. Friendly growers, eager to please, to sell out so they could go home to a warm breakfast.

"The best strategy is to look at everything first," Ellen said. "Go up and down the aisles to see what there is." Ever the consummate shopper, she cautioned, "Check the prices. Then go back and buy."

We split up, she in search of hanging baskets for her mom and annuals to fill her own porch, pots, and garden. I wandered among the vendors, looking, taking it all in. The coffee in my left hand was faintly scented with vanilla, and its steam rose in the early morning air as I rumbled my empty wagon around the booths, examining, touching, absorbing, astonished. I suppose there were vegetables for sale. Perhaps there were eggs, or even meat. I didn't notice. For me it was all about the flowers. I wanted to ask questions. I wanted to give advice to other shoppers. I wanted to converse with the growers. Heck, I wanted to *be* a grower.

Even the other customers were interesting. Ellen had been correct about the many conveyances they brought. Strollers minus babies, shopping carts absent groceries. Skateboards, bicycle baskets, wheelbarrows and dollies. All carried plant plunder. I stopped at a display of herbs, the dill and parsley as airy as a Dairy Queen ice cream cone. I rubbed my fingers over the peppermint and the sage and lifted them to my nose to sniff.

I moved on as my dilemmas grew. Should I grab the $7 flat of 'Accent' impatiens now, in the scrumptious shades of lilac and shell pink I coveted? If I went a trifle further down the line and didn't find a better price, would they still be there when I circled back around? How about those patio dahlias? At three dollars per pot, they were a steal, but would I have room for them in my cart, or, for that matter, in my garden?

And then I saw it. Abutilon. Flowering maple. I'd read about the half-hardy annual in magazines and seen an occasional pot in fancy nurseries. But the ones I saw before me at the Farmer's Market were exquisite. Eighteen inches tall, with dappled, textured, gold and green leaves and an abundance of dangling bell-shaped flowers shaded a rich coral. I had to have one. 'Gold Dust,' the label read. I purchased two, placed them tenderly in my cart, and was off to the next vendor.

As the morning wore on, the crowd expanded and dispersed like a ring on the surface of a pond. Parking spots surrounding the selling field opened up with departures and were quickly filled with new seekers. The sun rose higher, and the day warmed.

On the fifth circling, my wagon full, I found Ellen, triumphantly pulling her own cart crowded with morning glories, potted fuchsias and Martha Washington geraniums. I showed her my flat of *Salvia farinacea* 'Victoria', my five flats of mixed impatiens, and my abutilon.

We headed for the van, weary but exultant.

That was my first Market, but not my last. The offerings were different every year, though our pattern was the same. Go to Ellen's after work on the Friday before Mother's Day. Dinner. Some shopping at Nordstrom or Chico's. Early to bed, early to rise. Coffee at

Dunkin' Donuts. On to the Market, Ellen directing the way. (I never have figured out exactly where it is).

Some years on our appointed day a warm haze lay over the selling village, filtering the rising sunlight like layers of cheesecloth. Some years were chilly, rainy, and miserable, and I needed to wear my winter gloves. Still we went. One year my fingers grew numb halfway through the morning, and I kept returning to the car to warm myself. Some years a soft gray wall of mist, like an unrolling rug, crept in from the Connecticut River. We could hardly see the booths. Some years we caught only glimpses of a hammered-steel sky between the vendors. Splatters of hard rain drowned out the calls of the shoppers, and puddles soaked our shoes.

We sometimes ran across gardening friends and work acquaintances at the Market. Once I bumped into a psychiatrist I'd been employed by a couple of jobs before. His personality was still as tight as his haircut. We saw friends and foes from the state who'd heard us tell of the jewels to be had at the Market.

Over the years I drove Ellen and myself in a variety of vehicles to the Farmer's Market. Ellen had a BMW when we first met, then an Audi. My vehicles were more suitable to our endeavor. First the old minivan, next my husband's shop van, and much later, my very own pickup truck. No matter what I drove, there were years when we barely could fit all our purchases in, even when we'd jerry-rigged the back to hold double the indulgences. Some years we spent hundreds of dollars on plants, other years not quite so much.

But always, as we left, tired, cold, hungry, exhilarated and broke, we'd head our plant-laden vehicle towards the Olympia Diner on the Berlin Turnpike. There, amid the clatter of sturdy white china and the sizzle of bacon, we'd talk of the treasures we'd found. We'd tell each other where we planned to plant what, and what we'd search for next year. We might briefly discuss men, kids, or work, but our attention was focused on our gardens.

Over a decade, Ellen's career ascended while mine stagnated. I soon lost her as my supervisor when she was promoted. And increasingly I knew that I would leave social work to become a professional gardener.

The years go on. I've now entered my sixth decade of life, and Ellen is about to enter her fifth. She's still beautiful, composed and sophisticated, and still shops at Nordstrom. I now wear jeans and Muck boots instead of blue suits and sturdy pumps. I shop at Agway.

But though we are dissimilar, our garden rhythms are still profoundly linked. Beautiful Ellen, her hands elegant, her hair coiffed, still senses the siren song of Mother Nature. She responds to that call differently than I. But each April, when the days grow longer and the earth warms, we think of each other, and of the Farmer's Market, where garden promises come true.

Flowering Maple (Abutilon pictum)   Photo by Jerry Shike

Description: Half-hardy annual in most zones. Often grown as a houseplant and taken outdoors for the summer. May serve as a garden annual, in a hanging basket, or potted as patio or houseplant or trained to a standard.

Favorites: 'Gold Dust'.

Zones: 9 to 11.

Exposure: Sun, part sun.

Soil: Rich, well-drained.

Water: Average.

Fertilizer: If planting in pots, use good commercial brand with time-release fertilizer and water crystals incorporated.

Pruning: Prune for size. 'Gold Dust' grows to 8 feet if not kept in bounds. Abutilon is a self-cleaner, dropping its spent blooms.

Potential problems: None noted. Not especially attractive to deer, groundhogs or rabbits. Serious disease free, though some leaf spotting may occur in wet years.

Interesting Asides: Know as "Flowering Maple" due to the similarity of its palmate leaves to those of maples. Flowers are bell-shaped and borne all season except in exceedingly hot weather. Very popular as a parlor potted plant in Victorian times. Cousin to mallow and hibiscus. A happy abutilon will flower almost non-stop, in shades of white, pale yellow, deep coral and red. Easy to propagate by stem cuttings.

22

Lady's Mantle

Ann Tibbatts

"You want me on the church's garden tour, Ann?" I looked away from her earnest gaze. "I'm not sure the garden's good enough."

"Now, Colleen," she said, hands deep in the table of potting soil at Hollandia Nursery. "I've seen your place lots of times. This is the middle of April, and you already have color. I know you have shrubs and perennials and that new cutting bed. I think you'd be an excellent addition. And besides, it's all for the church."

Ann Tibbatts, her pretty smile and sweet voice notwithstanding, had me cornered. Our Methodist house of worship, fronting the main street of our small New England village, had graced the downtown for the past 160 years. But with changing times came dwindling membership and fewer financial resources. The tour presented an opportunity for the Bethel United Methodist gardeners to showcase their talents as well as raise funds for their church.

I agreed to participate.

Then I set to work. My garden, while pretty, was no showplace. Ann's plan called for three separate events, one in spring, one in summer, and the last in autumn. I was to be on the first leg. Darn. The date coincided with not only the painting of our clapboard house, but was scheduled for the day following a large party we'd planned for months.

Oh well, it couldn't be helped.

The painters labored for weeks and did a fine job on the house, but they made a mess of the foundation plantings. Ladders flattened the new boxwood and squashed the 'Angelique' tulips. An errant paint can rolled off the roof and crushed the ceramic toad guarding our front stoop. Spatters of paint decorated the bluestone walk and 'China Girl' holly. I sighed and groaned and complained, but what was done was done. The flower beds in the front and side yards were a different matter. I could control what happened to them.

I'd attended a few tours in previous years and knew that clean-up was pivotal, as were sharp edging, copious amounts of mulch, and judicious plantings of annuals. I ordered my Sweet Peet mulch early, edged all the beds with my handy-dandy half-moon edger, and weeded carefully, extracting all the pilea, sorrel and quack grass I could locate. I tidied up stray pots and garden debris. When Ann requested it, I wrote a brief description of my garden, highlighting what I figured visitors would most like to admire. Would it be the herb patch, with fluffy parsley and pungent basil? Or the perennial bed, with its carpet of snow-white cerastium, sprigs of blue forget-me-nots and late-day scent of hesperis? (Certainly not the foundation plantings, decimated by the painters.)

As The Big Day grew closer, I busied myself in the work. I calmed my anxiety by listening to the *kee-kee-kee* of the hawks, the whistling of the bluebirds, and the cheery notes of the robins as they built their nest high in the sugar maple. Mother Nature provided a warm, dry spring and cooling breezes. The scent of stock and mignonette carried over the yard as I worked.

On tour day the sun rose into a sky of rain clouds leavened by scraps of blue. I skipped church. Our party the prior evening had gone well, but at 8 A.M. I was still gathering wine glasses, stray napkins and dropped bits of hors d'oeuvres. Tour guests were due to arrive at noon. As the day wore on the increasing sunlight polished the hosta foliage and sparkled the scattering of raindrops bejeweling the lady's mantle. A perfect day to entertain visitors.

Proud of my garden, I escorted visitors around my yard and enthused about plans and plants, successes and failures, hopes and dreams. I answered questions, tried to recall cultivar names, and explained my deer repelling strategy, my pond intentions and my horticultural philosophy.

And my guests' favorites? My cutting bed, with its fragrant, colorful stock, vibrant snapdragons and annual *Salvia farinacea* 'Victoria' drew many oohs and ahhs as I showed it off. I related how I'd chosen the spot for its bounteous sun, how I'd double-dug the soil, then added fertilizer and peat moss, and selected flowers for their vase-ability.

Visitors recalled the movie *Shakespeare in Love*, which had been awarded Best Picture at the Academy Awards the previous March. They inquired about my herb and rose garden, which must have been reminiscent of those shown in the film.

The rhododendrons (those that had been spared by the painters) drew comments as well. Large specimens of 'Nova Zembla' and 'Roseum Elegans', unlike in many yards, had not become deer fodder and were in full lavender and red bloom.

The four hours went by in a flash. As the sun rolled down toward the horizon, I realized I'd been more than comfortable in the hostess role. I'd enjoyed myself. I'd learned a few things, and even had a few ideas on how the event could be bettered.

On a warm April day the following spring, Ann Tibbatts and I stood chatting in the church vestibule before the 10:00 service. The stained glass windows above us brightened and faded as patchy clouds blew against the sky. The bells from our belfry rang out over downtown. When the sound cleared, she asked, "Colleen, will you consider taking responsibility for the Garden Tour this year?"

"Oh, Ann, no," I answered quickly. "I'm still working for the state, commuting to Waterbury. Granted, I managed to get my own place whipped into shape for last year's event, and I did enjoy myself. But run the whole shebang? I don't think so."

Ann thought otherwise. "Look, Colleen, you can do this." She patted my arm. "You're a wonderful gardener, you're organized, you belong to the Garden Club, and you care about our church. You're the best person for the job. Think about it, will you?"

Later that afternoon I pondered her words as I spread composted manure around the emerging hosta. I thought about it some more as I wrote the daily entry in my garden diary. Maybe I *was* the best person for the job.

With Ann's initial help and encouragement, I eventually organized, directed and participated in three fundraising Garden Tours for the Bethel United Methodist Church. For several years to come I was fresh and full of zeal, but it was stop and go, two steps forward and one in reverse as I learned.

The first step was starting a mental list of possible plots. I looked for variety; maybe a vegetable patch, a perennial bed, and a collection of woodies. An in-town garden and a poolside one would be good, too. I eavesdropped on conversations at coffee hour, trying to catch a horticultural mention. I watched if anyone showed up at church events wearing gardening shoes. I observed who brought in altar flowers from their yards. Turned out there were a number of promising patches. However, their owners took some persuading.

To convince wary would-be exhibitors, I used Ann's wiles. "Look," I'd say, cornering the quarry at an unsuspecting moment. "You've got a great garden. There're all sorts of people who'd pay for the privilege of peeking in your backyard. How about volunteering to be on the tour?"

When they'd sputter, I'd add, "Think of it this way. You'll provide a delightful afternoon out for folks *and* raise money for our church. And remember, your place doesn't need to be exquisite, weedless, or an exemplar of the rare and expensive. Tourers value seeing modest offerings, too. After all, most gardens are precisely that."

Once I'd persuaded my target number of gardeners (securing an extra one or two in case someone dropped out), I was direct with them on dates and times and my expectations. They needed to be in the garden on Tour Day. They needed to set up a table at the entrance to their yard, for collecting tickets and distributing information sheets.

Early in the planning stages for my first event, I ran the ideas past our minister, Bob Whitfield. He agreed the first weekend in June would be a good time. "Before all the graduations and weddings, and after Easter and Pentecost."

He suggested that I set up a table in the social hall after 10:00 services to sell tickets. For several Sundays prior to the Tour I brought in a pretty lace tablecloth, stacks of flyers, and vases of purple lilacs, blowsy peonies, and classic, elegant lady's mantle, which had stood up well to the heat of that spring. *Learn How **You** Can Grow These Flowers!* my sign in front of them read. Intrigued, people paused.

"I wish I had more time for gardening," an older woman said, holding a tow-headed, squirming toddler's hand.

"A tour is a great way to learn labor-saving techniques, and to find out what grows best locally," I replied. "And it might be fun for your grandchildren."

"Either that or some peace and quiet for me," she said, smiling.

A young mother with a baby in a front pack touched the silken petal of a blood-red poppy and said, "My dad grows these; he'd like to see the gardens. And that's right around Father's Day."

"Here, I'll sell you two tickets; one of them can be a gift for your dad."

And so it went. The tickets flew off the table.

As tour time grew closer and gardeners' nerves grew more frayed, I reassured my garden volunteers, just as Ann had done with me years before. I advised them on planting colorful annuals such as marigolds, impatiens and snapdragons. I urged them to edge and mulch their beds. I proposed that they plant captivating perennials such as blue, spiky *Festuca glauca* 'Elijah Blue' and lady's mantle, with its charming chartreuse flower clusters. I offered to visit and make suggestions if that would allay apprehension. For many of my participants, this would be the first time their work would be on public display, and some did indeed need the reassurance of a visit.

Taking a cue from Ann for advance publicity, I'd placed a free notice in *Connecticut Gardener* magazine's annual list of garden tours around the state. And, as she had bid me do when I was on her tour, I made a brief announcement with handouts at the local Garden Club.

For the original tour, Ann had arranged for the local newspaper to come out and photograph my garden. I'd dressed in my best horticultural attire, posed over the pansies, and smiled awkwardly up at the camera while holding a trowel delicately poised for action. I looked ridiculous, but the picture must have worked, because a surprisingly large crowd mentioned it on Tour Day. When it came my turn to run things, I remembered Ann's lead and contacted the regional newspaper. They sent a photographer to several of the gardens and ran a cover feature article which blared the good news. On Tour Day we were inundated with guests from all over the locality, so many that cars studded the street and visitors lined up in the driveway. So many that we ran out of tickets and had to quickly manufacture more.

As I prepared for my first tour, Ann gave me a copy of the brochure she'd drawn describing her earlier tour, and I scrutinized it. Friends gave me pamphlets from tours they'd taken. My gardening pal Paul Young put me in his car and drove me across the state to a fancy tour in a seaside community. On the way I examined that community's leaflet, which had directions to each garden, drawings of sample plants and a list of sponsors. Since I had no sponsors, nor an elaborate budget, I wouldn't be able to create anything so detailed. But the brochure served as a starting point, an inspiration for the booklet I devised to advertise our tour.

As I pulled our event together, I asked each participating gardener to give me a brief description of his or her garden, along with parking requirements. These I incorporated into the brochure, along with a map of our town. As each ticket was sold, I handed over this packet of information, the idea being that the tourer could choose from the description which gardens to see.

I also learned from the tours given by the Garden Conservancy each year. This national nonprofit organization exists to preserve the best gardens in America, and they raise funds by opening fine private gardens on specific days each year and charging a modest fee to tour them. Each locale is heralded with advance signage and driveways marked with balloons. We did the same. Another idea borrowed from them was to have all visitors sign their e-mail addresses, if they wished, so they could be notified of future tours.

Ann congratulated me after my first solo tour, and laughed her tinkling, waterfall laugh when I said I wanted to write an article about my experience.

"Colleen, who better? Let me know how it goes, and don't hesitate to call if you need any information from me."

As the years went on, people came to anticipate the annual event and stopped me to ask when the next one would be held and whose garden would be included. I became the local expert. Just as Ann had advised me, I gladly advised others on the how-to's of a Garden Tour. Eventually the article idea I had mentioned to my mentor became one of my first published feature pieces, written for *Connecticut Gardener* magazine.

All of which I had no clue I could do when Ann Tibbatts asked me to run my first tour. I look back in amazement at my hesitation when she invited me, so long ago, to participate in the church's first garden tour. Her confidence nudged me in a direction I'd never have considered. She modeled leadership, and in doing so taught me a great deal. Because of her I dared display my precious plantings. Because of her I assumed a cloak of leadership in my church and in my community. Because of her I first imagined writing an article for a gardening magazine.

Ann is tender and strong, and pretty and feminine. She's not afraid to pass on hard-won knowledge or to gently guide those who come after her. She's full of enthusiasm and energy and natural beauty. Like the lady's mantle, she's a classic.

Lady's Mantle (Alchemilla mollis) Photo by Sue West

Description: Mounding, cup-forming, short, herbaceous herb. Bears chartreuse flowers on short stalks above the layered, scalloped foliage. Plant is especially pretty with dew or raindrops catching the sun.

Favorites: 'Thriller' is a more upright form. Dwarf form is erythropoda, which is delightful in between patio pavers.

Zones: 4-7.

Size: 1 to 3 feet by 1 to 3 feet.

Exposure: Part shade.

Soil: Rich, organic, though will tolerate less optimum conditions.

Water: Average to abundant.

Fertilizer: A spring scattering of 5-10-5 is sufficient.

Pruning: Blossom stalk may be cut for neatness after bloom. Plant may self-sow.

Potential problems: Slugs and snails may visit.

Interesting Asides: The name means "Little Magic One," perhaps referring to dew drops which in folklore have enchanted properties. Was used by herbalists to staunch bleeding and to treat menstrual difficulties and drooping breasts.

Asclepias

Colette Anderson

"The Pinkertons are coming!" my colleague shouted over to me. I was crouched above the campanula, trusty trowel in hand. "Quick, duck behind the wall!"

We hoisted our purloined plants and scurried to relative safety in the portico of the Administration Building. The burly Pinkerton guards, buttons gleaming on their black uniforms, heads swiveling in surveillance, drove slowly by the forlorn garden. We hadn't been seen.

Or had we?

My buddy and I were among the last few employees on the campus of a just-vacated state mental hospital. The shut-down process had been occurring over the past year. Patients had been shuttled to new homes, staff to community offices. But if one listened hard enough, echoes of the ill still sounded through the hollow buildings and across the windswept grounds. The smell of desperation and abandonment clung to the deserted structures. The stalwart buildings, home to thousands of the chronically mentally ill during the previous 70 years, would soon be either pulled down or metamorphosed into municipal agencies. They'd already been stripped of items of value, as well as nicked desks, sprung chairs, old light fixtures, and splintered bookcases.

Soon our network of services, temporarily stationed at the hospital, would be moving to the community as well. In our brief time there, however, several of us had noticed remnants of forgotten gardens. And as spring advanced, we couldn't help but see unpruned flowering shrubs snugged up next to the brick former dormitories and dining halls. Lilac trusses reached to the second story smoking porches, and hydrangeas in full bud threatened to obscure the first floor windows where for so long patients had gazed out of locked screens at the bucolic wonder unavailable to them.

We decided to do some horticultural liberating.

The first self-appointed mission was picking some of the deserted flowers for all of us to enjoy in our isolated offices. It seemed a shame, really, to have them go to waste. We located a ladder, and with much laughter, wavering balance, and old scissors, we cut armloads of aromatic purple lilacs to share among the staff.

The escapade had been sanctioned (sort of) by our supervisor, who shrugged and told us to go ahead. What harm could it do? We felt encouraged enough to reconnoiter the rest of the territory, and decided the next task in our life of garden crime would involve rescuing several large rippled-leaved hosta of unknown name that ringed the former central dining hall. We'd also salvage a stand of bicolor German bearded iris that stood sentry by the tumbledown sheltered workshop.

After those successes, we resolved to free the perennials in a once-lovely flower bed at the main entrance. The pinwheel-shaped garden had clearly been a showpiece in its time, designed, dug and planted by patients with the assistance of a local garden club. The project surely had been labor-intensive, and the perennials had bloomed in a frothy filigree for years. But since the hospital had been emptied of patients, caretakers had simply mown over the plants, which were now struggling to survive. Some had already passed to the Great Garden in the Beyond. We were determined to save the remainder.

On the appointed day we dressed for the task of appropriating plants (no suits or heels!). During lunch hour, accompanied by quiet cheers from the staff left behind, we tiptoed out of our build-

ing equipped with spades, trowels, and various wrappings to protect our findings. We weren't sure the Pinkertons, hired to protect
the deserted buildings, knew about the scheme, and we weren't taking any chances.

We dug out bellflower and balloon flower, deep-rooted asclepias, felted lamb's ears and rose campion. We found remnants of
phlox and a brave stand of lady's mantle languishing in the sun. We
took what we could dig. Then the Pinkertons loomed.

With our time clearly up and luck running out, once the coast
was clear we almost skipped back to the office. Arms stacked with
booty, we were laughing at our escape.

We spread the treasure out in the corridor.

"What a haul! Are you going to share?" the secretary asked.

"Of course, grab a pot. Or some damp newspapers."

We divided our loot then and there, slicing into the daylilies,
teasing apart the roots of the overgrown campanula, and separating
the scalloped-leaves clusters of lady's mantle. Off the perennials
went to various home gardens, to new lives where they needn't fear
beheading by an uncaring lawnmower.

Amid much self-satisfaction, we went back to work. Mission
accomplished.

Until the following day, that is, when we were firmly admonished that no more such folderol was to take place. That everything
on the grounds belonged to the state of Connecticut, not us, and
we were to take no more plants. We members of the Horticultural
Rescue Squad stared at one another for a few seconds. Busted!

"But Blanche," we said to the head honcho, "we were *saving*
those plants, you know that! The grounds crew didn't care. No one
does."

"I know, I know, but stay away anyway. No more liberating
plants. No more cutting flowers."

And so commenced my horticultural dealings with the Department of Mental Health and Addiction Services of the State of Connecticut. Despite the wrist-slap, our derring-do brought pleasure and plants to a number of would-be gardeners, and saved any number of items. Surprised at the interest, I vowed to continue the horticultural dialogue with my co-workers, just minus the pilfering.

The gardeners in my work cohorts quickly sorted themselves out. The finance guy who asked advice on proper care for the grapes clambering over an arbor at his new home. The payroll clerk who enquired about appropriate material for a long, shady driveway. The Utilization Review nurse who proudly displayed a photograph of her seed-grown Japanese irises. The staff members who chose vacation destinations based on their proximity to well-known gardens. The slightly-askew individuals who'd spend a windfall on new topsoil for the vegetable bed instead of new clothes for themselves. Those folks who'd spend years tracking down just the correct statuary for their shade garden. We had them all.

Our offices in the abandoned hospital closed the next year. We moved operations to the community. Sensing the interest in the new office, I began to bring in plant divisions, culls and extras on flimsy trays after long, satisfying weekends in my garden. These trays, put together with chicken wire and chewing gum, carried yearling columbines and divided daylilies and extra bundles of forget-me-nots. They held loose clusters of hosta, brittle clumps of bleeding heart and tiny asclepias. When I transplanted the rhubarb from my patio garden to the berm, I hauled into work pots of the ginormous, evil-looking red roots, causing off-color jokes and much mirth in the coffee room.

I toted my treasures down the sad, sunstruck streets of Waterbury, a city smelling of car exhaust and defeat, but which was nonetheless home to many of our mental health clients, and therefore to our services.

As a clinical social worker, my overarching goal with my clients was to make a positive difference in their lives, despite the spate of 1990s changes in the care of the mentally ill. Ever-escalating deinstitutionalization, welfare reform, and diminishing dollars for treatment, rehabilitation and employment training all made our clients' lives grueling and our jobs difficult.

My new supervisor, Colette Anderson, was also a social worker. She was of Italian heritage and not only cared deeply for our clients, but loved all things horticultural. Her ready smile supplemented a will of steel, and with her warmth and engaging, disarming manner she could charm a bird out of a tree. Full of humorous commentary at her gardening peccadilloes, she asked me for horticultural advice, brought plants in for identification, and listened when I talked gardening. Though the work came first, she'd always make time for gardening chat. Her bright, stylish clothes reflected the plants she grew both in her office and in her garden.

She was often first in line for the freebies. So as a good employee, I started reserving choice plants for her. I'd plunk them by my office door so our weekly supervisory session could open with an innocent topic, deflecting whatever unpleasantness might have occurred that week at work as we all strived to provide a network of services for the chronically mentally ill in our community.

Co-workers, including Colette, soon wanted to know more about the plants I carried in. I started composing small descriptive tags and pasted on photographs clipped from Wayside Gardens or Burpee seed catalogues. These were taped onto Popsicle sticks or broken-pointed pencils and stuck in the box of plants for identification. I'd bring in my weekend stash, and on Monday mornings, staff members were free to peruse the collection and take home their choice in donated yogurt cups stuck in a Dunkin' Donuts fiberboard tray.

Others got into the game. Rose Fogelman brought in plants to identify and give away. That's how I learned of the existence of bloodroot and yellow archangel. She shared culls of her iris and pointed out the architecture of peony seed heads. Leona Fraser gave away pips of ornamental strawberry and tips on how to grow pink-flowering oxalis. Our director offered advice on producing spectacular bloom on 'Jackmanii' clematis.

It wasn't long before co-workers began asking me to visit their gardens and the plants I'd given them. My fingertips left tiny dabs of perspiration on the clipboard the first few times I toured their gardens, answering questions and giving advice. But I rapidly learned how to diagnose issues and offer guidance in situ.

"There's the lilac you gave me three years ago," Leona said. "It looks good, but it doesn't bloom much."

I took a close look at the purple *Syringa vulgaris*, its leaves emerald green, tucked in between two small but thriving maples.

"Did it bloom more last year?"

"Yes."

"Here's your problem. It's getting shaded out by the maples. Lilacs need a lot of sun to bloom. It's never going to be happy crowded in there. I suggest you move it to a sunnier spot before it gets too big to handle."

"OK, consider it done. Now about these peonies?" She pointed to an anemic stand of stalks. "They send up just a few stems each year. And what's that vine all over them?"

The earth under my sturdy trowel didn't give as I bent to examine the setting. The few grains I was able to scoop were a khaki tan. I hesitated, massaging my forehead as if that would make the answer any more palatable to the eager gardener before me. "Well," I said. "Peonies are heavy feeders. This soil," I indicated the freshly-dug spot, "isn't giving them the nutrients they need to produce flowers. In other words, they're starving."

"What can I do?" She squinted at the errant perennial.

"First, take out some of this exhausted dirt. Be careful not to disturb the peony roots. And replace it with rich organic soil. Start composting and use the stuff to enrich your soil. Next, give them a good dose of Plant-tone twice a year. Last, mulch with an organic mulch like Sweet Peet or Agrimix."

"And the vine?"

"I don't recognize it, but I'll take it to the Cooperative Extension office. They'll know or can find out what it is. Let me have a chunk, OK?"

Back at the office, word spread that I was always willing to answer gardening questions. I didn't mind the interruptions at my mare's nest of a desk as coworkers stopped by. In between caring for clients, I lent books and recommended magazines. Eventually, though I certainly didn't charge for my advice, I had gardening business cards made, christening my enterprise *Morning Glory Gardens*, a name Kyle had composed. The card displayed a simple drawing of Courtney's that showed morning glories scrambling over a fence.

I was beginning to dream of a retirement career in horticulture. As a high school freshman, my vocational test had indicated I'd be happy as a forester. I'd strayed from that, but perhaps it was time to return to the land.

A few years later our offices moved yet again, this time to a spanking-new building where even houseplants were persona non grata. The plant exchange came to a halt. With Colette's permission, I segued to other aspects of horticulture. Teaching, for example.

The executive secretary poked her head in the conference room. "Colleen, it's time to set up for the staff meeting. Can we have the room?"

I hurriedly swept up my welter of *What to Do in the Garden This Week* list, plant descriptions, pictures cut out from catalogues, and tip sheets. "Oh, of course, Elena, I'm so sorry. I got carried away." I stowed my Scotch tape, used to paste up a picture of the Plant of the Week, and assembled my stack of papers on which I'd described potential garden pests. I smoothed my skirt, checked my face for traces of pollen, and mentally comported myself for the weekly staff meeting. The smell of the leatherette chairs, faux-wood table and morning coffee superseded that of the faint imaginary whiff of stock and snapdragons, of dirt and delphiniums. Though

I'd been allowed to conduct brief, before-work gardening classes, I was still a social worker, and there was work to be done.

An elaborate latticework of customs certainly surrounded state service, but I had carved out a bit of time to teach, and I loved it. I adored answering questions about water needs and what to do about predatory deer. About how to start composting and why. About reinvigorating poor, exhausted soil and how to obtain late season interest. I was keen on promulgating my belief that all gardeners should grow asclepias, since this plant, commonly known as butterfly weed, was not only a beautiful, hardy perennial, but an essential host and nectar plant to migrating monarch butterflies. The monarchs followed the vivid orange blooms down the Eastern coastline to their wintering grounds in Mexico. I was partial to informing folks that growing asclepias would make a positive difference in the butterflies' lives, that it was incumbent on us all to help them out.

I was becoming a horticultural educator.

But, despite research in my growing home horticultural library, there were the inevitable questions I couldn't answer. It was time to go back to school. Not for a Ph. D. in social work, nor a master's in public health, both of which my younger self had considered. No, the satisfaction gleaned from sharing plants and knowledge, information and suggestions was a powerful lure, and I began a course of study at the New York Botanical Garden leading to an eventual certificate as a gardener from one of the great horticultural institutions of our time.

Colette encouraged me every step of the way.

A year or so later I applied to teach gardening through Bethel's Continuing Education Program. With much trepidation I drew up a course description for a three-class series, complete with handouts, tip sheets and ultimately, a PowerPoint presentation. From there I eventually graduated to lecturing on gardening topics at public libraries, parks and recreation departments, and garden clubs.

Soon I was teaching at my alma mater, the New York Botanical Garden.

The latter days of my social work career coincided with my rapidly developing interest in gardening. I finally had a large enough (too large, perhaps) space in my yard to experiment with all sorts of plants. My children were increasingly independent. My husband was occupied with his business. The moment had finally arrived in my life that I could devote large chunks of time to my passion.

I was ready to retire from the practice of social work, and I knew the way forward, with the assistance of an understanding supervisor who cared not just about my ability as a clinician, but also my hard work and team participation. She knew me as a loyal employee of the state of Connecticut, but she'd allowed me, in my spare time, to flourish in my avocation as a gardener.

Near the end of my days with the state, in a role reversal of sorts, Colette brought in a bouquet of flowers at our weekly supervisory session.

"Do you recognize them, Colleen?" she asked with a smile.

I examined the deep green leaves, the bright orange cluster of flowers and the nascent oval seed pods. I felt the rough texture of the stems and the structure of the multi branching plant.

I grinned at her. "It's asclepias. Is it one of the...?"

"One of the seedlings you gave me years ago, yes. And even though I've mistakenly tried to pull it out a time or two, it's survived in my garden." She leaned forward, her eyes shining. "It brings the butterflies each year. And I wanted you to enjoy the flowers on your desk."

Colette was a special boss in a special passage in my life: the time when at the end of my long vocation as a social worker, I moved into a new stage of life, a deeply rewarding career as a gardener.

Bloom where you are planted, they say. I was fortunate enough to be allowed to bloom in state service while preparing for a new career. From rustling perennials at the hospital, through sharing gardening gifts with co-workers at lunchtime, to teaching gardening in spare moments at work, I passed through the phases leading to a new life.

I'm a professional gardener now. A garden coach, lecturer, educator and writer. Thanks in no small part to Colette, I make my living from the land.

Butterfly Weed (Ascleplias tuberosa) Photo by Jerry Shike

Description: North American native herbaceous perennial, also known as Butterfly Milkweed. It is the cultivated form of wild milkweed seen on roadsides. Known for its long-blooming, bright orange flowers. Grows easily from seed. Very attractive to butterflies, especially monarchs, whose caterpillars eat the leaves and lay their eggs on the plant.

Favorites: 'Hello Yellow'.

Exposure: Zones 5-9. Prefers full sun, but will grow and bloom in less. If happy, it self-sows, though not invasively.

Soil: Fertile, well-drained soil.

Water: Quite drought-tolerant. Water at transplant time.

Fertilizer: If grown in good soil, none needed.

Pruning: These 1 by 3-foot plants bloom from late June through July, and do not need pruning.

Potential problems: Has few insect or disease problems, as leaves are quite bitter. Has been known to be occasionally eaten by groundhogs, however.

Interesting Asides: The name *asclepias* comes from the Greek god of medicine, and tuberose comes from the knobby swellings on the enlarged root system, which enables the plant to be drought-tolerant. Fruits, similar to wild milkweed, are hairy, spindle-shaped pods which contain numerous tufted seeds, easily dispersed by the wind. During World War II, schoolchildren collected the silk from milkweed of all types to stuff military life jackets. Late to emerge in spring; mark its spot so it's not disturbed.

24

Canna

Dorothy Plimpton

"We hope you like it, honey."

February, 1999. Mother perched on the edge of a lobby sofa in a nondescript hotel in Binghamton, New York. Her hands a-flutter, and her voice pitched a shade too high, she watched me unwrap the small, rectangular box she'd just handed me. Its wrapping didn't quite meet in the back, one corner was ripped, and it bore the neglected look and stale smell of having been prepared years ago. I shook it gingerly.

Was it possible that my own mother was regifting me?

"This is your fiftieth birthday, after all. We wanted to do something special."

Dad said nothing as Mother repeatedly glanced his way.

What on earth?

I was present under mild duress. Mother had orchestrated the rendezvous halfway between my home in Connecticut and theirs in upstate New York, and I'd agreed that my husband, Jerry, and I would meet them for a celebratory birthday dinner. Our mother-daughter relationship, ever prickly, had improved in recent years. But as always, I prepared myself for the inevitable anxiety.

Jerry and I parked in the cramped hotel lot just down the row from my parents' eight-year-old black Chevy Cavalier. As we approached, Mother, wearing her good dress and carrying her second-best purse, spotted us through the glass wall and waved frantically, beckoning us inside.

She couldn't wait until dinner for the presentation. I'd hardly seated myself when she ceremoniously handed me the small package, her breath coming fast. I peeled back faded tissue paper and lifted the top of the used checkbook box. My hands dropped to my sides as the gift came into view.

Nestled inside was a thick wad of thousand-dollar U.S. Savings Bonds. I ran my thumb over them, uncomprehending. I looked at Mother.

"Do you like it?" She bit her lip, tears glinting. "I haven't insulted you, have I?"

My speechless hug was my answer.

"We've been buying bonds for years, your father and I, planning to give each of you kids $20,000 when you turn 50. We want you to spend it on whatever you want. Mad money."

My mother couldn't have coddled a canna if her life depended on it. Water lilies withered under her gaze. Hosta humbled her. Nonetheless, her $20,000 gift was instrumental in my becoming a pond gardener.

Dorothy Eleanor Kennett was an English teacher by trade, and what she excelled at was growing kids. She had four of her own, and she helped raise a foster brother, all of whom she shepherded, guided, and cajoled. She was a stubborn, opinionated, religious woman, and her faults were showcased as she dragged us into productive lives.

She cared nothing for the soil, but was a gardening mentor nonetheless. Three of her offspring became gardeners. What are the odds? In our respective yards, hundreds of miles apart, with no guidance from our mother, my sisters and I delight in cosseting our annuals, bulbs, perennials and shrubs. We glory when the lilacs perfume the air. We judge the temperature and texture of our compost. We lay out elaborate plans for our landscaping, every inch of which, of course, we'll implement ourselves (with maybe, as the years pass, a bit of adolescent hired help).

Despite herself, Mother is the reason I'm a water gardener as well as a dirt gardener. She's the reason I have a lovely hole in the ground which produces extra goldfish when I'm not looking, supports green frogs, water lettuce and a healthy crop of string algae. She'd be surprised to know that I consider those fish and frogs my livestock, that I take seriously my charge to provide them with adequate cover, sustenance and quality of amphibian life.

Her twenty thousand dollars in not-yet-mature savings bonds translated into $13,000 in the bank. I invested part of it, but $8,000 went to purchase a custom-designed ornamental fishpond which I lifted not a finger to build. For once in my gardening life, I hired it done.

I'd coveted a water feature for ages. More and more gardening magazine articles were dedicated to the joys of a fishpond. The Philadelphia Flower Show had shown them off for years. And most telling of all, my gardening buddies were beginning to install them. I could envision the splashing of the waterfall, the flash of the goldfish and the fascination of having wildlife visit the edge to drink. But with three teenagers, a full-time job, and a long commute, I had neither the time nor the money to install a water garden in my yard.

Mother's gift was exquisitely timed.

"Here, I think." Michael, young, muscular, and knowledgeable, had spent the better part of the spring morning in my yard, walking from venue to venue, selecting the perfect spot for my pond. He'd paused in the cutting garden, but rejected it. He explained that a pond would dominate such a small space. He'd examined the slope to the backyard garden, but stated his bias: a water garden really should be enjoyed by passers-by on the street, as well as homeowners.

At last he stopped on the house side of the main perennial bed that stands between our quiet street and our front door. "This is it. Not perfect, but pretty good. It feels right." He glanced up at the mature birches. "Problem is, these trees will drop leaves in the water every fall. You'll have to be on your toes and clean them out pronto."

The tradeoff appealed to me. From the site by the birches I could share my pond with the Starr Lane joggers, dog walkers and moms with strollers. I figured if I could keep the weeds out of my flower beds, I could keep the leaves out of my fishpond.

I agreed to his choice of placement.

The process of pond building was utterly absorbing. First sturdy workmen dug the 24-inch hole. Deep enough for fish to survive, not deep enough to need a town permit. Then they lined it with old carpet, next a thick layer of butyl rubber, draped carefully in and over the sides of the excavation. A rumbling dump truck unloaded a load of goodly-sized rocks into my front yard. Michael stood in the lined hole, directing placement of each boulder, each rock, as it was carried to the site by the sweating men.

"I'm making hiding places for the fish you want," he explained. "So they can hide from the cranes and the raccoons. And I'm giving you an interesting shoreline. Last but not least, notice how the rocks hide the liner."

I'd explained to Michael that I was increasingly an organic gardener and didn't want to treat my pond with chemicals. He suggested a biological waterfall and filtration system which would circulate and oxygenate the water. It was constructed as the rocks went in.

The final step was planting the surround. I'd sprung for soil and plantings. The nursery dumped a load of rich black dirt and planted some feathery pink astilbe, ugly yellow ligularia, and intrusive liriope. But at least they did it, not me.

The finished product, to my eyes, was indistinguishable from a natural pond. Only ten feet round, tucked in amongst boulders under the trio of birch trees, it did indeed have the appearance of a glacial kettle hole.

Then the capstone—we held our breath and filled the hole with the garden hose. The water stayed in the pond, right where it belonged.

A day later I made a ceremonial trek to the reservoir at the end of our road and ladled a bucketful of mud and water. I'd read that it was wise to inoculate a new pond with natural water and bio-organisms, both to suppress the growth of algae and to boost the health of fish and amphibians. I dumped it in my fishpond, uttering a small prayer to Nature for balance.

The next day the kids escorted me to the pet store, where each chose a fingerling goldfish. Courtney opted for a flowing fantail; Eddie preferred a bubble-eye; and Kyle, ever the simple soul, chose a plain gold goldfish.

The fish thrived in their new home. We fed them each day, sparingly, as per instructions on the box of food. We watched in wonder as the fish not only grew fat, but learned to swim to the edge of the pond and raise their gaping mouths out of the water at our footsteps.

One last improvement. I sprang for large pots of cannas, those huge, old-fashioned tropical plants beloved by Victorians, with their vivid leaves and vibrant, plume-like flowers. Cannas enjoy life at water's edge and, though they were initially expensive, my wallet has appreciated the fact that I've learned to dig and overwinter them. They and their offspring have brightened my pond for ten years now.

In retrospect, the whole pond endeavor was way too expensive. And worth every penny, especially when my parents visited in July. The pond had been in a month. They'd not known what I did with my birthday money, and hadn't inquired.

They also hadn't noticed the pond on their way from the driveway to the house.

Once safely inside, and after greetings and settling into the guest room, I gathered them in the hall. "OK, close your eyes. I have something to show you." Mother and Dad looked at each other, but did as they were bidden.

"We're going out the front door. I'll take your arm down the steps."

They gingerly stepped onto the grass and covered the 30 feet to the edge of the pond, eyes still firmly shut.

"I put the money you gave me into a hole in the ground. Take a look."

They opened their eyes, at first not understanding. They chuckled, then laughed, then spent a delicious few moments admiring the rush of the waterfall and the flash of goldfish. Dad insisted on feeding the livestock right then and there.

After a while we retired to the family room. There, windows open, the splash of water provided background for our conversation the rest of the visit.

The next morning I found Mother reading the morning paper ensconced on the bench by the pond, glasses perched on the end of her nose, entranced at the sight of visiting sparrows bathing in the drops spilled from the waterfall. We chatted a while, the soothing splash of water softening distressing topics such as the recent Columbine school massacre and ongoing presidential foibles.

Would I have gotten a water garden without the monetary assist from my parents? Maybe, eventually. Would I have enjoyed it half as much? No.

But trouble sometimes follows a water garden. It's not like gardening in soil. You have to clean out the leaves so the water doesn't sour, and keep the water oxygenated so the fish don't suffocate. You have to provide a winter haven for small amphibians who call your pond home. You have to keep the water level consistent, and balance plant and animal life. Too many fish and the water fouls. Too many green plants and the fish smother. You have to take out the algae that occasionally bloom no matter your efforts. In order to keep fish alive under winter ice, you need to keep a hole open all winter so gases can exchange. You have to fish out the dead frog carcasses in the spring thaw until you figure out how to winter frogs over in a pond that doesn't have a natural mud bank for them to burrow into in hibernation, but an impermeable butyl liner. And so on and so forth. I did all that.

I learned, for instance, that in order to protect my frogs, I let the leaves drift into the water in autumn, forming artificial mud. I learned to sink a dishpan full of white play sand into the bottom of the pond each fall, the better for frog hibernation. (It comes out with the spring cleaning). Also, hornwort works best as an oxygenator, but don't have too much of it. Bales or balls of barley straw make a fine organic water purifier. A long-armed net swirled clockwise with the waterfall going is needed to catch most of the dead, evil-smelling leaves that must be removed each spring. I learned that pond plants in pots are not worth the bother. Garden plants which frame the water serve the purpose best.

Was it worth it? You betcha. Not just because of the myriad of creatures that use my pond. Not just for the soul-calming sound of falling water. And not just for the sparkle of golden fish scales that I can see from my upstairs study.

It was worth it because, for as long as my mother lived, unlike with my other gardens, she felt a part of that pond. She never asked exactly what was planted around it, nor what the maintenance schedule was. But she never failed, each visit, to spend quality time by it. She never questioned my choice for her gift. She didn't have to.

The pond, the unexpected bestowal from a non-gardener mother to a gardener daughter, brought two disparate individuals together. We found common ground, literally, over a small body of water. It didn't matter to Mother if crocuses bloomed by the water's edge in April, or if raccoons came to drink and wash their food while fishing for my goldfish. What mattered, what we both felt, was the peace of the water, the pleasure of the gift.

Mother would never have chosen to spend money on a hole in the ground. But joy is where you find it.

Photo by Sue West

Canna

Description: Large tropical and subtropical herb with rhizomatous rootstock. Flowers are typically red, orange or yellow.

Favorites: 'Tropicana' (to 6 feet). Orange-striped leaves and vivid orange flowers. 'Lucifer' (3-4 feet). Dwarf, green leaves edged with red. Scarlet flowers.

Zones: To Zone 8.

Exposure: Full sun at least 6 hours per day. Will take less, but won't flower as well.

Soil: Moist, organic. Can grow in pot if kept damp.

Water: Lots! Will be happy in boggy conditions.

Fertilizer: Yes, cannas are heavy feeders, but use a low nitrogen product.

Pruning: Cut off dead flowers, and damaged lower leaves, if necessary.

Potential Problems: Leaves will lose coloration if allowed to dry out. Slugs may come to dine. Use organic controls.

Interesting asides: Easy to winter over in colder climates. Once frost blackens the foliage, dig rhizomes, allow to dry for a day or so. Shake off excess dirt and place in an unheated area, but keep from freezing. When weather warms in spring, replant.

25

Ageratum

Marie Meyer

On a bright August morning in the summer of 2004, during one of my all-too-frequent trips to town, a flash of blue behind a tidy colonial on Hoyt's Hill Road caught my eye. I was fairly sure the color was plant-related, but wasn't exactly certain to what domain it belonged. I looked for it each time I crested the rise on the historic street.

In my self-appointed role as garden-getter for the Bethel United Methodist Church Tour, I was always on the lookout for exceptional gardens. The azure I'd seen resembled that of morning glories, an uncommon sight given deer depredation in our corner of New England. I had to find out what it was.

A few days later I knocked on the front door, where visitors were greeted by a wooden bench and sheltering baskets of geraniums and impatiens. No answer.

The following week I tried again. This time the gardener was home. A regal, white-haired woman with kind blue eyes and capable hands came to the entrance. I introduced myself and explained my peek at what I had surmised were morning glories. She beckoned me forward.

"Yes, they are," she said. "Come in, come in. I'm Marie Meyer. Would you like to see them from the back of the house?"

She led me through to the kitchen, where a sumptuous view filled the window.

What I'd glimpsed was indeed a cluster of blue morning glories, jumbling over a metal arch leading into a magnificent oval flower bed in the backyard. From my perch indoors, queenly dahlias vied with a kerfluffle of daylilies. Agastache stood tall at the back of the bed, and purple ageratum was generously sprinkled throughout. Not only was the garden well-laid and stuffed with varied tints and shades of red, yellow and blue, but Marie clearly had an artist's eye, for slipped in here and there was ornamentation. Birdbaths, stone walks, a statue of St. Francis. The symmetry of the bed pleased me. She'd arranged it on the side of a rise, backed with stone and substantial plantings of spirea, grasses and roses.

I knew I'd just met an extraordinary gardener, and that she was a natural for both the tour and the local garden club. Marie agreed to consider both, and we coordinated a time for me to visit her garden at length.

A week later, clad in gardening shoes and gloves, Marie and I tromped around her yard, she explaining, me exclaiming. A venerable Japanese maple served as the focal point for the public face of the garden. The dooryard, edged in Belgium block and half bordered by a rock wall, boasted large- and small-leaf rhododendrons, pieris, and *Pennesitum setaceum* 'Rubrum'. Interspersed were azaleas, *Salvia farinacea* 'Victoria', coreopsis, and ageratum. New Guinea impatiens razzle-dazzled among 'Knockout' roses. Phlox subulata, small zinnia and trailing sedum tumbled over the edges.

Marie even tended to the hell strip between the sidewalk and the busy, hilly street. These narrow belts of dirt, notorious for their parched, infertile soil, are difficult to plant, but she'd established piebald houttuynia, goutweed and ajuga. Tall purple ageratum had leapfrogged into the patch. The long rectangular space said *welcome* to passersby in cars and on foot alike.

Amazed at the expanse, I asked where she shopped.

"Oh, I don't shop much." She waved an arm at the profuse splendor. "Most of the flowers I brought with me or started from seed."

"You brought this *with* you? No wonder your garden looks so mature."

"Well, most of the shrubs were here. But yes, I moved a lot of things."

"Where did you garden before?" I asked. "How far did you have to move them?"

"Garden City, Long Island. We were there for 21 years. My husband's a Lutheran minister, retired now. When we left our last church, the new pastor and his family didn't want to be troubled with the garden, so I was free to take some of it."

I glanced around. "That had to be a lot of work."

"Yes, but I really had no choice. Most of what came with us I'd had for years. Like the salvia and columbine seed I brought from our first churches, gifts of dear friends and good gardeners. The perennial candytuft and ever-blooming bleeding heart are from our congregation in Patchogue. And the sweet woodruff, the dahlias, the forget-me-nots; they were from gardening friends, too." She opened her hands. "I knew I couldn't take all the people I cared for with me, so I moved the plants that reminded me of them."

"Makes sense to me." I nodded. "But how'd you do it?"

"I started making selections as soon as we knew we were going to move," she said. "I chose the plants that meant the most to me, and took divisions, if possible. All the perennials I'd started from seed came along. I probably moved twenty-five percent of the garden, which gave me a head start here."

"Did you have a plan to get all that accomplished?"

"Yes. I'd transplanted a garden before, when we moved from Patchogue to Garden City. We'd been there 11 years. Essentially what I did this time was collect all sorts of pots, dig up the plants I'd selected, and borrow a friend's station wagon. We loaded it up and made several trips to the new house." She snipped a misbehaving rosehip. "I put the pots in the shade until the new garden was ready. But when I left my old garden, I made sure it looked good; I didn't leave obvious holes, for instance.

"Some things were easier than others. The purple ageratum I started in 1990 for my daughter's wedding, and it's been with me ever since. It pops up everywhere, it's tall, has staying power, and the deer don't eat it."

I bent to admire the fuzzy blooms. "This isn't something I grow. You say it seeds itself?"

"Oh yes, it's enthusiastic. You're welcome to take some when it's ready."

We meandered to the back yard, the hint of which had started our gardening acquaintanceship. Upon examination, I saw that the flower bed contained, besides the morning glories, zaftig dahlias and a frisson of edging campanula. Arabesque Japanese anemone cast a gimlet eye over daylilies and feverfew. A stone path meandered through the cleome, ageratum and roses. Agastache in heavy bloom hung pendulous over smaller daylilies and coral bells. In the center rested a cement steppingstone, the words "Mom's Love" spelled out in colorful glass chips. Though close to town, all was hushed in the garden, save for the tinkle of wind chimes and the rustle of maple leaves.

"And these Siberian irises, the ladybells and the feverfew?" Marie continued. "They all come with memories. Same with the rhubarb, the gooseberries and raspberries. So many things were given to me over the years by people I care for. I love to walk through my garden and remember them." She paused. "It's a joy to connect with people through plants."

I gazed off over the patterned flowers, catching the fragrant air. "Yes," I said, "yes it is."

The time spent with Marie had refreshed the memory of my garden move of some 15 years before. Though I'd not carried nearly as much as she managed to, I did transport a few daylilies and some campanula, a few irises and all the chelone. The principal plant I transported was Grandma's lilac. A piece dug from the lilac leaning over the farm fence at my husband's childhood home had been relocated from Illinois to New Jersey in 1986. My mother-in-law had received it from *her* mother-in-law in 1936. At our former home it occupied a place of honor in the sunniest part of the yard, close by the children's play set. There it bloomed in concert with the clove-like scent of the swamp azaleas and the blazing vision of late tulips.

When we moved to Connecticut the lilac was dug once again, roots wrapped and carried like the Joads from *The Grapes of Wrath* in our pickup truck to its new home. It's since lived in several different locales in our yard as trees have grown and shaded it out. But each May it produces fragrant lavender flowers (and suckers!) in abundance. One day its offspring will go to my children's homes, a living legacy of their past.

The afternoon with Marie also brought to mind a question. What compels certain gardeners to move their gardens along with themselves? Is it the same reason colonists brought yarrow and Queen Anne's lace to this country and African slaves came with okra? The same reason westward pioneers packed wildflower seeds as well as flour on their wagon trains?

Is it because gardening, that most ephemeral of the arts, is a never-finished project? Is it the challenge of the enterprise; to see if the plants will thrive in the new home as they did in the old? Or is the gardener accepting the time-honored challenge of replicating the compelling celebration and splendor of the former home?

For some, it's determination: *I worked so hard on this; I'm not giving it up now.*

For some, like Marie, it's a desire to take with us a dash of the love and memories of family and friends.

For some it's about saving money. *No need to buy new plants when I can take them from the old garden.*

For a small minority, it's selfishness. *No one else is going to enjoy what I worked so hard to create!*

But whatever the reason, before we uproot our gardens there's an ethical dilemma to consider. *Should* we take them? Or is what we've planted, loved, and nurtured intrinsically part of the landscape and should therefore be allowed to remain? Is it true that when we create with Nature, what we produce is never truly ours, but only borrowed? If that's so, then perhaps what we've grown needs to remain in place, despite questionable skill levels of the next homeowner, or the need to irrigate, or the dangers of deer. For, unbeknownst to us, the landscape may continue to provide shelter, loveliness, food for wildlife, inspiration to others. And conceivably we are obligated to allow it to do so.

There are other, more concrete reasons why some gardens can't be moved. Some states, especially the agricultural ones such as California, prohibit moving plant material across their borders without an inspection and often a quarantine. Then too, when a gardener moves from one climate extreme to another, it's often not sensible to transport material which may not be hardy. Also, when a gardener downsizes, or moves to an apartment, it may be time to surrender ownership of many beloved plants.

But if it's feasible and permissible to transport some of the result of our sweat and toil to the new home, then it's imperative to work with the realtor, and if possible, the new homeowners. Marie was aware, for instance, that the new pastor and his wife in Garden City did not want her perennials, so she was free to take them. When I moved from California to New Jersey in 1985, it would have been imprudent to take my garden of hybrid tea roses and camellias. I didn't know who would purchase our home, or if they'd be gardeners. I was certain the camellias wouldn't be cheerful in the zone 5 of northern New Jersey. So I left a detailed diagram of the plantings, what they needed, and the improvement proposals we'd drawn up but not yet implemented in the 18 months we lived in Danville.

It's not just plants we shuffle. We gardeners have been known to move compost and ornamental pinecones, seashells and driftwood to the new plot of land. Some of us even transport favorite stones, as I did with a particular type of purple sedimentary rock, shot through with white quartz, which appeared locally in northern New Jersey. When we moved to Connecticut I brought several specimens with me. Once there, I couldn't quite bring myself to place them in the garden for fear they'd get lost in the mulch and the marigolds. Thus, one stone became a landing for birds in the birdbath, and another now adorns a bookshelf. When I see them I'm pulled back to the warm autumn day when I first saw Puddingtone.

Our peripatetic society relocates on average every five years. All over the country, for all sorts of reasons. Newly-minted college graduates move for that first grownup job. Ambitious 30-somethings seek career growth. Retired folks go to warmer climes. We leave behind homes, friends, trees, neighborhoods, grocery stores, beloved church communities, and ways of life. And sometimes our gardens.

But gardeners remain a resilient lot—we're accustomed to being trounced by nature. If the slugs, snails and deer don't devour the fruits of our efforts, then disease or drought may visit. We learn to cherish what survives. We rejoice when our crops succeed. And we mourn our losses.

So when move we must, some of us will take part of the past with us. If we can't uproot our friends, neighbors and communities, we'll take their representatives, the plants. As Marie taught me, we can sow the seeds of new life in a new place. Seeds that link us to the tendrils of the old. For in our hearts and in our soil, we implicitly believe in tomorrow.

There, taprooted in our memory and in our gardens, they'll remain.

Floss flower (Ageratum houstonianum) Photo by Sue West

Description: Blue or purple-flowering annual used for bedding plants or in cutting gardens.

Favorites: 'Blue Blazer', 'Blue Horizon', 'Blue Lagoon'.

Zones: Annual. Hardiness varies, but does not withstand frost.

Exposure: Full to mottled sun.

Soil: Easy to grow in any good garden dirt.

Water: Average.

Fertilizer: A scattering of 5-10-5 at planting time is sufficient.

Pruning: Not needed, but may be deadheaded or sheared back lightly if plants become unruly.

Potential problems: Mites are a possibility in hot dry weather. If present, treat with insecticidal soap.

Interesting Asides: Ageratum is one of the few annuals with a truly blue flower, though it also comes in shades of white, lavender

and pink. It bears soft, fuzzy blooms of five to fifteen tubular flor-
ets that often cover the plants. Is not attractive to deer. It's a long
bloomer, from early summer to frost. The name derives from the
Greek *a geras,* meaning non-aging. Makes a good cut flower. Native
to tropical regions of Central and South America.

26

Japanese Painted Fern

Bernice Shike

In the autumn of her 90th year my much-loved mother-in-law left this mortal life. Born, raised and died in west-central Illinois, Mom was a farmer's daughter and a farmer's wife. A few months after her death, some treasures and mementos of her long life made their way to our home in suburban Connecticut. Among the candy dishes and photographs of well-spent decades were her diaries, covering the years from 1936 to 1980.

I had always known Mom was a diarist. The small, worn books stood in a row in the glass-fronted case behind her chair in the parlor. When I was a young bride, eager to learn more about my husband's childhood, Mom had allowed me to dip into these books to read the entries about my husband's birth in 1942, his childhood trips and adventures, and what life was like in mid-century farmland America. Jerry tells me that when he was a boy on the family farm, he remembers his father using Mom's diaries to check on weather conditions of a season or a year prior, to find out exactly when the south field had last been fertilized or when the sows farrowed. The books were endlessly useful.

And now, nestled in tissue paper in a box in our hallway, they were mine. Mom's prose was not florid. There in her spare writing were the outlines of a life richly led on the corn and wheat motherland. The small books with their faded ink were given a place of honor in our home. As I positioned them, I began to muse on what written chronicles I had of my life and times. I'd kept a diary in my teen years, recording thoughts on cute boys and upcoming dances. And of course, I'd started baby books when Courtney and Kyle were infants, and a photo diary when Eddie came to us.

But I knew that any true talent I had as a diarist lay in my garden journals.

Starting in 1989 with a now-tattered, spiral-bound 7 x 5 notebook, and ranging to this year's finely tooled, 392-page beauty, I have kept a record of my gardening journey. Thirteen different books, marked with coffee rings, smudged with garden dirt, and dog-eared where I have returned to a particular page time after time, these are my chronicle of life as a gardener, a gift to me, recording my toil and joy over the past 21 years.

At first I kept it simple. I wrote when I applied deer repellent and when I rebuilt the compost. I noted temperatures and the frequency of rain. I told my diary what I had planted and where. I observed the first crocus and its cheery yellow hello to spring. I scribbled what was in bloom, in bud. That initial book covered 2 ½ years and is decorated with the spontaneous drawings of my then-five-year-old. The next book was a petite, lovely journal, a gift from my friend Meta, illustrated with line drawings of delicate flowers. Its last entry records that the moving van carrying her belongings to the West Coast had just passed my driveway.

In subsequent books the entries got longer and more detailed and necessitated more room. By the middle '90s I was purchasing muscular composition-type books. And increasingly I found myself, in addition to writing down the dates of the first and last frost, recording thoughts and feelings about my garden and my life—the lack of time to enjoy the garden, the angst of middle age, the creative pleasure of seed starting, the rush of finding just the right granite rock in our woods. I had started to make a record of where I planted what bulbs, and where more would be needed in the fall.

I now keep a record of what I order from the catalogues in the dead of winter, and how much money changed hands. There's a running list of the Perennial Plant of the Year, grumbles about the groundhog, and things to be remembered underlined in red. I write down hawk sightings and where I need to kill the bittersweet. I speculate on the best way to control the voles. I give way to my thoughts on gardens I have toured and classes I have taken.

I use them for more personal musings, as well. I keep track of my sorrow at how far away my daughter lives, and a son's struggles with early adulthood. When the economy crashed I wrote ideas on how to garden more frugally. I sketch out my weekly newspaper column, and I outline my blog. I even keep track of my weight in my diary, for I know I'll always be able to lay my hands on the book.

I search for just the right pen to write my entries with. It must have smooth, dark ink and not be too expensive. And it must be available at Staples. When I discover that elusive perfect pen, I stash it either in the folds of the diary for safekeeping or hide it in a corner of the bookcase, out of the reach of my family. The book snuggles up beside me in my leather club chair each evening in the family room as I wait for a quiet moment to document in familiar dark ink my garden accomplishments of the day.

And everything on each page is useful. I dip into my journals again and again. My favorite thing to do of a long evening or a stolen somnolent afternoon is to retrieve the journals of years past. I will often search for the entries of the same time of year, just as my in-laws did concerning their life on the farm.

Unlike Mom, I could never share my diaries. They are simply too personal—too much of me is revealed on their pages. But perhaps Mom and I, and indeed all diarists everywhere, are alike. We seek to memorialize what is central to us. To commemorate and to celebrate. Those of us who write of the earth are part of recording the vast reckoning of the seasons. Most of us know that few eyes other than our own will ever see our efforts. But on we go, year after year, writing it down.

Photo by Sue West

Japanese Painted Fern (Athryium niponicum var. pictum)

Description: Herbaceous perennial fern with finely-cut foliage. Each frond is marked with burgundy, green and silver. Grows to 18 inches high and wide; will gradually colonize to form large stands.

Favorites: 'Burgundy Lace', 'Ursula's Red'

Zones: 3-9

Exposure: Shade to part shade; will burn in too much sun.

Soil: Rich, moist, well-drained to loamy.

Water: Appreciates generous amounts.

Fertilizer: None needed if grown in good soil.

Pruning: Not indicated during growing season. Cut dead fronds in early spring; new growth will emerge.

Potential Problems: Occasionally visited by slugs and aphids.

Interesting Asides: This low-maintenance, deer-resistant fern is one of the showiest plants for the shade garden. Chosen as Perennial Plant of the Year in 2004, it's a natural as an edger, in a container, or as a ground cover. Also very pretty alongside pond or stream.

Perennial Plants of the Year

(chosen annually by the Perennial Plant Association)

2010 *Baptisia australis*

2009 *Hakonechloa macra* 'Aureola'

2008 *Geranium* 'Rozanne'

2007 *Nepeta* 'Walker's Low'

2006 *Dianthus gratianopolitanus* 'Firewitch'

2005 *Helleborus x hybridus*

2004 *Athyrium niponicum* 'Pictum'

2003 *Leucantheumum* 'Becky'

2002 *Phlox paniculata* 'David'

2001 *Calamagrostis x acutiflora* 'Karl Foerster' (feather reed grass)

2000 *Scabiosa columbaria* 'Butterfly Blue'

1999 *Rudbeckia fulgida* 'Goldsturm'

1998 *Echinacea purpurea* 'Magnus'

1997 *Salvia* 'May Night'

1996 *Penstemon digitalis* 'Husker Red'

1995 *Perovskia atriplicifolia*

1994 *Astilbe* 'Sprite'

1993 *Veronica* 'Sunny Border Blue'

1992 *Coreopsis verticillata* 'Moonbeam'

1991 *Heuchera micrantha* 'Palace Purple'

1990 *Phlox stolonifera*

27

Pansy

Muriel Ridener

My best friend Muriel is a messy gardener. Not for her are neatly arranged beds of highfalutin' cultivars purchased from the finest nurseries. Her discount store babies and passalong plants are tucked in slap-dash around the patio. In her yard hastily-planted pots spill soil, and there are no carpets of mulch. Instead, puddles of Sweet Peet are lumped where they fell from her bucket or lie heaped into scattered piles by visiting possums.

Drives me nuts.

Muriel does believe in ground cover… as in no patch of earth shall be left bare. In her case, mint does the job. The visitor's nose, therefore, is delighted by the crisp scent of spearmint wherever she traipses, and smaller ephemerals are obscured by cascading mountains of spicy foliage. But there's always a sprig for iced tea.

And never mind about height, or composition, undue soil preparation or timely trimming. Tall weeds of unknown etiology *(Let's leave 'em to see what they'll look like!)* wage war with stately azalea. Transplanted heritage irises snuggle up against the house, thrust not into a soft bed of enriched soil, but dumped into a hastily-excavated hole in the grass. Bleeding heart sweeps its dwindling stems downward, obscuring the carex.

And yet, her garden works. The juxtaposition of colors, the riot of blossom and weed and wildlife. It's a friendly garden, a welcoming garden. A place where fireflies dance in the July air at dusk.

A place where birds never seen in my manicured acre visit regularly, resplendent against the jumble of the flowers. Indigo buntings, red-bellied woodpeckers and scarlet tanagers are drawn to the feeders plunked willy-nilly into the midst of her flowering abundance. Birds and squirrels and wild turkeys argue over the largesse of spilled seed. Caws and coos and squeaks and gobbles steal her attention from the tasks at hand.

Things are never dull in Muriel's garden, just as things are never dull in our friendship.

We came late to best-friendship when we met nine years ago. We still chuckle over our introduction via an 800 number posted by the State of Connecticut to promote car-pooling. We've been inseparable since the first tentative day in our local high school parking lot, when we oh-so-politely discussed who would drive and when, all the while protecting our individual turf. Our meeting occurred a few weeks after the attack on New York City's Twin Towers, and many of our conversations initially revolved around despair and terrorism, war and justice. Numerous people in our town worked in the city, and it seemed everyone knew someone who had died in the unspeakable violence.

Once we got past the shock and sorrow, not only of our community but all of America, and once we established our carpooling ground rules, our friendship steadily developed. We vetoed the radio in favor of chatting. We first discussed movies and books and politics. We counted the red-tailed hawks on the light posts above the highway. As we grew more trusting, we shared our experiences with the fortunes and misfortunes of men and marriage. We laughed ourselves silly over the escapades of co-workers. We cried and triumphed in turn with our children's foibles and accomplishments.

A year later I was diagnosed with non-Hodgkin's lymphoma. Staggered, I took a few months off work for my surgery, and to gather strength for the battle sure to come. Which, as it turned out, never arrived. My cancer was corralled with the initial operation. No chemotherapy was required, and I was back to work by spring.

But during the sojourn at home I received a lovely book from Muriel. *Garden Poems*, it was called. An Everyman's Library collection of fine garden poems from antiquity to the present. Never a fan of verse, I shrugged, and reluctantly, dutifully dug into the compact hardcover with the Rembrandt tulips on the frontispiece and deckle-edged pages. My eyes were opened as I became acquainted with Emily Dickenson and Edna St. Vincent Millay. Though I never grew as fond of poetry as my best friend might have wished, I did come to appreciate the singularity and significance of odes, sonnets and rhymes.

For we relished words. From deep in the recesses of Muriel's bookshelf we extracted *Hog on Ice*, Charles Earle Funk's compendium of English-language expressions. We joyfully delved into the books,

"Oh ho!" we hooted. "So that's what 'woolgathering' means!" We nudged each other, exchanging knowing glances. "I can think of a few people at work that applies to!"

"And Gordian knot? Who knew there really was one?"

"How about 'Charley-horse'?" Muriel said. "I wonder if the guys know what's behind that word?"

We vowed to use the words and phrases we'd discovered. And we tried to use them, at least with each other, in the hour we rode together each day. Convinced that outsiders would consider us daft, most of the colorful words and pithy sayings found little light of day outside of my Chrysler Sebring and her Honda Accord.

I should have known from her car that Muriel wouldn't be a neat-as-a-pin gardener. Even back then she was always on her way to or from a tag sale, or the library, or to her volunteer job with unwanted animals. So her backseat (and frequently the front seat!) was generally chockablock with scuffed furniture, well-thumbed books, and dog food. It didn't matter. If it was her turn to drive, she'd wedge me in somewhere and off we'd go down the interstate, laughing all the way.

At last came blessed retirement. First mine, then, eight months later, Muriel's. Our friendship shifted from a race to beat the time clock to leisurely hours spent at our local funky coffee shop, volunteer work at the library, and redecorating our respective homes.

That's when I really looked at her garden.

Oh my.

'Heavenly Blue' morning glories scrambled over tattered hemlocks. Too-big-for-their-space 'China Girl' and 'China Boy' hollies leaned into the driveway. A downspout dumped copious amounts of rainwater directly onto a flowerbed. But, upon closer inspection, the morning glories bore prolifically, unlike my meager vine's daily offerings. The hollies bloomed enthusiastically and shone with vibrant red berries come fall. In the damp downspout bed a swashbuckling array of impatiens and coleus fairly leapt out of the soil.

Clearly there was a lesson to be learned from Muriel's garden. It took me some time, but I learned it well. It goes like this: Life is messy. Kids, even grown ones, don't always do what we think they should. Husbands sometimes leave us, or die before their time. Money can be scarce, despite the best-laid plans. Illness and infirmity visit with regularity. There are no guarantees in life.

Enjoy every day.

And so Muriel and I choose to look beyond our differences. She doesn't cluck at how many hours I toil producing just the correct edge on my beds, or how precisely I arrange the mulch. I don't whimper at the sight of her flowers swooning in pretty pots on the deck. She knows I take pride in my straight-edged beds, and I know her violas will set seed that will produce carefree beauties in the cracks of the pavement next spring.

Gardens can be messy. So can life. There's symmetry in that. We're all different, we're all the same.

"Messy," it seems, is just a word.

Wild Pansy (Viola tricolor)   Photo by Jerry Shike

Description: Common wildflower, grown as annual or short-lived perennial.

Favorites: Johnny jump-up, aka Heart's Ease.

Zones: 7 to 10. In colder areas cultivated pansies are grown as annuals. Violas often self-sow.

Exposure: Shade to semi-shade.

Soil: Ordinary garden soil, prefers moist conditions.

Water: Supplemental water at planting, and in times of drought.

Fertilizer: No chemical if flowers are to be consumed.

Pruning: Deadhead to keep flowers coming.

In the Vase: Makes a nice dainty bouquet in a small vase, or use in lapel vase.

Potential Problems: Slugs, deer. Use non-toxic controls.

Interesting Asides: Can be coated with sugar and used as edible ornamentation or in tossed salads. Also useful pressed and displayed as table décor or on stationery.

28

Hosta

Paul Young

Never let it be said that a small group of thoughtful citizens cannot change the world. Indeed, that is the only thing that ever has.
                                                    —Margaret Mead

"I'd be delighted to be on the Garden Tour, Colleen." Paul Young smiled at me, his blue eyes twinkling, workaday hand extended. He clearly *was* delighted. The exiting Sunday worship crowd jostled us as we headed down the aisle toward Reverend Whitfield standing in the narthex. "And that's a real good idea for a fundraiser. When do you need me?"

I breathed a sigh of relief. Paul, a retired nurseryman and renowned gardener, had just agreed to be on the tour I was organizing for our small Methodist church. I hadn't even had to drag out my shaky botanical Latin to convince him I knew what I was doing.

Drat. I'd been practicing. *Sambucus, amelanchier, kalmia.* I'd gone to the extent of checking with an online pronunciation guide and had most of it down pat.

Paul's ten acres with its four-acre pond had been on my mind since I'd decided to arrange a garden tour. I'd seen his acreage just once, years before, and the memory of a thousand hosta, wildlife on the pond, specimen trees, collections of dogwoods, mountain laurel, iris and ornamental grasses was still vivid. But would such a gardener want to consort with the likes of an amateur like me?

Well, it turns out, yes. He would.

We arranged to meet at his Limewood Farm the following week. But not before Paul extracted permission to also visit *my* garden. I gulped and agreed, vowing to myself to get the mulching done, finish the edging, and tend to a thousand other garden matters before I'd ever let him set foot there.

Wednesday presented a clear, chilly early spring day. As Paul and I strolled around his domain, I absorbed hosta knowledge, admired the pond, stared up at the stewartia, listened to the returning finches and robins, smelled the sharp scent of broken sassafras twigs. As we rounded the last curve of the water and headed back toward the driveway and house, I motioned to a small path disappearing into the woods.

"Where does that go?" I asked.

"To 15 acres that's not mine anymore. The Bethel Land Trust owns it now."

I was intrigued and wanted to see it, to know more about the donated land.

"OK, let's take a look," he said. "I haven't been back there in a while."

A turkey vulture circled over the granite escarpment as Paul and I toured his former property. Tracks of wild animals pockmarked the still-snowy ground. Witch hazel tinged faintly yellow stood alongside an old logging road, while stone walls and a decrepit limestone quarry gave mute testimony to the farmers and tradesmen who had once used this corner of New England.

The property, on the divide of the Saugatuck and Still Rivers, had hosted Native Americans in antiquity. It was most likely used as pasture and woodlot by our hardy Connecticut forebears, prior to and for a century after the Revolution. Denuded in the 1700s to manufacture charcoal needed to fire the lime kilns for the production of iron, and in the 1800s for farming purposes, the oaks, hickories, maples and aspen have returned, as has the wildlife. Fox, coyote, turkey, opossum, and a variety of birds call these 15 acres home during part or all of the year.

It was difficult to believe that this property was within a stone's throw of Metro-North, the commuter rail line into New York City, deep in fast-growing, heavily populated Fairfield County, Connecticut. Open space in hurly-burly suburbia is an increasingly rare and unmitigated treasure. As land far from the sights and sounds of human settlement becomes ever more precious, land trusts such as Bethel's step up their efforts to acquire space to remain forever protected.

The land trust movement began about the time of the first Earth Days in the 1970s, when groups of citizens became concerned enough about the rapid disappearance of open space to take action. There are now more than 1600 land trusts in the United States; some are large and national in scope, such as the Nature Conservancy, but many are small, locally generated and run by volunteers. All are nonprofit and act as repositories for land to be forever protected. A national umbrella organization, the Land Trust Alliance, owns no land but provides guidance and information. Large or small, national or local, all land trusts have a common goal; to preserve the land as nature would.

Always.

The first few dedicated individuals in the movement—some of them landowners seeking a legacy, some of them professional communicators, some of them simply people who cared for the land and its future—got out the message through word of mouth, letters to the editor, public forums, and community organizations. Information spread, and several popular methods of acquiring land appeared.

Ten years ago Paul Young began working with the Bethel Land Trust to protect his parcel of wooded and rock-walled countryside. He employed a mechanism known as a bargain sale, in which the receiving trust covered the surveying expenses and legal costs he incurred in preparation for the donation. Land trusts come with

267

many benefits, not the least of which are tax advantages. Paul's tax burden has been reduced because the property, now undevelopable, is worth less on the open market. In addition, recent federal tax legislation has spurred more landowners to preserve their properties. As part of a pension-reform law enacted in the summer of 2006, and extended by Congress in 2008, landowners may deduct the value of a donation up to 50% of their adjusted gross income per year, up from the previous ceiling of 30%. A landowner with an adjusted gross income of $100,000, for example, would be eligible for as much as a $50,000 tax deduction per year.

There are other methods of preserving land. Outright donation or bequeathal. Conservation easements. Deeding. As more and more of green America is paved over, saving what's left becomes ever more urgent. Paul taught me that.

And much more.

Since that April day years ago, we've become great gardening buddies. We regularly visit each other's gardens. We share tips, advice and plant divisions. We go off on plant-purchasing jaunts and garden tours. As his guest I go to growers' symposiums. He good-naturedly scolds me for not labeling my hosta adequately. I remind him with a laugh that he needs more russets and vermilions and aquamarines among his thousand hostas and woodies.

He's gotten me addicted to the genus hosta and persuaded me to join the Tri-State Hosta Society. I've brought him into the local Garden Club. Together we pulled out and replanted the overgrown yews and poison ivy that comprised the "garden" in front of our Methodist church. I convinced him to let me nominate his garden for inclusion on the national Garden Conservancy Tour. (It took two years of paperwork, photographs, nudging, and a visit by the state representative, but he was accepted.)

Our friendship has grown to include the rest of my family. Paul is a mentor to both our boys: Kyle, who's interested in studying sustainable agriculture, and Eddie, who's overcome so many obstacles. Paul is a friend to my husband, with whom he works in the woodshop and on church committees. Paul's a cheerleader to my daughter, who lives in China and is considering the next exciting steps in life. We're all invited to Paul's frequent lawn and garden parties, ranging from the croquet party on the Horseshoe Garden, to the apple-cider mini-festival in October, to the kalmia party each June, when his 40 varieties of mountain laurel are in lush bloom.

Though of different generations, Paul and I see eye-to-eye on the key things. Love of the land. The freedom and felicity of growing things. The importance of wildlife in the garden. The necessity and reward of hard physical labor.

Paul had already assembled a lifetime of gardening friends and professionals by the time I asked him to join my Garden Tour. He certainly didn't need to take me under his wing. But he did.

In doing so, Paul taught me about pragmatism in the garden, how to plant a collection, and the importance of labeling. He introduced me as a colleague to horticulturalists throughout the state and encouraged me to experiment with my planting. He pushed me to professionalize. Paul taught me to scan the sky for birds and the water for fish. He taught me the joy of day-long plant trips, the child-like pleasure of viewing another's garden, and how to join professional organizations. He taught me how to believe in myself as a gardener.

And Paul Young taught me a lesson that Native Americans knew well, but which we today have by and large forgotten. It is this: We don't own the land. Oh, it may be ours for a brief time. We may till it and grow on it and even call it ours. But the imprint of our individual footfalls will be gone in a trice. It knows no permanent owners.

The land is entrusted to us all.

Hosta   Photo by Sue West

Description: Herbaceous perennial, growing from roots or rhizomes. Most are clumping, and can range in size from several inches to several feet. Flowers are produced on erect scapes, but most hosta are grown for their attractive leaves, which come in colors ranging from blue to green to gold and many permutations in between. Red stemmed cultivars have been very popular in recent years.

Favorites: 'Sum & Substance', 'Blue Mouse Ears', 'Great Expectations'.

Zones: 3 to 10.

Exposure: Dappled shade.

Soil: Rich, organic, moist.

Water: Ample at time of transplant and in drought. Otherwise, no supplemental watering needed.

Fertilizer: If grown in rich soil, none needed. Use Milorganite as both deer repellent and fertilizer.

Pruning: Seldom needed, though spent flower stalks can be removed for aesthetics. In the autumn, after frost, remove old leaves.

Potential problems: Slugs love the thin-leaved varieties. Use organic controls such as Slugg-O or Escar-Go. Diatomaceous earth or ground eggshells work also. Entire bed can be ringed in copper sheeting. Deer relish hosta. Use a good-quality deer repellent regularly. A new virus has been spotted on hosta; to avoid this disease, purchase only from reputable growers.

Interesting Asides: Hosta is America's favorite perennial. There are thousands of cultivars, and more coming every year.

29

Daylily

Sydney Eddison

In the 1950s at St. Rose Parochial School, my art project was usually chosen to hang in the very back of the room, tight by the window casing, where few could see it. I could not draw, and therefore my dowdy pictures were frequently out of kilter, unfocused and badly proportioned. Construction paper was often smudged with effort, corners torn and, upon one memorable occasion, tear-stained.

"It doesn't matter," Mother reassured me. "I never could draw, either, Colleen. Remember, you have other talents."

There *was* an artist in our midst, however, and the nuns were quick to recognize Ann Spencer's aptitude. Her paintings, illustrations and sketches were displayed front and center, year after year, above the dusty black chalkboards of the wooden-floored classrooms in our six-room, two-story schoolhouse.

Every gardener is at heart an artist, wishing to bring splendor, vibrancy, light and design into their yards and into their lives. As I matured as a gardener I became faintly aware that color was important. I played with it, unsure what I was doing, and seeking direction. On a years-ago visit to the Gertrude Jekyll Garden at the Glebe House in Woodbury, Connecticut, I observed how that master orchestrated the rhythm and flow of the hues of the natural world and then some, encircling the parsonage with ribbons of color, using annuals, perennials, shrubs and vines. From the cool whites and blues at either end through the warm yellows and oranges to the central fiery reds and back again to cool colors, she wove the rainbow. On the back of my museum program I jotted some plant names. Although intrigued, I was also daunted, and I knew I could never hope to imitate such prowess.

In 2003 I noticed in the New York Botanical Garden catalogue the offering of a color seminar with famed gardener Sydney Eddison. Celebrated for her lyrical books that touch not only on horticultural expertise but also on the lessons of life, I knew Sydney to be an artist by profession as well as a writer, and I leapt at the opportunity to study with her.

At the New Canaan Nature Center, the moist air of the nearby conservatory enveloped us as we sat at battered tables. A worm composting box and rolled posters of horticultural pests jostled us for space. The class followed Sydney's lead and conversed about the color wheel. We tried to use the language of tone and hue, contrast and harmony. We discussed nature and art and the freewheeling seasons of New England. Sydney exhorted us to look beyond plants and think about color itself. She elicited comments from us on problem combinations. Then she requested us to choose a method to draw and illustrate our own gardens. One woman, the Ann Spencer of our group, used tiny, fluffy pieces of multihued tissue paper to exemplify hers. As the class crowded around, enchanted, I asked myself, *Why couldn't I have been so creative?*

I went home, looked at my garden, and dashed out to purchase Sydney's recent book, *The Gardener's Palette*. I skimmed it, looked at the beguiling pictures, underlined passages, made margin notes, and tried to sort out what I'd learned both from her class and the book. It was slow going, though, in part because of leftover childhood messages, and also because my rawboned garden seemed to lack not only color, but grace and cadence.

Nonetheless I picked up a thing or two, if only the need to be more confident in my choices. And I realized I knew more than I thought. I'd inadvertently already chosen a color scheme. My garden exhibited the pure whites of *Phlox paniculata* 'David', impatiens and iberis; the clear yellows of daffodil, kerria and coreopsis; and a multitude of blues, purples and lavenders. I obviously thrilled to Virginia bluebells, scilla and silky, papery morning glories. I apparently couldn't get enough blue salvia, purple petunias and allium. Froufrou pink lamium, lavender-and-white columbine and maiden blush vinca also made my heart skip a beat. I'd already learned that yellow crocus provide a landscape "pop" when placed among their pastel brethren and backlit by white birch. But I shunned the hot colors. Not a speck of red or orange had I allowed in my beds. No brilliant crocosmia and nary a scrap of screaming orange marigolds were in sight.

It was a start. I understood which colors I preferred. But I also sensed that I'd chosen a limited palette and that there was much more to discover on the whole topic of color.

A year or so later I stood in an undulating line at the Mattatuck Museum on Waterbury's city center green. A garden symposium was underway, and Sydney Eddison again was a highlight. In a high-ceilinged room, amidst the mingled essence of ink and wool and beeswax, she graciously autographed her latest book, *Gardens to Go*. I needed a copy for my ever-expanding gardening library and to serve as an inspiration for my ever-increasing collection of patio pots. When my turn came, I introduced myself and explained that I'd read much of her work, taken a color class with her, and was still challenged by the subject matter.

She smiled sweetly as she signed. "It's all about learning to look, Colleen. Pay attention to what you like, and trust your own instincts. You know more than you think you do."

She made it sound so simple that once home, I decided to give color another try. I pulled *The Gardener's Palette* off the shelf, bought a color wheel and filched a paint chip album from my husband, the cabinetmaker.

This time, using Sydney's color wheel, it took only a few minutes to appreciate that the circular arrangement is based on the rainbow. I found this reassuring. Rainbows, Nature's celestial color fling, I could understand. They demonstrate that adjacent colors, which share pigment, are harmonious, and that opposite colors contrast. This grasped, I was launched. Harmony was why, for the front porch, the pot of strobilanthes I had underplanted with pink and white impatiens stood out as a pleasing welcome. I wasn't quite as comfortable with contrast, I realized, which was why the sight of *Salvia farinea* 'Victoria' next to red 'Knockout' roses jarred my eye.

I knew that if I wanted to discuss plant combinations intelligently, learning the proper words would be mandatory. But I shuddered at the thought. Surely only true artists had a handle on the vocabulary!

Not so. I soon memorized the simple terms in Sydney's book. *Hue* refers to a color. *Tint* is simply a color lightened by white. *Shade* is the opposite, a color darkened by black. And a *tone* is one dulled by gray.

I began to get it. No longer did my eyes glaze over at the gardening articles on the use of color. I could learn something from the pictures and the text. No longer was I flying by the seat of my pants. I understood why I did what I did in the garden, and why some arrangements pleased and others distressed.

Certain things I did instinctively, as Sydney had said we would. I loathed the combination of pink bleeding heart and orange tulips that bloomed together one spring. So I learned to stay away from that combination. Alternatively, accidental pairings lent charm to my front garden. A leftover six-pack of two-toned small marigolds got planted under a chartreuse spirea one June and delighted me the rest of the season. In the Mailbox Garden, obedient plant shone against purple perilla and *Aster novae-angliae* 'Alma Plotschke'. Maybe I did know what I was doing.

It wasn't just color in the garden that was important, I discovered. As I replanted my deer-devoured woods edges, I looked for trees and shrubs that not only were hardy and native in southern New England, but also colorful. Trees like sassafras and sugar maple, swamp maple and sourwood. Shrubs such as spicebush and amelanchier and viburnum. My forest edges began to light up the Indian summer days of October.

That experience led to my ability to see the beauty of late color in the backyard garden. Instead of mourning the passing of the phlox and daylilies and boltonia, deep into October I'm able to appreciate the bronze, cinnamon and purple of oakleaf hydrangea and notice how it stands out from the apricot and buttery-yellow of fading hosta leaves, and is bracketed by the glow of amelanchier leaves and sweeping red of a 'Crimson Queen' Japanese maple.

Perhaps it was because of the orange of the autumn trees and the hosta leaves, but I eventually softened up on using that secondary hue. The year I accidentally planted a 'Tropicana' canna some middle distance behind asclepias sealed the deal. When they bloomed, the orange flowers provided a punctuation point in the backyard garden.

As I worked, memories of color came flooding back.

"Your eyes are so blue, Colleen," Mother had said. "They match your gym bloomers, you know."

I hadn't known, and wasn't sure I was thrilled to match the dreadful one-piece outfit the nuns mandated we girls wear for physical education. But from that day forward I'd always loved blue. And when having one's colors "done" in the '80s was de rigueur, I discovered that raspberry and magenta and rose went well with my complexion. It's probably no accident that when I began to garden in earnest, these were the colors I chose. And though wearing green, gray or white is never my first sartorial choice, they are the colors that stitch my gardens together.

Increasingly less intimidated and more confident, I began to pay added attention to color besides that of plants. Our colonial-blue house presented an opportunity. I began to collect blue outdoor ornaments to go with it. Blue birdhouses, birdbaths and a few pots. Not too much, just enough to spark the yard. I jotted in my diary what went well with what. I kept my eye on a café-au-lait concrete statue of a flower-bedecked girl at a local garden center. When she went on sale I snapped her up, named her Rosa, and now she resides among the grasses along the front walk and peeps out from the *Panicum virgatum* 'Shenandoah'. Her color matches that of the *Chasmanthium latifolium* seedheads and the flower panicles of the *Miscanthus sinensis* 'Variegata'.

On I went. The backyard garden, viewed from the gazebo, needed height and color. *Amaranthus tricolor*, also known as Joseph's coat, proved just the ticket, and garden visitors never fail to exclaim, "What *is* that tall, red and white and yellow plant?"

Hardscape interested me as well. I made sure the two arbors leading to the backyard were painted the same misty beige as the gazebo, and that the pavers under them were a complementary russet to the large, neighborly pots of coleus. When we acquired a garden shed and tucked it in under a mature Norway spruce, the color chosen was a neutral gray, to blend in with the surrounding woods. But the window boxes got planted with bright pink, white and lavender impatiens.

Along the way of my search I discovered that there *are* shortcuts for the truly color-challenged. Catalogues offer complete color-coordinated, height-sorted and season-themed collections of everything from seeds to bulbs to perennials to trees. One can go to the Web and download drawn-to-scale, color-themed gardens. No-muss, no-fail gardening. But where's the fun in that?

On a summer day circa 2005, as I drove along the winding country road to Sydney Eddison's home, admiring the countryside, it was difficult to believe I was deep in suburban Connecticut—and only 14 miles from my home! It was an earlier era, and the 18th century farmhouses shaded by century-old oaks only added to the bewitching out-of-time sensation. The road terminated in a sign for the Paugusset State Forest, and for a moment I was certain I'd lost my way. Then I saw the yellow colonial tucked into a rise next to the woods and realized I was there.

I had arrived early for the tour and was admiring the captivating abundance of pots, containers, charming yellow furniture and bubbling water feature on the terrace, all previously seen in her books, magazine articles and on television, from *House Beautiful* to the *New York Times* to *Martha Stewart Living.* The scent of freshly-mown grass mingled with the pungent aroma of the marigold and peppery nasturtium spilling over the edges of the wall, and the very air seemed suffused with gardening delights.

And there were the color lessons. My eye was drawn to a combination of chartreuse geranium and red-leaved coleus and a welter of *Zinnia angustifolia* hard by stalwart brugmansia. A daring display of abutilon and sweet potato vine embraced pots of ivy geraniums and pansies. Brugmansia also dominated a scene complemented by canna 'Pretoria' and multihued, scalloped-edge coleus. Licorice plant, lantana and trailing vinca overspilled their boundaries and softened the contours of the terrace. The array of plant material filling the small space was stunning.

When Sydney approached, I complimented her on the mass of color and delightful design in the small enclosure. She replied with a small gift snipped from a pot. Though I was thrilled, I wasn't surprised.

"Just take this and tuck it away before the others get here." She smiled at me, a trailing piece of purple tradescantia in her hand. I thanked her, knowing that the smoothed-leafed annual with the fleshy stems would be perfect in a container in my nascent Connecticut garden.

Her patio garden and brief conversation held my attention, but having seen it so many times in magazines and books, I deliberately delayed the pleasure of looking directly at the main perennial border. As Sydney was called to guide the other guests, I strolled over for my first sight of the mature, east-facing hillside garden, stuffed with perennials, shrubs, annuals, and small trees, rising from and contrasting with the level green of the lawn. It took my breath.

It certainly had a familiar cast, but to view it in person! There was the edging of lamb's ears for which her garden is famous. There were the daylilies, limned so lushly in *A Passion for Daylilies*. There was the cutleaf Japanese maple, the incised foliage of the peonies, the graceful arch of the poppies. There was the whole of the garden laid out, just as it had been illustrated on the inside cover of *A Patchwork Garden.*

Standing in awe, I remembered to look for the lessons in color in the yard. The blue ceramic ball, rough-hewn and settled into the earth, was easy to spot, next to a silvery cluster of lamb's ears and sitting sentry to a spiky green-and-gold yucca. The daylilies, terracotta and vermillion, whisper-soft pink and brilliant yellow, were underspread and softened by a filigree of coreopsis. And always green, the buffer: in the lawn, the backdrop of forest and foliage of resting plants.

I didn't know where to walk, what to examine closely, or how best to absorb the marvelous sights. My glance skipped from the mature rhododendrons backing the border, to the quiet coves of beautyberry and hellebore; the scattering of sprightly corydalis and the symphony of limbed-up forsythia and chartreuse spirea. The hush of the surrounding woods was dispelled only by the quiet chatter of fellow garden enthusiasts. "Look at the daisies!" and "How long do you suppose that oakleaf hydrangea has been in?" and of course, "How many daylilies do you think she has? It's her favorite flower, you know."

I pootled around alone, from the fieldstone wall to the leaf mold compost area, from the terrace to the lower lawn. I examined the deer fence and the stubby rough wood of the barn. I gazed up at the mature maples in the forest beyond and imagined their vibrant color in autumn. I rambled among the daylilies, from 'Lullaby Baby' to 'Mary Todd', reading the labels, drinking it all in. I roamed down the swale to the primrose path, next to the summer-dormant stream. Though the primroses, which I knew to be another of Sydney's favorite flowers, were past, the bones of that garden were clearly visible. Another lesson for another day.

The last time I visited with Sydney, we sat at the kitchen table while her Jack Russell terrier, Phoebe, snoozed on her lap. Classical music from a radio atop the refrigerator blended with the sound of turning pages of horticulture books and the clank and earthy clatter of a workman outside on the lawn. Vases of late flowers—ginger-colored dahlias, *Chrysanthemum compositae* 'Sheffield Pink' and *Salvia farinacea* 'Victoria' adorned the tables and bookcases. Cuttings cluttered the sink surround, awaiting their winter treatment. Sydney served tea in charming, oversize cups attended by floral napkins. I felt welcomed and listened to. We discussed gardens, garden people, and her long career as a notable writer, gardener and artist. She spoke of family history and the poignancy of loss. We commiserated on the difficulties of growing older and the joy of pets.

When it was finally time to go, I asked her to sign my well-thumbed copy of *The Gardener's Palette*. She opened it to inscribe, noted the tricky color of the inside cover and offered one final lesson of the day.

"Look at this," she said, stroking the blood red of the page. "Have you got a minute more? I'd like to show you something, if you can come upstairs."

We climbed the steep stairs in her antique farmhouse, up to her study, Phoebe scrambling at our side. When I stepped into the slanted, white-walled, compact space, I gasped.

"I've seen this! The article in *Fine Gardening* years ago on your indoor workroom. Your husband built these shelves, right? And the bookcases and counter?"

"Oh, yes. He was such a help. I miss him so."

Above me in the skylight fluttered the first few flakes of October snow. Windows on two sides of the room poured gray early-winter light into the room. Books abounded, and a computer occupied much of the desk space.

"It's a wonderful place to work," Sydney said. "But here, let me show you what I mean about color." She rattled through a storage area and selected a watercolor she'd painted decades before, a stage set of a living room, done in shades of burgundy and deep pink with a splash of chartreuse. This she set on a low shelf. In front of it she laid a copy of *Gardens to Go*. In front of that, she placed a piece of bright fabric with dashes of the same colors.

"See how the hues are essentially the same? The watercolor I did years ago, the book cover three years ago, and this fabric. They all appeal to me. One's eye for color doesn't change."

I saw. I really saw.

And then I knew that I'd always seen it. From my childhood love of peacock blue morning glories and free-spirit-white Easter lilies. From the amethyst of a backyard lilac to the blazing oranges and reds of a transplanted sugar maple, through the strawberry-ice-cream pink of turtlehead and silvery-purple of painted fern.

The colors of my life had always been within my grasp.

Daylily (Hemerocallis)

Photo by Sue West

Plant Description: Herbaceous perennial with spray of sword-shaped leaves and flowers borne on scapes. Highly varied in form, size and color due to extensive hybridization from original orange plant. Each bloom lasts only a day, but a single plant may bear hundreds of blooms. A favored plant in the ornamental garden. Some are scented, others are reblooming.

Favorites: 'Lullaby Baby', 'Ruffled Apricot', 'Lady Liz'

Zones: 1-11, depending on species and cultivar.

Exposure: Happiest in full sun, though will grow and bloom in less.

Soil: Rich, organic.

Water: Roots are fibrous, so are drought tolerant; water well at time of planting/transplanting.

Fertilizer: If planted in amended soil, only a handful of fertilizer once per year is needed. Dig in around base of plants.

Pruning: Deadhead daily, cut stems when each scape is finished. Cut leaves down to ground at close of season.

Potential problems: Deer find the plant delectable. Apply repellent or use fencing.

Interesting Asides: Native from Europe to China, Korea and Japan. The name *hemerocallis* comes from the Greek, meaning "beauty for a day." There are over 60,000 registered cultivars. The flowers, shoots, and buds of some species are used in Asian cuisine. However, the common orange daylily is listed as a noxious weed in some areas.

30

Passing It Along

Jenny Bailey

"Colleen, got a minute?" Young, pretty Jenny Bailey appeared at my elbow during a hectic church-basement social hour one Sunday last May. I smiled, two-stepped over the pair of eight-year-olds skidding across the wooden floor, and lifted my cardboard cup of lukewarm Methodist coffee in her direction. The mingled smell of church perfume, Sunday school paste and homemade chocolate-chip cookies scented the air.

"I'm all yours, Jenny. Need my atonal comments on the choir? How about musings on membership?"

"None of the above. I'd like you to be my garden mentor."

Hearing the words "garden" and "mentor" in the same sentence is a magical occurrence for a devoted gardener. Still, I stepped back, startled. In her early 30s, a single career woman living in a new condo, Jen had heretofore never given me a clue that she was even interested in the toils of the soil.

"I couldn't help but overhear you talk about your garden at the Philips' dinner last night."

Oh, yeah, come to think of it, I *had* run my mouth. Complaining about the nasty wet April, the dry hot May, germination failure on 'Heavenly Blue' morning glory, and the usual lack of time to get everything done. I hadn't realized she was listening.

Hoping my voice didn't betray my excitement, I answered, "I'd be delighted, Jen. What kind of flowers do you have in mind?"

"Not flowers, vegetables. I want to grow peppers and tomatoes and pumpkins, herbs and beans. Maybe some artichokes and eggplant, too."

The cacophony of Sunday social hour swirled around us as I listened, my cardboard coffee going cold.

"My company, PepsiCo, has garden plots available for employees. First come, first serve. The section is fenced, they'll plow it, there's a water source, and it's accessible. But I've never really gardened. I don't know where to start."

Now, not only did I no longer know diddly-squat about vegetables (it'd been 13 years since I'd produced a one, and even then I'd specialized in *perennial* vegetables such as asparagus and Jerusalem artichokes), she wanted to grow some of the northeast's most difficult veggies. Eggplant, indeed!

"I primarily do flowers," I said tentatively, "but I'm sure I can help. But why vegetables?"

"It's on my life list. Flowers are beautiful, and I've grown some. But for me, having food to show for the work seems to be the most real form of gardening."

"*Square-Foot Gardening*, a classic how-to book by Mel Bartholomew," I said. "That's what you need. It shows beginners how to maximize their space, combat problems, and ramp up production. I've got an extra copy you can have."

Jenny's face lit up.

"And let's get you out to my place," I added. "The finest vegetable garden in Bethel just happens to be right next door."

We talked for the next 20 minutes while I gauged her level of interest, her skill, and her dedication to the non-combat sport of gardening.

It was mid-May, however, and if she was to grow anything this year, time was of the essence. So later that same week we trod the soft mulched paths of Chris Minor's colorful vegetable patch. A handsome wooden fence, fortified with chicken wire and covered with sweet autumn clematis, ringed the garden. Mature 'Bowl of

Beauty' peonies in full bloom marched around the exterior. A hose lay neatly curled in the midst of the cabbage and rhubarb. A stately row of tomato plants adorned with small green fruit stood supported by dark-green curved metal stakes, which I recognized from the Gardener's Supply catalogue. Netting covered a swath of almost-mature strawberries. The heady scent of a manured compost pile arose from a shaded corner. Majestic swamp maples, white oaks and tulip poplars formed a backdrop on the downslope woods.

"Wow." Jen shook her head. "How long has it taken you to do this?"

"Years," Chris replied. "I add a few new things, experiment, and try to improve each season. But it's a labor of love. I can't wait to get out here after work, and it's tough to tear myself away for dinner some evenings."

We asked question after question, and finally, filled with resolve and knowledge, Jen and I strolled back to my garden and adjourned to the compost. I pitchforked into the rich darkness, uncovering scattered crumbles from last year's leaves, shredded paper and peanut-butter sandwich crusts. "In order to get your garden to produce as much as Chris's, you need lots of this stuff. The rule is, the darker your soil, and the more organic material, the better your garden will grow."

"I'm not sure how much organic matter I've got in my plot."

"And you won't know until you get your soil tested," I said. "Contact the Connecticut Cooperative Extension Office. In the meantime, let's put some of this in your new garden, OK?"

We filled several five-gallon plastic buckets and hauled them up the backyard to her car. There, sweating with exertion and redolent with Mother Earth, we carefully placed them in her hatchback.

Jen wiped her hands on her jeans, thanked me for my gift and drove off to her new adventure. It'd been a successful day.

By the next week, when I visited her company plot, Jen had not only clearly absorbed Mel Bartholomew's and Chris Minor's lessons, she'd built herself a reasonable facsimile of a square foot garden. Orderly sections were laid out, in which were centered transplants of rosemary and basil, cherry tomatoes and beans. Supportive trellising stretched upward in hopeful anticipation of a harvest load of squash vines. A bevy of tomato plants awaited staking.

I oohed and ahhed. "Yeah, in general I'm pleased," she said. "But I'm concerned about these." Jen pointed to a yellowing row of parsley plants.

"Give them a bit more organic granular fertilizer," I said. "Scratch it in around the base, water them, and those plants will bounce back."

They did.

Spring passed into summer and, except for a small plague of mildew on her summer squash, Jen's garden thrived. She visited her patch several times a week, even when there weren't chores. She weeded, and carried water in a small plastic container when the heavens didn't provide. Every Sunday I'd get updates as we discussed various problems. There were few, thankfully.

It was time, I decided, for the watering can.

Over the years I've developed a few recommendations for watering, which, during the process of mentoring, I'd imparted to Jen. They are as follows:

* Keep the soil composted and mulched, the better to retain whatever moisture is present.

* Water early in the day, to avoid evaporation and disease.

* Keep the hose handy, and the watering cans full.

Jen had started her garden with composted soil. She was willing to water in the morning, and a company hose was available. But she had no practical container in which to carry water.

Ahhh, a French Blue! The Cadillac of watering cans, the slim, blue, heavy-gauge plastic cans are attractive in the garden, balanced in the hand, and hold an impressive three gallons of water. The brass rose on the spout gentles the spray, and the slim line of the can enables it to snug up against the fence or wall.

Originally I had three. One still resided in my garden. The second one had gone to my sister when she embarked on her life's gardening journey. On a warm Sunday in August, I gave the third to Jenny Bailey.

And so went Jen's first year in her very own garden. Watching seeds turn into carrots, beans and pumpkins amazed her. She chatted with newfound gardener friends and brought fresh vegetables into the office to share. When her parents came north for a visit in September, they helped her pick tomatoes and black beans, and that night dined on fresh pesto with roasted cherry tomatoes. Towards the end of October, Jen gleefully showed off a genuine, if tiny, jack-o-lantern produced from her square foot plot.

Plans are already underway for next season. No longer a non-gardener, she's eager to try her hand at growing spinach and broccoli as well as the squash, beans, tomatoes and herbs she grew this year. She's thinking about, and asking about, solutions for the mildew. Some year, she says, she'd love to have a yard to landscape, and room for berry bushes, fruit and nut trees.

And so it goes.

Jen Bailey, similar to many of us, gardens because the very act stirs her soul. She gardens because now, having been introduced, something mystical in her blood each spring will demand it. Deep in the winter she'll go through the garden catalogues I've saved for her, and come spring she'll sow her seeds of tomatoes, peppers and squash.

And the thrum of the eternal rhythm of life will start anew.

31

Jerry Shike

He minced no words. "This thing is rock-bottom ugly." Jerry and I were standing at the lower edge of our backyard on a cool, damp May day in 2004. The woodland soil, covered with trout lilies and bloodroot, yielded slightly under our feet as he kicked the warped plywood and the peeling finish of our son's forgotten skateboarding halfpipe. "Kyle hasn't used this in months."

"Not since he got his driver's license, no," I said. "But you guys had fun planning and building it, and he had a lot of good times on it with his buddies."

"Well, it's gotta come down now. It's a mess."

I saw my advantage and pressed it. "You know, this is where I've always wanted a gazebo." I glanced at my husband. "It'd be a perfect spot to gaze out over the garden. And our garden's on the church tour again next month. Do you suppose…"

My patient, understanding husband looked at me as if I'd lost my mind. "You want me to tear this down and put up a gazebo in four weeks? No way, Colleen, I'm too busy with work. Plus, we haven't budgeted for it."

"Oh, Jerry, please. It would look so pretty. I can help."

He hesitated.

"And," I said, "it only has to go in once. It'll be here long after we're gone. Then the backyard is finished, I promise."

He crumbled like a graham cracker.

It took some time to find the perfect gazebo. We visited the local business that sold sheds, gazebos and jungle gyms. When the salesman reviewed our yard, he said, with an emphatic shake of his head, that it was impossible, due to the incline, to have a truck deliver a ready-made edifice to the site. The offer was made, half-seriously, to helicopter one in, but the $5,000 cost was way out of line for us.

Time was ticking away. The tour loomed.

Jerry searched the Internet and found a Mennonite company in Pennsylvania that sold attractive, sturdy gazebo kits. The price and the delivery window were perfect. And it came in the medium beige that matched the arbors and wooden fences elsewhere in the backyard. It was a go.

My bit of architectural wonder arrived on a flatbed truck on a gauzy, hazy day in late May. The hearty driver with the broad hat, full beard and wide smile helped us offload the pallets of eight sections of gazebo at the top of the driveway. Azaleas patterned the sloping backyard with pink, and forget-me-nots laid a swath of blue alongside the paths as Jerry, one of his employees and I, along with assorted kids, hauled chunks of gazebo down the hill to the prepared building site. We sweated, labored, smashed fingers and gnashed teeth as we dragged, hoisted, and lugged every last piece. Big pieces, smaller pieces, the railings and the floor. The benches that would circle the inside. The ornamental trim. And finally, the cupola. It still all had to be hammered together, and that would take us another two days, but it was in place.

Those two days turned into five, but we did it.

Tour day dawned hot and bright. In the gazebo we served ice tea in floral paper cups to our guests, who were grateful to be out of the sun, and enchanted by the sweeping view of baptisia, rhododendron and lilac up the slope.

The gazebo was the highlight of the tour.

Scores of colleagues, companions and collaborators have accompanied me on my life's work as a gardener. But central to my identity as a plantswoman is Jerry Shike, who married me in the shadow of my 30th year, and ever since, wherever we've lived, has dug holes, put up fence, laid soaker tubing, installed bird feeders, unkinked hose, hauled trees, listened to a litany of garden woes and joys, given advice, rubbed sore limbs, bought me gardening tools and rain barrels and fertilizer.

And built me a gazebo when I had to have one.

He's done without dinner many a day while I tucked in a pine tree or mulched one last corner of the shrub bed. He's put up with garden books strewn over the coffee table and all 100-plus issues of *Fine Gardening* stored in the cabinet where his DVD's were meant to live. He watched our babies while I tucked in tulips in New Jersey, encouraged me to plant leatherleaf viburnum in Indiana, humored me when I wanted a ton of pea gravel for the backyard in West Virginia. He bought me my first truckload of mulch and fought the pocket gophers alongside me in California. He accepts birdseed scattered on the front walk and back deck. He's dissuaded me (so far) from keeping chickens. He measures, purchases and installs lumber for raised beds and wire for enclosures. He tolerates my frequent afternoons spent on garden tours and classes, and appreciates the fact that I don't drag him along.

I'm sure Jerry didn't know what he was getting involved with when he entered into a life partnership with this gardener, but he's always been more than supportive. When I longed to retire from the practice of social work to become a professional gardener, he was there. When I tangled with the intricacies of the digital projector essential for my garden lectures, he patiently taught me its ways. When I need advice on invoices or brochures or billing, he's there. As he always has been. Without a mumble or a murmur. And though there have been years when my garden apparatus has taken up garage space belonging to his Harley, we worked it out. He doesn't complain when I fish out compostables from our garbage or shanghai used paper goods for our compost pile from parties we attend. He might roll his eyes, or grin in slight embarrassment, but he doesn't criticize, protest or nitpick. He's my gardening bulwark, my soulmate, my helpmeet.

We were young and strong when we started our gardening life together. Now December is closer than April; arthritis hampers my hands, and Jerry's back isn't what it used to be. The children are grown and gone, scattered to Asia and Florida and New York City. Change, like aging, is inevitable. So we hire more help, and relax a few rules. But we still share the work. We continue to learn from and teach each other. And what we've shared and garnered along the byways of our life together, we know we must pass along in the fullness of time.

Thus it ever was, with gardeners of tomorrow and gardeners long gone:

Louise Schoonover, flapping her apron at the chickens on her beloved farm.

Arthur Kennett, completing his life cycle in my childhood backyard.

William Kennett, teaching his grandchildren a lesson of compassion with a gnarled apple tree.

Mary Maloney, her outstretched hands offering garden gleanings.

Dorothy Kennett, unknowingly presenting her middle-aged daughter with a much-desired water feature.

Muriel Ridener, reveling in the dizzying bounty of her whimsical garden.

Paul Young and his dog, standing proud over ten precious acres of kalmia, cornus and hosta in suburban Connecticut.

Jerry Shike, a bemused smile on his face, building one more fence, sharpening one more tool.

And so many others, too numerous to count. All these and more have mentored me. Some, undoubtedly, no longer remember Colleen Plimpton. Some now sleep the sleep of the ages, their work complete, their skilled hands forever stilled, their knowledge safely bequeathed. Inevitably, their names and talents will fade with the decades. Unless we choose to remember.

I am the grateful recipient of their generous wisdom. But it is mine only for a short while. Nature demands that I pass the enlightenment on.

And so, with a happy heart and dirt under my fingernails, I do.